Praise for *Africa Is Not a*

"[Dipo Faloyin] is a smart, often scathingly funny writer. . . . [*Africa Is Not a Country*] brims with the sort of outrage that speaks of hope, of change." —*BookPage*, starred review

"With clarity and incisive wit, journalist Faloyin explores the origins of the 54 countries of Africa. . . . *Africa Is Not a Country* [is] a forceful rebuttal of erased histories and simplified imagery as well as a celebration of a continent already living its dynamic future." —*Booklist*, starred review

"A spirited critique of Western misrepresentations of Africa. . . . [E]xuberant and informative." —*Publishers Weekly*

"Trenchant. . . . A well-researched, cleareyed deconstruction of highly flawed conventional wisdom about Africa." —*Kirkus Reviews*

"A brilliant, prescient exploration of a richly complex continent. An antidote for our times." —Irenosen Okojie, author of *Nudibranch*

"An impeccably researched work, brimming with humor and intellect. A necessary read." —J K Chukwu, author of *The Unfortunates*

"A triumph of a book. A charismatic and hugely enjoyable read packed full of essential information—revealing a huge, vastly diverse set of stories, situations, and histories that really do pop the balloon of lazy stereotyping of Africa. You'd be doing yourself a disservice if you didn't read this book." —Nels Abbey, coauthor of *Think Like a White Man*

"This book should be on the curriculum." —Nikki May, author of *Wahala*

AFRICA IS NOT
A COUNTRY

AFRICA IS NOT A COUNTRY

Notes on a

Bright Continent

Dipo Faloyin

W. W. NORTON & COMPANY

Celebrating a Century of Independent Publishing

For information about permission to reproduce selections from this book, write to
Permissions, W. W. Norton & Company, Inc., 500 Fifth Avenue, New York, NY 10110

For information about special discounts for bulk purchases, please contact
W. W. Norton Special Sales at specialsales@wwnorton.com or 800-233-4830

Manufacturing by Lakeside Book Company
Production manager: Beth Steidle

Library of Congress Cataloging-in-Publication Data

Names: Faloyin, Dipo, author.
Title: Africa is not a country : notes on a bright continent / Dipo Faloyin.
Description: First American edition. | New York : W. W. Norton & Company, 2022. |
"First published in the United Kingdom by Harvill Secker, an imprint of Vintage, a part of
Penguin Random House UK under the title Africa is not a country: breaking stereotypes of
modern Africa." | Includes bibliographical references.
Identifiers: LCCN 2022017536 | ISBN 9780393881530 (cloth) |
ISBN 9780393881547 (epub)
Subjects: LCSH: National characteristics, African. | Africa—Foreign public opinion. |
Africa—Politics and government—21st century. | Africa—Social conditions—21st century. |
Africa—Social life and customs—21st century.
Classification: LCC DT3 .F315 2022 | DDC 960.33—dc23/eng/20220411
LC record available at https://lccn.loc.gov/2022017536

ISBN 978-1-324-06589-0 pbk.

W. W. Norton & Company, Inc., 500 Fifth Avenue, New York, N.Y. 10110
www.wwnorton.com

W. W. Norton & Company Ltd., 15 Carlisle Street, London W1D 3BS

1 2 3 4 5 6 7 8 9 0

Dedicated to the nations of my continent:

Olufemi, Olutosin; Vero, Temitope, Yewande;
Feranmi, Sekemi, and Olivia.

Buku.

AFRICA IS NOT

A COUNTRY

Author's Note

I.

Assume any mention of the actions of an ethnic group refers to the leadership of that group at that time and does not reflect the majority beliefs of the entire community.

II.

I'm not generically African. I am Nigerian. This book reflects my viewpoint as such.

[Insert generic African proverb here. Ideally an allegory about a wise monkey and his interaction with a tree, or the relationship between the donkey and the ant that surprisingly speaks to grand gestures of valour. Sign it off: Ancient African proverb]

If all I knew about Africa were from popular images, I too would think that Africa was a place of beautiful landscapes, beautiful animals and incomprehensible people, fighting senseless wars, dying of poverty and AIDS, unable to speak for themselves.

— Chimamanda Ngozi Adichie

Contents

Identities

IDENTITIES form specifically.

I come from a place that exists somewhere between a pot of Jollof rice in the busiest kitchen in West Africa and a living room full of revolving main characters. I delight in discussion because I am forged from my family's most consistent ritual: gathering too many people in a confined space and arguing about nothing – each person giving their opinion on each person's opinion. I was born to people with conflicting recollections of events where they were both present. I grew up surrounded by family forever complaining that someone else is not telling the story right, either in accuracy or with the requisite flair. In our home, history isn't written by the winner but by whoever speaks first.

My mother is a people person, a crowd-pleaser. She is never more comfortable than when she is uncomfortable, cocooned by unfolding events out of her control, where the solution is always a family meeting. From her I inherited my love for living in highly dense populations, ensconced in noise and all-round activity; a deep joy at being boxed in by a jukebox of experiences and an extensive bus network. My mother always stays for one more song. I always stay for one more song.

My father is an extrovert on his own terms, extremely at ease in his own skin, with an urgent need to just be. His current pace is a counterweight to motion. If he could design a perfect day, it would involve a morning nap.

From him I take a tranquil disposition: things are probably never as bad or as good as they seem at first. At our fastest, we are slow walkers; at our slowest, as my sister once noted, we may as well be strolling backwards.

I am half Yoruba and half Igbo. They say Yorubas just want to have a good time and Igbos just want to have a good life, which means I am programmed, anytime anywhere, to never automatically turn down an invite without, at the very least, asking some follow-up questions. I have three older sisters, which means 23 per cent of my life has been spent mourning the points I wish I had brought up in a long-finished argument.

I come from a confusingly sublime matrix of who is actually a blood relative, and a deep appreciation of heat, both in taste and touch, and the healing powers of pepper soup. I was raised with a strong belief that it is an aunty's duty to mind your business and that it is impossible to have too many cousins – two concepts I'm triggered to defend. I am from a home with an open-door policy. I am from a belief that to visit our home is to eat at our home, because food is the ultimate love language; food forgives sins and dispenses grace.

I was raised to get up early for church and stay up late for election nights. I am from a family that has never willingly gone on a beach holiday, and values intuition over organisation; a home where decisions are based on emotion rather than practicality. A strict childhood diet of arriving at events and airports too early has made me allergic to arriving at events and airports too early. Bedtimes were set, as was the understanding that children should be heard.

I am descended from a long line of bad poker faces, a clan genetically unable to hide the frustrations or joys etched in our hearts, however temporary. I am from silence being the ultimate punishment, and appreciating the eternal value of a dance floor bursting with people you love as the greatest man-made invention. I am from a philosophy that questions why you would ever order something new off a menu when you know exactly what you want; why order something new when you understand precisely who you are?

*

We are all the sum of a specific set of known knowns and more subtle influences that clash, combine and occasionally curdle. They are the intangibles that drive our most honest intentions and shape the essence of our personalities – something that is often too intricate, too elastic and too personal to ever give full voice to accurately, however hard we try.

Instead, in all our interactions, we leave tiny breadcrumbs as clues to the inner sanctum of our complex identities. It's an unwitting, uneven collaboration between the big things: the genetics we inherit from our parents, and the life decisions we take after careful calculations; the subconscious things – degrees of eye contact, automated anxieties; and the millions of things that thrive in the middle, whether it's checking the weather before stepping outside, the perfect storage place for condiments, a commitment to coordinating socks.

Small patches of persona stitched together until they form someone real.

Not everyone is allowed a complex identity. Throughout history, individuals and entire communities have been systematically stripped of their personhood and idiosyncrasies, often to make them easier to demean, denigrate and subjugate – and, in some cases, eradicate. Being able to define yourself openly and fully is a privilege; it is a grace many take for granted. The ability to walk into a meeting or an interview, or to interact with a police officer, and be given the respect and opportunity to present yourself without pre-judgement, can be life-defining, life-affirming and life-saving.

To strip an individual of that privilege is destructive enough. But when you apply this reductive treatment to an entire community, country or race, you create a poisonously false narrative that permeates for generations, until the fiction becomes fact, which in turn becomes an infected shared wisdom steadily passed down – in schools, at family dinner tables, in words pressed into books, and in the images that populate our popular culture.

Few entities have been forced through this field of distorted reality as many times as Africa – a continent of fifty-four countries, more than two thousand languages, and 1.4 billion people. A region that is treated and spoken of as if it were a single country, devoid of nuance and cursed to be forever plagued by deprivation.

For too long, 'Africa' has been treated as a buzzword for poverty, strife, corruption, civil wars, and large expanses of arid red soil where nothing but misery grows. Or it is presented as one big safari park, where lions and tigers roam freely around our homes and Africans spend their days grouped in warrior tribes, barely clothed, spears palmed, hunting game, and jumping up and down with ritualistic rhythm to pass the time before another aid package gets delivered. Poverty or safari, with nothing in between.

No matter how hard I try to explain that I was raised in a sprawling metropolis with all the twists and tricks of a sprawling metropolis, too many can only imagine what they've been programmed to believe. They cannot picture my mum's primary school, with happy, well-nourished children bursting through the gates every morning, because various international charities have them convinced that to be young in Africa is to be surrounded by flies and fuelled with nothing but contaminated drinking water; that to be African is a daily exercise in barely escaping the clutches of a rotating cast of free-roaming warlords in dirty fatigues, hanging off the back of 4x4 Jeeps that whizz along dirt jungle paths.

In reality, Africa is a rich mosaic of experience, of diverse communities and histories, and not a singular monolith of predetermined destinies. We sound different, laugh differently, craft the mundane in uniquely mundane ways, and our moral compasses do not always point in the same direction.

This book is a portrait of modern Africa that pushes back against harmful stereotypes to tell a more comprehensive story – based on all the humanity that has been brushed aside to accommodate a single vision of blood, strife, and majestic shots of rolling savannahs and large yellow sunsets. It will unspool the inaccurate story of a continent, dragging this bludgeoned narrative towards reality.

Real challenges exist on the continent. To ignore them would be just as grave a distortion. Many do live in destitution; some governments have failed their citizens; and in parts, the gap between the wealthy and the forgotten continues to grow. But when you infuse this story with context, you see the bigger picture and understand why what has happened has happened. When you remember the cards the region was dealt as a result of colonialism, and the way European empires divvied up the fruitful and fertile land, tore apart 10 per cent of all ethnic groups – forcing grossly different cultures to form singular nations against their will – and stole 90 per cent of the continent's material cultural legacy; when you remember all this is recent history, and that my parents are older than the country they were born in; when you discover the high prevalence of dictatorships is a multifaceted tale of colonial powers deliberately playing tribal groups off against each other, with Western nations propping up their favourite strongman, and it's not that we are naturally bloodthirsty and ungovernable; when you taste

Jollof rice for the first time, or see the work that activists and generations of reformers have put in since the independence era, you begin to
understand that Africa is a region that is fundamentally rooted in
human stories – which, like everywhere else, can be anything and everything, from a celebration of greatness to an act of barbaric cruelty. The
continent constantly surprises, because every country is just trying to
make the best of – to put it mildly – an awkward situation.

Each chapter of this book will bring the context that is often missing in
discussions about Africa to the fore. You will discover how each country
was formed by people with poor maps and even poorer morals. I will
analyse the harmful ways Africa is depicted through cheap stereotypes
in popular culture, and in the imagery used by charitable campaigns to
elicit quick-fix solutions that often do more harm than good, by pushing negative typecasting. You will understand the story of democracy
across the continent through seven dictatorships; the ongoing battle to
have the artefacts and treasures that were stolen during the colonial
period returned; and the impact food culture from across the continent
has had on rituals throughout the world. Identity also requires a healthy
rivalry, and you will discover the fabled Jollof rice wars and the strange,
incongruent beauty of the Africa Cup of Nations. In the final section, I
explore the present, and how locally led, on-the-ground activists, movements and emerging creative and business cultures are shaping the
future of the continent, speaking to how communities are actually
built – efforts that represent more than just dusty savannahs, civil wars,
and a people without a voice of their own waiting for someone to speak
for us, for others to swoop in and save.

But first, before we dive into the history of the continent, I want to
take you to Lagos, my familial hometown, to show the present-day realities. Though this book is no travel guide of places to stay and sights to
see, it is important to understand the varied specificity of the region. It's

vital to immediately ground yourself in an environment; see, smell and envision yourself in the everyday, not hovering a mile above ground or surveying through a pair of binoculars. And no place is more distinct than the continent's most populous city: the blackest place in the world, sewn together by little more than optimism and vibes.

There is a fundamental misunderstanding as to what is happening in this great expanse of land. This book aims to fill that void, while showcasing a deep and enduring love of the region – as a concept, as a reality and as a promise. And should you come away with just one thing, then I want you to know, for certain, deep down in your innermost core, that the continent is a coalition of over a billion individual identities that structure specifically.

That Africa is not a country.

Part One

Lagos

LAGOS is full.

At any moment, Nigeria's unofficial capital is certain to burst, revealing it's been hiding a smaller, more functional metropolis this whole time. By population, it's London, New York and Uruguay combined, with room to spare for any Latvian curious to sample the world's most perfectly seasoned chaos. It's three times Johannesburg and Nairobi, double Cairo, and could fit everybody in Namibia twenty times over. Ghana is a great nation – but no one would notice if you swapped Ghana's entire population size for the Lagos metropolitan area.

Lagos is the punchline to a joke that could start: 'Twenty-one million people unburdened by self-doubt walk into a bar . . .' The point is: there are a lot of people in Lagos. None of them are shy.

Lagos is loud and plagued by joy. It sounds like impatience and over-familiarity. It moves like a culture built on faith and certainty being the same thing. It's stitched to the same vague tones of a dream, where imagination seems to outpace movement, and progress is grounded in intention, if not reality. You're hearing a never-ending scream of car horns, reminding you that, at their core, Nigerians love nothing more than to warn you of their presence. Here in Lagos it's understandable, though – everyone is either driving too fast to be preoccupied with your safety, or fixed in the bumper-to-bumper traffic that scars every inch of the city; threading through the region's two main hubs, the Mainland and Lagos Island; crawling past districts soaked in wealth and culture, and neighbourhoods where families are literally living in swamps. Traffic, in fact, is the city's official sport – an unavoidable discipline for everyone, from waiters to the CEOs of multinational banks. One of the hundreds of government officials that litter Lagos Island could try swapping the city's upmarket restaurants and shopping centres for a trip to Rwanda's Kigali or Abidjan in the Ivory Coast, to discover how road travel does not have to be the enemy of joy.

For everyone who is not an elected official in Lagos, thinking small is a sin, as is arriving anywhere on time. You will come to reason that, if everyone is running late, then everyone is actually early. Many of your habits will change. You will become possessed of a passion for using your outside voice at all times, regardless of location and in spite of circumstance – to welcome, to explain, to pray, to haggle, to wish someone well, to wish someone great harm. Live in Lagos and you will learn to speak the local dialect – 'Please hurry up; I don't have time' – sooner than you wish. You will learn to feign offence when someone tries to hustle you, because you understand that the game is the game, and in the end the house always wins.

Lagos smells like fresh fruit and diesel. On the weekends, you're never more than half a mile from an MC begging for silence from a crowd dressed in Technicolor fabrics that were intricately tailored to scream: 'Do you know who I am?' Never answer that question, or in time you will discover Lagosians understand the devastating effects of bottling up a grievance. Plan it right, and you can hit three wedding receptions on any given Saturday. Time it to perfection, and you'll hear Davido sing 'If I tell you say I love you, oh . . .' no fewer than eight times.

Everything in Lagos is negotiable. It's just up to you to draw the line. Exhibit A: Upon realising that they had lost our beloved family dog, our vet tried offering us someone else's dog as a replacement, confident that we might grow to love this substitute. The fact that it very much did not belong to us was a minor detail, as was whatever arrangement they would later try to make with the family on the other side of this pact. We politely declined the offer and forcefully encouraged the vet to keep looking, until, eventually, they tracked down our good boy.

Lagos is highs of 40 degrees and lows of persistent power cuts. Its vistas are framed by large palm trees and an almost 100 per cent Black demographic. Every day, the piercing sun sprays across the city's natural grey filter, through a swarm of bright yellow buses, past the tall buildings and high walls that divide Lagos into tiny economic destinies, and sticks to what science believes to be the happiest people on earth. If the sun catches right on a relatively calm weekend morning – though 'relative calm' is a warped concept in Lagos – you can take a slow drive nowhere in particular, just to taste the city without letting it consume you – an easy mistake to make.

I have never seen an elephant in Lagos, or a leopard, but I have seen a fight break out at a party over the uneven distribution of souvenirs. You will not spot any of the Big Five game animals here – a safari tour of Lagos would be an adventure to spot the shrewdest car mechanics on the planet, multistorey housing blocks, and large bountiful markets that will sell it or make it or find it, if only you can describe it. Wind down and hear strangers converse as if they were family, because in a city where you need the favour of others to survive, you never know where you can acquire those favours.

The only guaranteed equality in Lagos is Suya – small strips of grilled meat at once turbulently spicy and graciously sweet, sliced on the side of the road, served with a side of onions and thick slabs of the northern Nigerian dialect Hausa, then wrapped in sheaths of newspaper and best consumed immediately after unwrapping, still hot, still coated in thick, burnt-charged smoke. Suya kisses every corner of Lagos life, because it's cheap and unreasonably delicious. It's broken up traffic jams and has made more palatable thousand-strong weddings that make you question the abstract of family. It's served at kids' birthday parties and used to give bougie hotels a semblance of authenticity.

Suya is a dance of still and sudden. You could say the same for Ikeja, the neighbourhood I grew up in. At times turbulently spicy, then graciously sweet. The roads that snake through our neighbourhood were peaceful enough for me to learn to drive on, but to walk alongside them, unprotected by a mesh of metal, was to play a game you would ultimately lose.

Every country has one city that soaks up attention and attracts origin stories and myths that are repeated back in smaller hometowns, by those bragging about all they have achieved under the floodlights. You either live in it or resent it. Lagos is no different: the city commands waves of raw energy that require you to adapt or stay at home. It's a magnet for people ready to hustle, to make it or keep it. It's New York if New York actually committed to not sleeping. Thousands of people arrive each day. You can escape Lagos, temporarily, but nobody seems to leave it.

Lagos is a place for outsiders willing to immediately become insiders. You're welcome – regardless of race, ethnicity and background – just don't expect to be given a starter pack. This inwardness breeds a specific pace, but also means the city is too stubborn to realign itself for tourism. Still, it would do well to embrace the work of Marrakech or Algiers in institutionalizing the preservation of their greatest hits, for their own and others to enjoy. In the early nineteenth century, for example, free slaves from Brazil returned to Lagos, bringing back with them physical and religious aesthetics from the new world, which they used to build a Brazilian quarter in the city that features some of the most beautiful architecture in the country – much of which has been allowed to degrade, rather than being optimised for the city.

In all this, it's hard to know whether the city is a concept or an experiment – but whichever it is, Lagos remains truly humbling; big enough to dwarf any ego. Something about being in Lagos forces you to be *of Lagos*. It has a way of moulding its own intentions for your life, over and around whatever misguided ambitions you had. It's a sentiment easy to romanticise but can often be exhausting. The city's unknown physics are not poetic, but a consequence of nobody taking the time to design it with intent. So instead, Lagos is governed by confidence – an innate, unshakeable certainty that the city is home to the continent's finest; a system of deep faith born from having the world's highest ratio of people to good dancers, and a palpable belief that *God dey*.

The overall effect is this constant sense of imbalance. Lagos has everything it could ever need to be *the* great city. Lagos has no idea what it wants to be when it grows up.

Megacities are traditionally motivated by an urgency to be the next big thing invading your timelines. Accra. Kinshasa. Nairobi.

But Lagos is in no such rush, instead betting on the city's main informal economy – optimism – and that no other city in Africa will ever surpass it in size and cult of personality. Still, Lagos Island has always offered clues to the best version of the city's future. Three large concrete bridges bind Lagos Mainland to a cluster of islands collectively known as 'the Island'. Large plazas tower over high-walled mansions finished in faux-gold, because here a show of wealth and status, real or imagined, is far more lucrative than money.

From the neighbourhoods of Ikoyi, Victoria Island and Lekki, a thriving arts and nightlife scene has emerged, and this has nourished a new wave of new-media-savvy creatives who are no longer trying to mimic American artists, but proudly creating work in their own accents. Now the Island provides your fix of art galleries, club nights, and overpriced smoothies flavoured with local spices that were never intended for crushed fruits. It's where you go for artisanal donuts and to hire boats that will speed you and your friends along the Atlantic Ocean to one of the many party beaches dotting the coast.

Ultimately, Lagos will only be able to say it's truly made it when the majority of the metropolis can dip into this pool of prosperity. When thousands of people are not living in houses perched on stilts stuck in a lagoon. Meanwhile, the city's identity remains fractured, in sharp, oddly shaped pieces – 21 million individual fragments that, when stitched into a somewhat coherent canvas, show a Lagos that is, if anything at all, remarkably full.

*

Of all the truths about Lagos and the many complex cities on this complex continent forced to find their feet in no time at all, one speaks loudest to the current realities: these places are the products of an aftershock from the time Europe's most powerful countries conspired to divide and devour an entire continent.

The colonisers' plans required many steps. The first of which was to draw a map.

Part Two

By the Power Vested in Me,
I Now Pronounce You a Country

The white man is very clever. He came quietly and peaceably with his religion. We were amused at his foolishness and allowed him to stay. Now he has won our brothers, and our clan can no longer act like one. He has put a knife on the things that held us together and we have fallen apart.

— Chinua Achebe, *Things Fall Apart*

I.

A map is a divided thing.

To imagine a map is to picture a clean rendering of colour-coordinated division. Boundaries split seas from their source, towns from their twins, and people from their destinies. When performing at its best, a map should help locate individual entities that, ideally, exist in those locations. A generous spirit might allow a map some margin of error. But should you arrive at a desired spot and find a molehill where you needed a mountain, then what guided you there was not a map, but a fable in which you were, unsuspectingly, the main character.

THE MAP WAS LARGE and wrong; impressive and inaccurate. By height, it was sixteen feet of topographic nonsense, outlined by men who had never set foot in 90 per cent of the land it claimed to portray. The drawing was largely based on reports of adventures around the region's coastline, where humans were weighed, shackled, then traded away into slavery; stories of vast pools of water; tales of regions where the sun was hot but agreeable, and where local diseases were believed to be sufficiently mild that it was possible a white man would not die within ten hours of his toes landing on hard soil.

Many of these white men – whom history requires we politely call 'explorers' – did die quickly, because diseases are complex mutational organisms, the sun is rarely loyal to strangers, and some local rulers realised that maybe, just maybe, these White Men In Khaki did not have their community's best interests at heart. But the White Men In Khaki who did manage to survive knew they were on to something special; and they were, because for centuries the native population had worked to make it so. Undeterred, they kept searching and exploring, unaided by the inconvenient trivialities of rules or a moral compass.

However, just as disappointment strikes a teenager who discovers his favourite band has gone mainstream, these travellers soon realised that their 'discovery' was not solely their own. They weren't concerned with the presence of the actual local people – mothers, fathers, children, doctors, teachers, poets – who lived on the lands they were trudging through for the very first time, in their wide-legged boots and sweat-drenched nostalgia for great explorers of the past. That didn't seem to bother them at all. What struck fear into their innards was that rival European nations were also sniffing around, looking to carve out sizeable chunks of empire for themselves. The explorers worried that everything would soon be claimed. And so rivals from all corners of Western Europe – names that are still taught with glory in schools, such as Livingstone and Stanley – started a race, later coined the Scramble for Africa, to own as much of somebody else's continent as they could.

This scramble was competitive, involving multiple heavyweight nations of the age of empire building. With that came the threat of a damaging international conflict. Not with local communities across the African continent – with their inconvenient hopes and dreams and physical bodies – but among the Western nations who wanted a piece of the pie.

In an attempt to avoid all-out war over who got to wage war on Africa, the mighty colonialists decided to meet and hash it all out, to come to a communal understanding as to how they could perfectly calculate their siege. And so the White Men In Khaki gathered at the Berlin Conference on the snowy afternoon of 15 November 1884, where they sat under a large map.

The drawing loomed large over a horseshoe-shaped table at 77 Wilhelmstrasse, the official residence of the German chancellor, Otto von Bismarck. The men who had gathered there had no real idea of what they were looking at; they had no concrete understanding of the intricacies of the map's interior; their knowledge was constricted by their previously singular interest in shipping off slaves from the coast. Looking now to the future, it was the promise of Africa's vast natural resources that made confiscating its fate such a tempting prospect. Some of them referred to Africa as the Dark Continent, recognising that, to them, the region was unknown. Nevertheless, knowing how little they knew didn't deter them. It wasn't knowledge they were in Berlin to devour.

The men in the room represented the interests of fourteen nations: Britain, France, Portugal, the Netherlands, Denmark, Spain, Italy, Belgium, Austria-Hungary, Russia, Sweden-Norway, the Ottoman Empire, the United States and Germany. They were there at Bismarck's invitation; the chancellor worried that the scramble for the continent was leaving Germany behind. He needed to slow things down and ensure that his country had a fair grab at the loot.

For the next three months, these men worked towards an amicable agreement for exactly how to partition the African continent without starting wars with each other. To do that, they needed to understand what was yours and what was mine. They had to establish if it was enough to just say they wanted a certain area, or if they had to be in close proximity to a region when they claimed it; if they had to plant a physical flag, or if they needed to kill every dissident ethnic group that stood in their way before it was truly theirs.

This formal procedure wasn't convenient for everyone. Some preferred a more relaxed approach to the conquest of indigenous peoples. But one thing almost all agreed on was that it was their natural right to explore the region and to take what they wanted. Or, as the prominent academic John Westlake elegantly said at the time:

The inflow of the white race cannot be stopped where there is land to cultivate, ore to be mined, commerce to be developed, sport to enjoy, curiosity to be satisfied. If any fanatical admirer of savage life argued that the whites ought to be kept out, he would only be driven to the same conclusion by another route, for a government on the spot would be necessary to keep them out. Accordingly, international law has to treat natives as uncivilised. It regulates, for the mutual benefit of civilised states, the claims which they make to sovereignty over the region and leaves the treatment of the natives to the conscience of the state to which the sovereignty is awarded.

More simply: if you were civilised people like us, you would be able to protect yourself from the sudden arrival of an invading army that wanted to rule you and claim everything you possess. That is the true measure of a cultured people.

Eighty per cent of Africa was still free when Bismarck rose to stand in front of that map at around 2 p.m. on the first day of the conference. (Within thirty years of that moment, 90 per cent of Africa would be controlled by Europe.)

Until then, the continent had been made up of vast ancient kingdoms, smaller nomadic communities, and everything in between. The European view had been that Africa's interior was largely to be avoided. If the climate didn't kill you, malaria and other tropical diseases would almost certainly do the required heavy lifting. The region was a place you stopped in briefly, to pick up strong Black men and transport them to slave plantations in exchange for sugar or whatever else you could weigh a person's life against. But by the mid- to late-nineteenth century, medicine had developed to such a point that Africa had lost its greatest defence against the sort of debilitating incursion that leaves a scar.

Bismarck began his welcome speech by reminding everyone that they were all good people. Good people with noble aims. He reinforced the notion that it was the uncivilised African natives and their uncivilised land that would benefit most from being served the three Cs that Livingstone had previously prescribed, and the conference aimed to bring: commerce, Christianity and civilisation. By opening up the vast continent to colonisation, they would help the natives become wiser and better.

Nobody disagreed.

From the very beginning, the conference pretended to be concerned with the economic development of the region for its people. Of course, any benefits to the helpful Western nations would simply be a fortunate by-product. Mutually guaranteed success for them as they mutually agreed to someone else's destruction.

Hovering over the conference was the inconvenient question of whether any of this was even legal, according to well-established international law. As a sidestep, Bismarck announced that the conference wouldn't bog itself down in discussions about the legal quagmire of sovereignty, or whether any of the gathered delegates actually had the authority to claim inhabited land for themselves. They would, instead, just focus on establishing guidelines that would govern everyone's behaviour when it came to picking which bits of prime-cut Africa they wanted for their respective empires. Bismarck laid out the aims of the conference, which were:

> To regulate the conditions most favourable to the development of trade and civilisation in certain regions of Africa, and to assure to all nations the advantages of free navigation on the two chief rivers of Africa flowing into the Atlantic Ocean [the Congo and the Niger] . . . to obviate the misunderstanding and disputes which might in the future arise from new acts of occupation on the coast of Africa . . . [and to further] the moral and material well-being of the native populations.

It's important, at this point, to recognise a small contradiction in Bismarck's stated aims – the little nuisance flapping in their ointment of reality. By the end of the conference, the fourteen assembled interests wanted a future for the continent that allowed far-off strange nations to freely fuel their pleasures with Africa's most lucrative resources, all while keeping the local people happy by developing their perceived undeveloped minds with a copy of the Bible, a smile and weapons. That was a lot to achieve, especially considering not a single person from the African continent was invited to take part in the Berlin Conference.

If African representatives had been invited, perhaps they would have objected. Or, at the very least, pointed out that drawing random straight lines on an inaccurate map might lead to some long-term internal frictions that would inevitably take generations and generations and generations to untangle from their cursed roots. Perhaps African representatives would have chosen to identify on the map which communities spoke which languages and worshipped which gods. Some thought might have gone into how dangerous it could be to run a border through proud, ancient kingdoms and cultures, and how forcing disparate ethnic groups to live under a single banner might make governing these wholly invented nations somewhat complicated. Perhaps a discussion might have broken out about what constituted civilised and uncivilised, savages and cultured, the developed and undeveloped world.

Perhaps.

But that didn't happen. And it was by design; it wasn't as if they couldn't find anyone from the continent willing to influence the future dealings of their own region. The Sultan of Zanzibar had explicitly asked to attend. He was not invited.

The diplomats at the conference were happy to avoid discussing the moral implications of apportioning someone else's land and property. Except for, it turned out, the representative of the United States, who wanted to understand whether in the future they needed the 'voluntary consent of the natives whose country is taken possession of, in all cases where they had not provoked the aggression'. He wanted to know this because 'modern international law follows closely a line which leads to the recognition of the right of native tribes to dispose freely of themselves and of their hereditary territory'. What they were doing was illegal, and they all knew it. However hard they dressed it up as a humanitarian or Christian attempt to rid

African natives of their so-called inherent backwardness, it was, by the standards of then – and now – grossly illegal and ethically indecent. They knew this when they shot down the American's question and reminded him that the conference did not intend to discuss sovereignty. To admit to the reality of the gathering would ruin a perfectly good opportunity to literally divide and conquer an entire continent, trading cards like it was all a game.

Still, they clearly needed to find a way of talking about sovereignty and flag-planting without talking about sovereignty and flag-planting. To achieve this, they devised more ephemeral notions of 'presence' and 'control'. Just enough to ensure that, later on, they would be able to resolve any misunderstandings amicably.

From there, they arrived at the most important item on the agenda: setting the actual ground rules for the slicing and dicing. You couldn't, of course, just have fourteen nations rushing in to grab whatever they wanted. That would be rude and uncivilised.

They eventually settled on the 'principle of effective occupation' – a phrase that was deliberately broad, and could be moulded to include all kinds of meanings and intentions. It essentially created a permission structure for countries to confiscate large swathes of land. Under this principle, European powers could claim authority over a region for a host of reasons that were in no way limited to having signed an agreement with local rulers. Whether their presence was welcomed or not made no difference. To colonise an area, you needed to: i) inform the other European powers of your claim, and ii) prove you'd established some governance, forced or otherwise.

You couldn't just point at the map and say you wanted something; you had to explore it and secure it by any means necessary. The 'necessary' means were often military. You could claim effective occupation of an area by setting up a police or military force that was, in some way, able to keep the peace (though the definition of 'peace' was clearly rather fluid). Another European power could not then come in afterwards and steal what you had stolen.

That was largely it. Keeping the rules deliberately loose meant countries did not have to put much effort into territories whose long-term value they were uncertain of.

After negotiations, the conference finally finished on 26 February 1885. Bound by their commitment to avoid any talk of sovereignty, the group didn't draw physical borders on the giant map and hand out portions of destiny right there and then. They decided to deal with the details later. But what they did instead was just as impactful. They devised the General Act of the Berlin Conference – a document that codified the end of Africa's right to self-determination, and accelerated the rush to gorge on the continent until it was picked clean. The document may not have been the starter gun for the Scramble, but it would spark the all-out mission of occupation.

Yet even then, at the tail end of the nineteenth century, world leaders were mindful of public perception. So the General Act, in a pretence of humanitarian concern, vaguely promised that the Europeans would work to end the slave trade in the region. Of course, they weren't bound to this promise in any way. Anyone paying attention could see this was a sham, and nobody on the continent was tricked. The reviews of the conference in Africa were not, to say the least, glowing. 'The world had, perhaps, never witnessed a robbery on so large a scale,' was the *Lagos Observer*'s verdict. 'A forcible possession of our land has taken the place of a forcible possession of our person.' A newspaper on the Gold Coast (modern-day Ghana) reworked a popular hymn to read: 'Onward Christian soldiers unto heathen lands / Prayer books in pockets, rifles in your hands / Take the happy tidings where trade can be done / Spread the peaceful gospel with the Gatling guns.'

And in an article in the May 1915 issue of the *Atlantic Monthly*, the legendary American civil rights activist and writer W. E. B. Du Bois noted:

> Before the Berlin Conference had finished its deliberations they had annexed to Germany as an area over half as large again as the whole German Empire in Europe. Only in its dramatic suddenness was this undisguised robbery of the land of seven million natives different from the methods by which Great Britain and France got four million square miles each, Portugal three-quarters of a million, and Italy and Spain smaller but substantial areas.
>
> The methods by which this continent has been stolen have been contemptible and dishonest beyond expression. Lying treaties, rivers of rum, murder, assassination, mutilation, rape, and torture have marked the progress of Englishman, German, Frenchman, and Belgian on the dark continent. The only way in which the world has been able to endure the horrible tale is by deliberately stopping its ears and changing the subject of conversation while the deviltry went on.'

When it came to signing and ratifying the General Act, the United States was the only country which declined. Everyone else agreed on the vague, difficult-to-enforce rules that came out of three months of haggling. Africa was now officially for the taking; it was right there in writing.

Moves to colonise the continent had started way before anyone sat round that table or hung up that map in Berlin. But here at the conference, almost every European nation conspired to cross into a new world that was not their own, and to open a door they did not build, plant flags on soil that scorched their feet, and keep a peace that was disturbed by their presence. The expansionist direction Europe was moving in was clear.

Some historians have argued that because the Berlin Conference didn't actually hand out land in some raffle-esque prize draw, the meeting was limited in its impact. But as the journalist Patrick Gathara writes: 'It did something much worse . . . with consequences that would reverberate across the years and be felt until today . . . in the process legitimising the ideas of Africa as a playground for outsiders, its mineral wealth as a resource for the outside world not for Africans and its fate as a matter not to be left to Africans.'

That Africa's fate should not be left to Africans has been the West's go-to strategy in the region for almost every one of the 137 years since. It's how modern treaties are organised and charitable donations are shared. It's the attitude on display when governments, themselves struggling with democracy, release patronising statements about how African countries should respect democracy. This mindset simplified the complex ecosystems of a landmass that covered more than 11 million square miles and was home to hundreds of millions of people as blank spaces on an atlas that could be claimed by turning up and alerting your friends to your presence, and declaring authority over the bodies and traditions of everyone who had existed there for generations. But Africa is more; it's always been more. The Berlin Conference did not see this because they allowed a large, inaccurate map to hover over every decision they made. They honed in on what Africa could be for them.

And what it could be for Europe turned out to be a lot. For Africa, it turned out to be everything.

*

II.

A border is a divided thing.

A series of cursive entanglements, built to both contain and separate; encourage and scare away. A border should be malleable, taking into consideration the delicate specificities of the things it is trying to group together, and the things it needs to keep apart. Visibility is important; intent is vital.

THE FIRST COUNTRY TO BE CREATED after the Berlin Conference was a product of the personal passion of King Leopold II of Belgium – a monarch deeply frustrated that his position came with very few actual responsibilities. His simple request to the other European colonialists was that they would allow him to rule a large portion of Central Africa that seemed to hold very little value to the other men. In return, he promised to work towards ending slavery, and to stick to the plan of civilising the African people who fell under his rule through Christianity and commerce, while allowing free-trade access to everyone else.

Back in their own countries, nobody raised objections because none of them knew enough about the area to justify putting up a fight. And at least for now, they figured, if anyone was going to have this large chunk of territory, it was probably better to give it to the Bored King rather than a powerful rival.

Little did they know that, a decade before the Berlin Conference, Leopold had hired the British-American explorer Henry Morton Stanley to scout the region on his behalf. They both liked what Stanley found, especially the natural resources – rubber and ivory – and access to the Congo River. The explorer had quickly started the process of deceiving local rulers into giving up their land, forcing them to sign treaties they didn't understand in exchange for worthless gifts of beads and other accoutrements.

The Belgian government didn't want the colony, however. Instead, they passed a resolution that gave it to the Bored King to do with as he pleased. And so, just like that, in 1885 a region five times the size of Belgium and home to what was then an estimated 25 million people became the official private property of a jaded fifty-year-old man with nothing to do. Leopold would combine the separate ethnic groups across this portion of Central Africa under his singular rule, and call the amalgamated region the Congo Free State. In time, this invented reality would become the country that we now know as the Democratic Republic of Congo (DRC). Today, the DRC is the eleventh-largest nation by area in the world.

The newly established Congo Free State did not go well. The Bored King soon realised that running a country as your personal side project was extremely expensive, especially when personal profit was your only measure of success. Leopold was losing money fast, and the Belgian government was threatening to force a sale if he couldn't find a way to turn things around. He needed his newly acquired subjects to start making him rich(er).

Having promised to help end slavery, the Bored King put the previously free Congolese people to work as slaves, forcing them to extract rubber from wild vines to feed the growing global tyre industry. When workers sliced into the vines, the rubber would splash out onto their bodies, creating a thick layer that was painful to remove. To maximise labour, much of this work was leased to private companies with low morals and dubious working practices to administrate.

Any Congolese who refused to work was shot dead by Leopold's private army. Anyone who didn't work fast enough to hit their quotas was shot dead. To ensure his army was policing the slaves efficiently and not wasting their expensive bullets on anything other than murdering locals, officers were required to produce a severed hand for every person killed, as proof that Leopold's brutal regime was economically prudent.

In the twenty years following the Bored King's purchase of the

DRC, it's estimated that around half the population – 10 million people – died as a direct result of his reign. When word spread internationally of the atrocities being committed, Belgium eventually took the Congo Free State from the king in 1908, turning it into the Belgian Congo until the Congolese secured independence in 1960.

Leopold died without ever once going to Africa. His gruesome reign should have been a lesson to the other participants involved in the Scramble. Instead, it was a premonition of what was to come.

With the same energy as rival grifters receiving the coordinates to an unlocked bank vault in a heist film, the colonial powers raced from Berlin to steal as much land as they could grab, with France and Britain turning out to be the most gluttonous competitors.

Before the conference, the French had made some early moves, invading Algeria in 1830. Through the slave trade, they also had an established presence in the area that is now Senegal. All they had to do was expand their on-the-ground presence there, fully colonising the region in 1854 by combining multiple local kingdoms into one area under French control.

After Berlin, France really accelerated their land grab. While Leopold took the larger chunk of the region, below the Congo River, France secured control of the north-western side, now known as the Republic of Congo, and they had also been permitted to pop over Algeria's northern border to take Tunisia, under the pretext that Tunisia was harbouring rebels. France was particularly interested in consolidating its power in West and North Africa, with multiple military generals forcing local leaders to sign treaties to hand over their lands, using violence when deemed necessary. 'Our possession on the West Coast is possibly the one of all our colonies that has before it the greatest future; and it deserves the whole sympathy and attention of the Empire,' French general Louis Faidherbe, who became the governor of Senegal, said at the time.

By the time the Bored King of Belgium had really upped the violence in the Congo Free State, France crossed from Senegal into areas that were home to disparate ethnic groups and communities – which would later be clumsily demarcated to become Mali, Burkina Faso, Niger and Benin – right until they crashed into what we now know as western Nigeria, where the British were busy marshalling their own strongholds. In an attempt to avoid their simmering mutual resentment turning into full-fledged war, it was at this point that the British and the French decided it was a more fruitful idea to throw down some lines, to create borders and then countries out of thin air, so each knew exactly what belonged to them.

This series of private agreements between France and Britain, signed between 1880 and 1898, effectively created nations out of nothing. Neither was completely happy with the outcome, so from time to time they would swap bits as they pleased, cutting out large chunks of territory and handing it to the other based on whatever natural resources each coveted at that moment. Colonial moulding in West Africa produced for France: Guinea, Ivory Coast, Mali, Burkina Faso, Niger, Senegal and Benin; while Britain carved out the Gambia, Nigeria, Ghana and Sierra Leone. As described by a historian in 1911, the region was sliced up as such:

> Gambia was to comprise 10 kilometres on both sides of the river and to extend as far into the interior as Yarbatenda. Sierra Leone was to end at 10 degrees north latitude, Gold Coast and Lagos at the 9th degree and Dhomey and Lagos to be separated by a line from the intersection of the meridian of the Ajarra creek and the coast to the 9th degree . . . the western limits of the British Lagos-Nigeria protectorate were left indefinite north of the 9th degree north latitude; and various other vital matters were not seriously considered.

A similar set of treaties expanded France's influence in Central Africa, winning them land that now constitutes Chad, the Central African Republic, and the part of the Congo in which Leopold was not then murdering half the population – though France was obviously doing some butchering of its own to secure all this land at such speed.

All France wanted from here was to secure its hold on North Africa by capturing Morocco and the land to the south – bordering Mali and Senegal – now known as Mauritania. It achieved the latter in 1904, when Britain recognised France's claim in exchange for France recognising Britain's grip on Egypt.

The British were old hands at this business. You could argue they invented the sport – they understood the plays and could execute under pressure when required. For centuries, they had been empire-building across Asia, the Americas and Australia; collecting trophies that ranged from gold to flesh.

Unlike the French, the British government preferred leasing much of the work involved in picking up colonies to private companies, before buying back the land from them later. It was a cheaper method, and the government could avoid the difficult administrative task of physically invading the different regions and forcibly extricating land from its historical ownership. To do this in West Africa, Britain leaned on the United African Company. Formed in 1879, it would rebrand two years later and become the National African Company, before changing its name again to the Royal Niger Company in 1886.

The Royal Niger Company focused its mission on the territories around the lower half of the Niger River. The agreements the company collated gave it control over a series of ancient local empires, which the company eventually sold to the British government, who later amalgamated them to form Nigeria in 1914. Incidentally, in the 1930s, the

Royal Niger Company would go on to take a final form, becoming part of a prominent multinational: Unilever.

Britain had a long history with the Gold Coast – an area along coastal West Africa where for centuries Europeans had fought over the control of two main commodities: slaves and gold. Over time, the British took charge of as many of the trading forts as possible, until by 1874 it controlled what is now Ghana.

On the other side of the continent, both Britain and Germany wanted slices of East Africa. As was now the accepted recourse, the two nations came to an agreement in 1886 to apportion it between themselves. Certain it was the source of the Nile, Britain wanted Lake Victoria and its surrounding fertile land. It got Lake Victoria and its fertile land, and with it an area that now encompasses Kenya, Uganda and parts of Tanzania. This was all secured by the British East African Company, which soon realised that it was expensive to run countries consisting of tens of millions of disparate people. It sold the region to the British government in 1895 for £250,000 (£33 million in today's money).

Meanwhile in southern Africa, the British mining magnate Cecil Rhodes (whose statue still stands at Oxford University, and who once said of the English: 'We are the first race in the world, and the more of the world we inhabit the better it is for the human race') was focusing on the betterment of his personal wealth. His dream was to build a railway that would connect the Cape Colony, which is now part of South Africa, to Egypt, with every bit of land in between owned by the British.

Rhodes had made his money from diamonds mined on the southern coast of Africa, and used that fortune to acquire land. His British South Africa Company – using a private army equipped with the latest advances in human-slaughter technology – spread itself across the Cape, forcing ethnic groups to hand over their territories. An 1891 border agreement with Portugal gave the British South Africa Company control over land Rhodes would later name after himself. The British also took what would become Malawi, while Portugal took control of Mozambique and Angola.

In an attempt to placate the Afrikaners – white Dutch settlers who had created their own states in the region and were frustrated at the British taking land that in their view they had rightly taken from others – Rhodes helped introduce a form of imperialism that would give the minority white community constitutional rule over the majority Black community. In Southern Rhodesia, white settlers made up less than 3 per cent of the population but were given more than 50 per cent of the land.

The Union of South Africa was created in 1910 by combining other southern colonies, and the white minority would institutionalise bigotry, implementing laws such as the Natives Land Act that gave the tiny proportion of white South Africans legal ownership of 87 per cent of the land, a discrepancy that effectively continues today. The laws seeded in this infant nation were cultivated, sprouting into the apartheid regime that would grip South Africa for decades.

The result of all this village-storming and treaty-signing was an Africa that was largely bought and designed by France, Britain and Belgium – three nations that had redrawn the boundaries of fate for tens of millions of people.

But others were playing, too. As well as picking up ground that would be squashed and bracketed to create Mozambique and Angola, Portugal had long-established control over a sliver of West African coastline between French-owned Guinea and Senegal that held a prominent port for the slave trade. Portugal would slowly gain more control inland, with the territory becoming known as Portuguese Guinea, and later, after independence, Guinea-Bissau. They were also able to control the adjacent islands of Cape Verde.

Germany's cut was focused in East Africa, though it lost almost all of it after World War I. A private arrangement with Britain secured its rights to the areas that would later become Burundi and Rwanda.

Compared to everyone else, Italy was not so quick on the draw. After the opening of the Suez Canal in 1869, Italian shipping companies started to purchase land around the port city of Assab, along the north-eastern coast of the continent. The British didn't mind, as it blocked some of France's moves in the region. Italy was able to send in troops and buy the land from the shipping companies, declaring it Italian Eritrea. It then spread its sphere of influence further eastward, into the tip of what is now northern Somalia. Italy also went to war with the Ottoman Empire in 1911 to claim the two colonies of Cyrenaica and Tripolitania, merging them to create Libya.

Arrive, manipulate, negotiate with a European adversary, conquer, move on. That's how 90 per cent of an entire continent was reformed by a handful of determined countries. All that was left was to draw some physical borders with the same care and consideration that brought the conquest in the first place.

A note: if you ever find yourself in a rush to invent an entire country because you fear all the good land will soon be taken by others, you may discover it's easy to overlook certain details that at first glance appear inconsequential. Yet, in time, after you've moved on to new adventures, they will begin to moulder and rot away, collapsing everything you built on top of them.

You don't need to know the difference between a river and an estuary until you absolutely need to know the difference between a river and an estuary. Estuaries famously detest being referred to as rivers, because they are the large body of water that multiple rivers flow into: the Grand Central Station of the maritime world.

The British and the Germans needed to know this information back in 1884, when it was time to agree exactly how they would forcibly partition hundreds of separate societies into just two nations: what we know today as Cameroon and Nigeria. Unfortunately, they wrongly identified the Akwayefe River as an estuary. This matters, because the two European countries decided on an invisible boundary, marked by the Akwayefe, to separate the areas of land that would make up British Nigeria and Germany's Cameroon. It matters because the exact shape of the Akwayefe determines whether the Bakassi Peninsula belongs to Nigeria or Cameroon. It matters because the Bakassi Peninsula is one of those rare regions of the world touched by the divine providence that says ye shall forevermore refer to it using the term that, translated into any language, means good times: *oil-rich*.

Unsurprisingly, since this boundary was imposed, both West African nations have tried to claim this well-resourced region as their own – so much so that they almost went to war over it in the '80s and '90s. To avoid this, they took their case to the International Court of Justice. Neither nation, however, could cite any historical or cultural claim to the land, because they were two arbitrary states effectively created as part of a business deal they didn't sign. Instead, both nations pored over the dusty old maps and treaties hidden in European archives that had been created by their colonisers, many of whom had never been to the Bakassi Peninsula. To understand the flavour of this quality material, here is how a British colonial officer in Nigeria described the method he used to shape the destiny of two future nations: 'In those days, we just took a blue pencil and a ruler and we put it down at Old Calabar, and drew that blue line to Yola ... I recollect thinking when I was sitting, having an audience with the Emir (of Adamawa), surrounded by his tribe, that it was a very good thing that he did not know, that I, with a blue pencil, had drawn a line through his territory.'

A hundred years after those rough blue-pencil marks hit paper, all Nigeria and Cameroon – two nations that collectively house the fortunes of 230 million people – could do was to present those etchings to a neutral body to translate and rule who got the oil. Cameroon won. But these two countries are not alone in facing the ramifications of poorly demarcated borders.

Uganda and the DRC share a border, part of which is meant to be delineated by the Semliki River, which flows from Lake Albert to Lake Edward. That's fine, until the river changes direction, of course. And thanks to global warming melting nearby mountain snow caps, the Semliki has shifted its course a hundred times in the past six decades alone. 'We never had an official boundary,' Mary Goretti Kitutu, Uganda's Minister of Energy and Mineral Development, told *The Independent* back in 2009. 'The colonialists just said "use the river" and that is what we had always gone with.' Communities that live near the river have switched over time from being Ugandan to Congolese and back again, because of a decision made by the Belgians over a century ago.

The border also cuts through Lake Albert. Oil has been discovered under Lake Albert. It's not hard to imagine what happened after a treasured resource was found near a mythical water border. Both countries, as anyone would, claimed it for their own, and an enduring conflict erupted along the fishing islands on the Albert.

Only 30 per cent of all borders in the world are in Africa, yet nearly 60 per cent of all territorial disputes that have made it to the International Court of Justice come from the continent. What's fuelling all this simmering tension is genuine, widespread confusion as to where one country ends and where another begins. Two-thirds of African countries have been involved in some fight over their shape and what exactly constitutes their nation. Many of these disputes have been deadly. Others have required the translation of inaccurate borders drawn using the precision of an Etch A Sketch (and an Etch A Sketch is far easier to erase).

*

The interior structure of modern Africa was built on greed rather than an informed reality. It's the same strategy my eleven-year-old nephew uses in negotiations: ignore the well-established rules and parameters, and demand a fairy-tale outcome that brings short-term joy, with the long-term consequences relegated to a problem for a future version of yourself to deal with.

Unfortunately for my nephew, he doesn't have an army at his disposal to force his will upon the world, nor has he successfully developed a way of enticing any adult apart from me to hand over large portions of their authority.

The colonial European powers very much did have the requisite power at their disposal. In the years following the Berlin Conference, they used their swords to sharpen those blue pencils and turn a fevered hallucination into a painful reality, creating problems for a future version of these colonies to deal with. They scribbled down treaties they would later break, using local translators who were not fluent in the ancient language of bad faith to negotiate the seizure of land from regional community leaders. One local translator would later reveal: 'I was not aware that "ceding" meant giving over the rights of government, and I dare not have made this suggestion to him.'

As the colonial agent A. F. Thurston put it:

I had a bundle of printed treaties which I was to make as many people sign as possible. This signing is an amiable farce, which is supposed to impose on foreign governments, and to be the equivalent of an occupation . . . A raggedy, untidy European, who in any civilised country would be in danger of being taken up by the police as a vagrant, lands at a native village; the people run away, he shouts out after them to come back, holding out before them a shilling's worth of beads . . .

The so-called interpreter pretends to explain the treaty to the chief. The chief does not understand a word of it, but he looks pleased as he receives another present of beads; a mark is made on a printed treaty by the chief, and another by the interpreter; the vagrant, who professes to be the representative of a great empire, signs his name . . . The boat sails away, and the new ally and protege of England or France immediately throws the treaty into the fire.

And when all else failed, they mounted up machine guns and fired at towns until there was nobody left to object.

All the European leaders knew the treaties were meaningless, often signed through coercion or agreed with someone pretending to be a local king. But it didn't matter, because the treaties showed their colonial rivals that they had conquered that piece of land, and fended off the competition. This approach continued until we arrived at the current configuration of states that collectively comprise the African continent.

The geographical arrangements of the late nineteenth century and the early twentieth century largely still stand. The damage this caused can be seen by casting an eye down a map of the continent and observing the outlines of each nation. You'll find an assortment of geometrical shapes that bear no relation to the topography, culture or languages of the land they apportion. Today, about 30 per cent of all African borders are straight lines. Just long, straight lines, purpose-built to cut through everything in their way. Borders – a border expert will tell you – should curve around real mountains and communities and landscapes. A border should be flexible enough to consider the delicate specificities of what it is trying to group together, and the characteristics of what it needs to keep apart. Though a straight line has its uses, a border, more often than not, should not be one of them.

But the aim of these demarcations was never to accurately acknowledge bonds among unified peoples whose common identity had been forged from centuries of the delightful mix of familial hope and tragedy that creates shared histories and mythically entangled futures.

These borders were not designed after long, considered consultation with experts and ethnic groups who could identify those of their own kin and congregation; individuals who could have explained their traditions and histories, and why it was important for their livelihoods and happiness that they be allowed to maintain their nomadic lifestyle and freely stroll on an autumn evening through their lands as they had always done, with their cattle by their side, busying themselves doing what cattle do to keep entire generations of a people fed.

If you were given the responsibility of creating a border that forever tied millions of people into a shared destiny, you might think to ask which ethnic groups have a dangerous history of going to war with each other.

That wasn't what happened, as the Nigerian academic Professor Anthony Asiwaju writes:

> Boundaries were drawn across well-established lines of communication, including: a sense of community based on tradition concerning common ancestry, usually very strong kinship ties, shared socio-political institutions and economic resources, common customs and practices, and sometimes acceptance of a common political control. In many instances . . . the boundary has separated communities of worshippers from age-old sacred groves and shrines. In other instances, well exemplified by the Somalis, the water resources in a predominantly nomadic culture area were located in one state and the pastures were in another.

The straight-line border drawn from Mount Kilimanjaro to Lake Victoria, for example, forced the nomadic Maasai to permanently divide between Kenya and what became Tanzania. Equally, the border between Sudan and Ethiopia caused the nomadic Anuak ethnic group to wonder why they were, for the first time in centuries, unable to wander where they pleased.

Separating ethnic groups in this way proved to be pivotal, and, in some cases, deadly. Take the Kakwa, for example. The British created a border that split the Kakwa ethnic group between southern Sudan and northern Uganda. When the Sudanese Kakwa joined southern Sudan in the civil war against northern Sudan, they were actively supported by the Ugandan military – as the then head of the army, a general by the name of Idi Amin, was a Kakwa.

Later, in 1971, when Idi Amin needed help in his power struggle against Ugandan president Milton Obote, the Sudanese Kakwa didn't hesitate to join his fight, with some five hundred guerrillas crossing the border to be by his side as he successfully orchestrated a coup. They were rewarded: by 1973, twenty-one of the top twenty-four positions in Amin's military were held by someone who was Kakwa or from southern Sudan. And of course, when Amin needed to flee the country after his government was toppled, he found refuge with the people he saw as his own, in Sudan. 'The long-ago partition of one small ethnic group,' wrote the Harvard professor Alberto Alesina, 'had terrible consequences for two separate artificial states – Uganda and Sudan.'

This pattern is replicated consistently across the continent. Researchers estimate that somewhere in the region of two hundred ethnic groups were forcibly split into multiple countries. This created nations born of a melding of adversaries, not genuine neighbours sharing a common spirit of understanding. And crucially, the boundaries that cut through their identities were forced upon them, opening a portal to a new world that could never be shut cleanly.

The only thing worse than having an arbitrary border is having an arbitrary border that nobody can see. Many countries are required to adhere to demarcations that were never laid down in reality. In a rush to make those boundary agreements with each other, the colonial powers skipped over surveying unknown territories. Instead, they often turned to shady treaties organised by agents on the ground who were more interested in getting regional rulers to sign their communities away than mapping out the depths of a hill or the curve of a river bend.

This has made it impossible for countries to fully understand the parameters of their own nations, especially when those ephemeral borders come close to a desired natural resource. Border communities, which are often poorer, continually suffer the most from the consequences of those fights. Far from creating bonds of unity, the colonial borders forced groups to compete for treasured prizes, not only for personal enrichment but to survive.

Before these arbitrary boundaries were made, communal loyalties on the continent were complicated. There were few urban centres as we would recognise them today. Societies were considerably smaller, and allegiances were linked more to the political authority that governed your specific clan or village than the land you lived on, making it easier for you to move around if required.

It wasn't until disparate communities were grouped together under the singular banner of an entirely invented nation that the local people were forced to recognise that resources and power might be limited, and it could be in their best interests to gather everyone who spoke the same language to form a nation within a nation, to formally organise and lobby for power in their assigned country.

This view was accelerated by a new invention, created miles away from where most people lived. The White Men In Khaki called this invention a 'capital city'. As far as most people understood it – many even to this day – a capital city was a mysterious enclave where powerful men who spoke a language unlike your own gathered to ration everything there was to ration within the country.

These Powerful Men In The Capital were given the authority to allo-
cate shares of life and death to whomever they pleased. Miraculously,
they often allocated the more desirable 'life' to a select few; firstly, to the
White Men In Khaki, then to those who looked and sounded identical
to These Powerful Men In The Capital.

It became clear that to beat These Powerful Men In The Capital and
take control of allocating life and death, you and your nation within a
nation had two options: become The Powerful Men In The Capital, or
build your own border around yourselves and establish your own
capital.

What's left from all this calculating is a continent of fundamentally
fragmented people adhering to agreements they had nothing to do with.
When independence eventually became possible in the twentieth century, countries were left with a choice. Stick or twist.

*

III.

A state is a divided thing.

Femi waited. Then waited.

His eyes darted between his classroom door and the clock hanging askew above it, anticipating. Waiting. Without a teacher to soak up their attention, his classmates wandered the room at ease, sitting on desks and exchanging rumours of what was to come, not just later that day, but in the future. Tales of a new beginning.

'My father said soon all the money the British have been stealing will return, and we will use it to become great,' a student offered to a congregation of attentive eyes.

'I heard every Nigerian will soon be given a house and a car to celebrate,' another countered.

Femi had heard those stories, too.

His family lived on a large rubber plantation. A rural respite fifteen miles from the nearest town. In the evenings, as the sun dropped behind the white man's house on the hill, his father would jostle the large antenna on their battery-powered radio, twisting and craning until the deep, crackling voice on the radio was clear.

'It is our belief that the people of western Nigeria in particular, and of Nigeria in general, would have life more abundant when they enjoy freedom from British rule,' the man on the radio proclaimed one evening. 'In our view, the rule of one nation by another is unnatural and unjust. It is maintained either by might or by complete subordination, through crafty means, of the will and self-respect of the subject people to the political self-aggrandisement of the tutelary power. There can be no satisfactory substitute for self-rule,' the same man professed on another night.

'Awolowo is just too much!' Femi's mother would smile whenever the de facto head of Nigeria's Yorubas finished one of his speeches.

Femi was seven. He didn't need to understand what Chief Obafemi Awolowo meant by 'political enslavement'. He didn't need to know who exactly was 'riddled with unspeakable ignorance', or even what 'riddled' meant. It didn't matter. Children have a way of extracting enough from tone and intent to grasp when they're about to be smothered in joy. For months, he could sense that intoxicating happiness expand and solidify until every adult around him was floating on it. And eventually, he was sure, he too would be high in the air, gliding, reaching towards the gloried 'soon' everyone spoke of.

The future eventually came, leaving Femi and his classmates staring at their classroom door until their teacher, Mr Chinedu, walked in carrying individual flags bearing the emblem of the independent country they had woken up in, and plates that would later be stained by molten red rice.

After everyone had grabbed a flag, Mr Chinedu led Femi's class in single file out of the room and through the school's main gate, until they reached an imposing football pitch where what seemed like the entire town had gathered to watch the students wave their flags and parade around the pitch, backed by musicians blasting on their talking drums and hawkers selling plantain *and Akara. Three-quarters of the way around the pitch, Femi turned and spotted his parents and younger siblings on the side. They exchanged broad smiles and blessed thoughts. Femi waved his flag even harder as he broke their gaze and continued on with the parade.*

Occasionally, an MC would call for silence as local politicians took turns to step on stage and speak and speak, each wanting an opportunity to establish their place at the beginning.

Later that evening, the entire neighbourhood squeezed into Femi's living room. I. K. Dairo's 'Ise Ori Ran Mi Mo Nse' sweetened the air. Cold bottles of stout did what cold bottles of stout do.

Outside in the courtyard, Femi sat alone in the evening heat, distracted by the words of the new national anthem swelling in his imagination, the words he had been made to practise for months and recite earlier that afternoon as a flag marked in green and white was hoisted up a pole. With his third and a half plate of Jollof rice balanced precariously on his lap, he stared unknowingly into the night, unable to fully envision what exactly was meant to come after an Independence Day. Not able to picture the factions that would form or the civil war that would unravel the optimistic origin story. He could not know at such a young age how far away 'soon' could truly be when committed interests align against it. He could not know how, even decades later, when his son would call to ask him to recount all he remembered from that day, he would still be waiting for that full measure of promise to arrive.

What he could do was quietly sit and hope that his parents would never stop dancing, and that the stories his friends told would come true, and that the man on the radio was right. Femi guided another spoonful of rice towards his face. And he waited for 'soon'.

As INDEPENDENCE MOVEMENTS swept across the continent in the '50s and '60s, newly formed African nations had no experience to guide them on how they should scour their manufactured identities for a unifying national soul. They were choked with the same headiness that grips your senses as you wait on the threshold of the perfect house party, doorbell rung, internally juggling hope and unknown possibilities, anticipation and courage and the smooth grace of chance.

They soon found it impossible to look beyond what was directly in front of their faces. Reckoning with their current state proved to be a full-time job. Many of these nations were strange, awkward things, with autonomous limbs that didn't really fit, guided by a multitude of brains working at vastly different frequencies, each controlling a wide array of powerful extremities. No wonder walking in a straight line proved a daily struggle. At their inception around sixty years ago, these nations were weak, unbalanced states, forever threatening to topple over and crush 1.2 billion people; states unable to recognise themselves, or their neighbours who were facing the same challenges.

The private agreements made by the European powers between 1884 and 1919 had blitzed and blended what were once proud, individual kingdoms, and as a result, African countries were faced with a difficult choice when they won their freedom: either to forge ahead and make the best of what they had, or redraw the entire map.

Nobody was fooled into thinking these borders were an act of divine inspiration. Everyone understood that they were part of a complex creation story that was selfishly messy and prone to plot holes that would certainly collapse under the weight of repeated viewings. Ethnic groups had been ripped apart, families had been ripped apart, languages had been ripped apart – a reality that was widely recognised across the continent. 'It was unfortunate that the African States have been broken up into different groups by the Colonial powers,' Nigerian prime minister Tafawa Balewa said in 1963. 'In some cases, a single tribe has been broken up into four different States. You might find a section in Guinea, a section in Mali, a section in Sierra Leone and perhaps a section in Liberia. That was not our fault.'

It wasn't. It was their responsibility, however, to carve out a path forward. The first obstacle was how to keep these nations culturally intact. This has arguably remained the region's biggest challenge. Back in the '60s, once the demographically varied inhabitants of these nations no longer shared a common foreign enemy, they had the time and clarity to realise that, apart from wishing their coloniser gone, ethnic groups shared almost nothing else – not a belief system, common language, morality structure nor deity. They had skipped the foundation of organic trust and understanding that is rooted in centuries' worth of nation building. And there certainly wasn't a strong bond between the rulers and the ruled, especially when the citizenry came from a different ethnic group. This made it hard, at first, to instil patriotism for the national collective over an individual allegiance to those who spoke, dressed and worshipped the same way.

But what were these new countries meant to do? It was the 1960s and the rest of the world was forging ahead, not willing to wait for Africa to reconfigure once again. Our parents and grandparents went to sleep one day and woke up bathed in promise. Their nations' births were not of their doing, but the future could be.

It was to solve these inconsistencies that the Organisation of African

Unity (OAU) – formed in 1963 to foster cooperation across the continent, and offer support to independence movements – met in Cairo in July 1964, hoping to agree on the best approach to take towards the continent's deficient borders.

By the time of the conference, thirty-four nations had gained independence, with Ghana the first among a fresh cohort to free itself in the late '50s and early '60s. Pre-conference, Ghana had already found itself in dispute with its neighbour Togo, which had just gained independence. The fight was over the border they shared that split the Ewe people, putting around three million of them in Ghana and two million in Togo. This particular topographic failure was caused by an agreement between Britain and France in 1919, after Germany lost Togoland at the start of World War I. Both Ghana and Togo were advocating for their countries to be made bigger, to incorporate the entirety of the Ewe. Ghana – which is considerably bigger than Togo – was effectively asking to swallow up its neighbour almost whole. Meanwhile, in North Africa, Morocco was also hoping to expand, claiming rights to Mauritania and the Western Sahara region. And looking towards East Africa, similar disputes were taking place, with Somalia hopeful of redrawing the constituencies that made up the Horn of Africa, struggling with its borders with Ethiopia and Kenya.

In an attempt to salvage Africa's fledgling harmony, it was thought at the meeting that tinkering with borders would only lead to more strife and conflict at a time when countries were just coming off a big fight for independence. It was unlikely, anyway, that with so many vested interests you could ever find a configuration that would work for everyone. It also wasn't clear how nations would go about arranging the new borders and who would be appointed to administer this work. The colonial powers had created such a mess that African countries couldn't change their boundaries without the knock-on effects being potentially devastating. One wrong border line and an entire nation could vanish, making what you did in your country very much everybody else's business.

People were also wary of the influence far larger nations with considerably more financial and military power – South Africa, Ethiopia, Nigeria, Egypt, Kenya – could have over the smaller countries. The initiation of an in-house scramble for land would certainly benefit a select few, and that was widely understood to be wrong. If only Europe had shown such restraint.

'I am not unaware that, when our colonisers set boundaries between territories, they too often ignored the frontiers of race, language and ethnicity,' President Philibert Tsiranana of Malagasy, now Madagascar, said in an address to other leaders. 'It is no longer possible, nor desirable, to modify the boundaries of Nations, on the pretext of racial, religious or linguistic criteria . . . Indeed, should we take race, religion or language as criteria for setting our boundaries, a few States in Africa would be blotted out from the map.'

The president of Mali: 'We must take Africa as it is, and we must renounce any territorial claims, if we do not wish to introduce what we call Black imperialism in Africa.'

In other words: splitting up into thousands of smaller ethnic groups was a predicate to chaos, and the enemy they knew was preferable to the villain they feared they would unintentionally create if an attempt to dismantle these unsustainably large countries went wrong.

Finally, it simply wasn't in the personal interests of the first generation of presidents and would-be prime ministers to break up the continent. They hadn't spent years leading the struggle for independence just to throw away a clear path to maintaining power. Wiping the Etch A Sketch clean did not guarantee them a prime position in whatever was drawn next.

This is why they ended up in Cairo in July 1964. After admitting that the 'border problems constitute a grave and permanent factor of dissension', the states signed a continent-wide agreement, pledging to 'respect the borders existing on their achievement of national independence' instead of recommending that the mapping begin afresh. The *New York Times* applauded the organisation, writing at the time about the importance of the OAU's 1964 conference: 'The OAU has brought together 34 African nations of 240 million people who speak 800 languages and occupy a continent four times as large as the United States. Some of the new states are divided both against each other and within themselves by tribal rivalries.'

There were then – and remain – some reasonable arguments for breaking up the entire existing arrangement – or, at the very least, reconsidering how the region approached the difficult battle for cohesion.

'Unity can only be based on the general consent of the people involved,' President Julius Nyerere of Tanzania argued in 1967, after his country showed a willingness to support secessionist movements, including backing the push by the Igbo of Nigeria's south-east to break away and form the nation of Biafra – a move the Nigerian government would oppose, leading to a bloody three-year civil war. 'The people must feel that this State, or this Union, is theirs; and they must be willing to have their quarrels in that context,' Nyerere continued. 'Once a large number of the people of any such political unit stop believing that the State is theirs, and that the Government is their instrument, then the unit is no longer viable.'

Demanding through decree that people feel a deep, patriotic love for a country has made a number of ethnic groups across the continent feel isolated, and that their specific needs have been ignored by their country's dominant ethnic groups, who at times have openly threatened their safety. This has, in part, fuelled secessionist movements in Uganda, Sudan, Angola, the Central African Republic, Chad, the Democratic Republic of Congo, Somalia and Nigeria.

*

The ideal formulation isn't clear: just take two examples of states that have taken two very different paths to realign their borders.

In the Scramble for Africa, the British negotiated control over the northern region of modern-day Somalia, while Italy secured the south. The two countries governed their colonies very differently. Britain – who only wanted the region so France couldn't have it – was happy to keep its distance, leaving it for local ethnic groups to run. This arrangement was made easier by the fact that British Somaliland was predominantly made up of one ethnic group: the Isaaqs. Italy, however, considered its cut of Somalia to be a key part of its relatively small empire, and was aggressively involved in administering a colony that was home to dozens of different ethnic groups.

Just weeks after both regions won independence in 1960, they merged together to form a united Somalia. United, that is, in the loosest possible sense. Within a decade, an already-volatile political equilib-rium was shattered by a military coup that saw Siad Barre, a southerner, take power. Over the next two decades, the dictator's harsh regime would favour his own ethnic group. Feeling ostracised, and like they were under effective occupation, the Isaaq set up a national movement to fight back. Things quickly escalated into a brutal civil war, as Barre unleashed the full might of the state to punish the Isaaqs for their per-ceived insubordination. In just two years, from 1987, the Barre regime killed an estimated 200,000 people. An investigation commissioned by the UN concluded: 'Based on the totality of evidence collected . . . the crime of genocide was conceived, planned and perpetrated by the Somali government against the Isaaq people of northern Somalia.'

In 1991, northern Somalia, under the name Somaliland, declared itself an independent state. It has lived that way ever since, despite the refusal of the international community to recognise it as a legitimate nation of its own, fearful that they may spark a series of secessionist movements. Still, today, Somaliland has its own flag, currency, military, judicial system, peaceful democratic elections, and a constitution. Some experts argue they now enjoy more political stability than their neighbours to the south, because they enjoy two unique advantages not shared by the vast majority of African nations: they are made up of one ethnic group, and their colonisers had minimal involvement. Somalia, meanwhile, with its multitude of ethnic groups, has been plagued by a never-ending civil war between ethnic factions and terrorist groups, with the added involvement of other East African nations.

Then there's the case of the world's newest country, the very much internationally recognised South Sudan, whose independence was actively celebrated when it was achieved back in 2011. Before then, there was a deep divide between the predominately Muslim north and the primarily Christian south. When Sudan initially became independent from British and Egyptian rule, the north gained power – and, similar to the situation in Somalia, the powerful built their authority around elevating those of the same heritage as their own. This sparked tension with the south – and, eventually, a decades-long civil war, which ended with the southern Christian region voting almost unanimously to break away and form South Sudan.

Unlike Somaliland, South Sudan is made up of dozens of ethnic groups, whose differences were ignored and put to one side as it focused on extricating itself from the north of Sudan. Initially, life as a new country started off well, with the two largest ethnic groups – the Dinka and the Nuer – coming together to lead the government. But things soon turned, as South Sudan's first president, Salva Kiir, a Dinka, and its vice-president, Riek Machar, a Nuer, began vying for sole control of the oil-rich region. Kiir accused Machar in 2013 of plotting a coup. Machar, meanwhile, claimed the president had allowed power to corrupt his mind. Neither was afraid to fan the flames of ethnic tension to build their own supporter base, in the process burning national unity and leading their country to a disastrous civil war that plagued South Sudan until the ceasefire in 2020.

Hundreds of thousands of people were killed and around four million displaced as a result. The instability continues as millions remain homeless, housed in insecure camps marshalled by UN peacekeepers. Meanwhile, the government continues to insist it has done nothing wrong. 'The current state of South Sudan in terms of Human Rights is okay,' Michael Lueth, the Minister for Information, told VICE in a recent interview. Lueth has personally been accused of orchestrating the killing of 140 civilians and three UN guards.

Both Somaliland and South Sudan got what they wanted without getting what they wanted. One remains in a state of unsettled limbo – ignored, hovering as a warning to others who choose to be bold with their own fate. The other is free, yet trapped in a cycle of requited vengeance. Neither offers a clear roadmap for the rest of a continent to follow.

For many, this represents the continent's forever plague: damned if you stick, damned if you twist. A study in 2011 by a group of Harvard and NYU professors tried to measure whether artificial states are more prone to political and economic instability. They defined artificial states as nations whose 'political borders do not coincide with a division of nationalities desired by the people on the ground'. They measured two different functions: the effects of straight-line borders, and the erratic separation of ethnic groups.

The researchers discovered that countries with unnatural borders and divided communities tend to have greater economic problems and political violence. Using their metric, they also found that nine of the thirteen most arbitrary states in the world are in Africa – Chad, Equatorial Guinea, Eritrea, Mali, Morocco, Namibia, Niger, Sudan and Zimbabwe. The other countries are Pakistan, Jordan, Ecuador and

Guatemala. All former colonies delineated to bring wealth and power to some, and subjugation to others.

*

Modern Africa was designed against its will to be a divided thing. A continent of fifty-four houses built on sand, poorly anchored to business deals written using Victorian definitions of civilisation. The irregular births of its nations, and the short time they've had to deal with the ramifications, underlie why so many are still fighting to overcome deep, foundational challenges. It is not because Africans are savagely ungovernable or too ignorant to lead a successful country. Even though most people would not say so out loud, such thoughts permeate our subconscious when we do not understand the context, the founding of the current configuration of states, and how their conflicts are fuelled and exploited by their foundational make-up.

'It is the weakness of the state in Zambia which allowed Frederick Chiluba to divert state resources while president toward his fellow Bemba,' argues Professor Pierre Englebert, senior fellow at the Atlantic Council. 'It is the weakness of the state which made it possible for Charles Taylor to use the revenue of the Liberian International Ship and Corporate Registry to fund arms trafficking in the late 1990s. It is also the weakness of the state that allows militias and gangs to organize drug, mineral and arms smuggling at the Liberia-Guinea-Côte d'Ivoire border area or in the Ituri region of Congo.'

The danger is that a significant number of people carry the silent bigotry that there is something inherently wrong and indecent about Africans as a collective that must have caused this continued scuffling. This is where discrimination breeds something more lasting, more insidious, and quickly, before you realise it, you're gathered in a room, under a large map, scheming, creating a thing with arms and limbs it cannot control, and an undefined soul divided into a million pieces.

In a final twist, the colonial powers responsible for Berlin would later return, determined to *save* Africa again. This time they brought a new brand of paternalism, replacing fake treaties and rifles with a modern, potentially more dangerous weapon: a camera crew.

Part Three

The Birth of White Saviour Imagery

or

How Not to Be a White Saviour
While Still Making a Difference

INT. AFRICAN FARM, MORNING

Close-up shot of a crying child, flies orbiting his head.

FAMOUS VOICE

Matombu is eight years old, but he doesn't look like it.

He doesn't. He looks malnourished. The camera pulls back to take in Matombu's full body. His stomach is bloated. In the corner of the room we can now see a parent, lying helpless. Let's just assume they are dying.

CUT TO:

EXT. DRINKING WELL, MORNING

Matombu is trying to drink from a dirty tap, but the only trickles of water are stained filthy black. Still he drinks anyway.

Stepping into the shot, we see our narrator for the first time. An extremely famous Oscar-winning actor, with bright blond hair, unblemished by the toils of Africa. We immediately recognise the famous actor.

FAMOUS NARRATOR

There is a good chance he may not see his ninth birthday. But for just £2 a month, you, yes you, can change his life.

Our narrator turns to Matombu and smiles. He reciprocates. There is hope, again.

I REMEMBER THE MESSAGES. More specifically: I remember ignoring the messages, dozens of them, each one carrying the exact same YouTube link. Hidden behind that link was a video that was clogging up the attention of my Facebook and Twitter feeds.

From the thumbnail alone, I couldn't decipher the video's content. And the title – aside from the date, the year we were then living in – meant nothing to me. Still, it would be easy to claim, ten years later, that the reason I initially avoided watching the video was because I knew the internet, and understood I should encounter every viral moment with a healthy dose of content scepticism. That I had learned to question the transience of our online culture, preferring to engage in a more comprehensive relationship with life and self.

In reality, the truth is I dodged the link because the video was thirty minutes long and growing up with the internet has quite simply destroyed my attention span. Then – just as now – I'm unlikely to watch any piece of content forwarded to me that lasts longer than four minutes. Longer than two minutes, and I'll have to think about it.

But thirty minutes? No.

Truly viral content has a way of latching on to everyone it encounters. You sense a shift in the force, as all other ambient distractions make room for it to emerge and have its moment under the bright sun. That is part of its joy. For a brief moment in time, it feels as though the world is engaged in a shared experience that connects us to something bigger than our own singular existences. That randomness alone can be worth the adventure.

But thirty minutes? No.

The video wasn't going away, though. And fighting the internet is one of life's more futile endeavours. Breaking point usually comes when the conversation suddenly shifts dramatically from 'Check this out' to 'So, what do you think?' At this final stage, you're expected to have an informed opinion on the snowballing discourse. Ideally, something smart and witty, with witty taking precedence if you must choose between the two.

By my memory, I resisted for several days. Looking back through the messages, however, it was a mere twelve hours before I eventually admitted defeat and clicked on the mysterious phenomenon curiously titled *Kony 2012*.

In 2003, three filmmakers – Jason Russell, Laren Poole and Bobby Bailey – travelled to Uganda. There, in the northern city of Gulu, they met a young teenager called Jacob. Along with hundreds of other children, Jacob was on the run from the rebel group the Lord's Resistance Army (LRA) – an organisation that had spent nearly thirty years terrorising the region, kidnapping and sexually assaulting tens of thousands of young children and forcing many of them into their child army.

Jacob detailed to the filmmakers his personal experiences of being brutalised by the LRA, explaining some of the atrocities the group had committed, including murdering his brother – an act Jacob had witnessed.

As you'd hope, Russell and his team were deeply moved and shocked by the teenager's account. They had never heard of the LRA or its leader, Joseph Kony, and they certainly knew nothing of the vast scale of violence perpetrated by the rebel group or the broader Ugandan civil war it was entangled in. But right there and then, in the middle of the

Ugandan jungle, Russell, Poole and Bailey committed to doing whatever they could to bring Kony to justice.

Jacob's circumstances were indeed horrendous. What he had described was certainly worthy of shock and restorative action. The natural response to encountering something awful should be to take whatever action is within your power to stop it from happening, especially when it's happening to someone staring right at you. So taking the filmmakers in good faith, their instinctive commitment to improving the situation was both the human and humane response to what appeared, at first sight, to be an ongoing tragedy.

The solution was given form a year later, when the filmmakers created the charity Invisible Children, with the goal of highlighting the plight of kids like Jacob – whose suffering they considered invisible because Americans knew nothing about it – for the rest of the world. As a coping mechanism, it's often easier to assume our personal ignorance is widely shared. And so, just as they were shocked into action, the filmmakers figured the rest of the world would be too, if only people knew about the terrible things that were happening in Africa.

After nine years of work, Russell, Poole, and Bailey's efforts culminated in a film that they envisioned would finally bring down a war criminal.

The first few seconds of Kony 2012 are not subtle. Deliberately so. The symbolism is there to be seen and not deciphered: a powerful quote about taking action, now, is followed by the sight of the Earth spinning slowly from space, as we go from dusk to an emerging dawn, full of possibilities.

'Right now there are more people on Facebook than there were on the planet two hundred years ago,' the narration begins. 'Humanity's greatest desire is to belong and connect,' it continues, interspersed with footage of people sending emails, Arab Spring protesters toppling brutal regimes, children Skyping their technology-literate grandparents, and long-separated lovers reuniting at the airport.

The opening sequence does what it is meant to do. It opens our spirits to onrushing waves of hope, instilling within us a longing for the sturdy power of human connection and innovation while working towards a shared goal: the betterment of our planet by realising the impossible.

Next, Invisible Children sets the urgent tone of the film, the approach the charity will take to secure our immediate support – and, crucially, the action they will eventually need from us. A countdown timer appears on the screen, and we're told that the next twenty-seven minutes are an experiment, 'but in order for it to work, you have to pay attention.'

Moments later, we're in a delivery room watching the first crying seconds of an infant's life, reminding us of the great lottery of our existence – none of us choose to whom we are born or what circumstances we are delivered into. The infant's name is Gavin and he is the son of our narrator, the co-founder of Invisible Children, Jason Russell. Gavin is adorable. All you want in life is good things for this five-year-old whose idea of dancing is doing cartwheels, a truly underrated dance move. Russell reveals that he just wants a better world for his son. And it's impossible to get this far into the film without wanting that, too.

Emotionally, you're ready to solve a problem, any problem. You're just waiting to be told what it is.

'Who is this right here?' Russell asks his son, four minutes in, pointing to a photo stuck on their family's fridge.

'Jacob . . . our friend in Africa,' Gavin replies.

From here, Kony 2012 takes us back nine years to Russell's first trip to Uganda, and the night he met Jacob and glimpsed the harsh realities of his life.

Jacob wants to be a lawyer – but more than that, he reveals, he wants to be dead, so he can stop suffering and reunite with his brother who was killed by Kony and the LRA. It's this statement that compels Russell to make him a promise. 'We are going to do everything we can to stop them,' he assures Jacob. 'We are going to stop them.'

Russell admits that, at the time, he made the pledge not knowing what it would mean. But now, he has mapped out a strategy, and he needs the world's help to immediately fulfil it because – for reasons never fully explained – the film 'expires on December 31st, 2012'.

The 'only purpose' of *Kony 2012* is to stop Joseph Kony and the LRA. The film is blunt about that. The 'why' is explained through a series of animations. Kony has been kidnapping children 'just like Gavin' for twenty-six years, turning the girls into sex slaves and forcing the boys to fight in his rebel army, where they learn to mutilate the LRA's enemies and kill their parents. Around 30,000 children have been recruited by Kony, including Jacob, who managed to escape.

'We should stop him,' Gavin tells his father, as we cut back to the US. The subtext: if a five-year-old gets it, so should you.

From Uganda in 2003, Russell and his team flew straight to Washington, DC, to lobby members of Congress, who were initially dismissive of their requests for the US government to intervene.

Undeterred, Invisible Children organised rallies across the country, spoke at schools and colleges, and even invited Jacob to the US to educate people on the crisis. The charity also raised money to build schools in Uganda and created a network of early warning signals to let villages know if a rebel attack was imminent. As a result, Russell narrates, 'the unseen became visible'.

They took their growing movement back to Washington, to continue the push for the US government to take military action against Kony and the LRA. In 2011, Invisible Children got their wish, at least partly:

the government deployed a small training force of around a hundred officers to Uganda to 'provide assistance to regional forces that are working toward the removal of Joseph Kony from the battlefield'.

That could have been that. However, months later, Kony remained at large, and Russell feared international pressure was waning. They needed a new approach. This is where *Kony 2012* came in – and, twenty minutes into the film, we discover what the filmmakers need from us.

Watching it again now, the 'how' is remarkably simpler than I remembered it. Russell narrates:

> In order for Kony to be arrested this year, the Ugandan military has to find him. In order to find him, they need the technology and training to track him in the vast jungle. That's where the American advisers come in. But in order for the American advisers to be there, the US government has to deploy them. They've done that, but if the government doesn't believe that people care about arresting Kony, the mission will be cancelled. In order for people to care, they have to know. And they will only know if Kony's name is everywhere.

That was it.

Make Kony a household name in America and around the world, and his arrest would be imminent, the charity envisaged – bringing to an end a complex, decades-long conflict.

The easiest way to make the LRA leader pop-culture famous, of course, was to convince celebrities to amplify the 'catch Kony' message. To achieve this, *Kony 2012* asked fans to put pressure on their favourite artist, politician or actor to raise Kony's global profile. Alongside that, viewers were encouraged to buy $30 action kits, each one filled with posters, bracelets, stickers and yard signs, which the organisers hoped would blanket the planet in the warlord's likeness, and make him so ubiquitous it would be impossible for the US government to focus on anything else but capturing him and ridding the world of his influence.

All this action was to culminate two months later, on 20 April, with a plan to 'cover the night' – an evening when society would 'meet at sundown and blanket every street in every city until the sun comes up'.

With posters.

The fast cuts, ascending rock anthems and portraits of Hitler, combined with an action plan that involved little more than accessorising your outfit and sharing a link – it all made changing the world feel so attainable; justice seemed so malleable to whatever your imagination could dream up. And all without leaving your home? Ideal.

In theory, the filmmakers had succeeded in making Joseph Kony one of the most famous people in the world. Millions of young people demonstrated a never-before-seen commitment among this generation to capturing a grotesque war criminal who had terrorised extensive areas of Central Africa for three decades. *Kony 2012* may not have been perfect, but at least it was something – and Africans should have been grateful for the help. Right?

We were not. And we made it known. The movement never did manage to 'cover the night'. The initial positive response that made it go viral soon shifted in ways Russell and his team never imagined. The criticism – led predominantly by Ugandans and Africans across the diaspora, but also minority groups who recognised some of the tropes used in the film to drive attention – soon engulfed the entire movement and overwhelmed Invisible Children.

Ten days after the film's release, Jason Russell was arrested outside his home in San Diego. He was allegedly screaming, running in and out of traffic in his underwear. The result of a stress-induced breakdown.

Kony 2012's honeymoon was short, but nobody can deny there was a honeymoon. Hour after hour, in the days following its release, the film's viewing figures skyrocketed. Ten million views quickly became forty, which rapidly rolled into fifty. Thirty-two million people watched it on 7 March alone.

By the end of that week, around 70 million people worldwide had taken the time to watch a thirty-minute film that wasn't a sitcom or a meme, with the charity raising more than $30 million. #StopKony trended on Twitter for three days, with 10 million tweets dedicated to the movement in the first week. It became the most viral YouTube video in history.

Its initial success was partly down to how quickly celebrities jumped on board, though they hardly had a choice. Those who were not directly called out in the film by name and photo still had millions of their fans, high on change, demanding action. Overnight, Joseph Kony became one of the most infamous people on earth. All that remained was for the filmmakers' theory to be tested: now that college students in Palo Alto knew who he was, it was certainly only a matter of time before Kony faced justice.

While the world waited for the imminent destruction of the LRA, an alternative interpretation of the charity's campaign was starting to surface, threatening to burst the nascent euphoria. It was charged by pent-up frustration at a depiction of Africa that has plagued the continent for decades, under the guise of charity.

Three days after the film's release, Nigerian-American author Teju Cole wrote a series of tweets in response to the campaign. He called out figures like Jeffrey Sachs and Nicholas Kristof, as well as organizations such as Invisible Children and TED, for contributing to what he called the 'White Savior Industrial Complex.' He described how widespread the phenomenon had become in the US and pointedly critiqued its self-serving nature, ridiculing the white saviour's tendency to oversimplify serious world issues.

In the context of Africa, there is a longstanding frustration with the West's very specific need to portray Africa as functionally helpless in battling its own problems – using stark imagery of death and devastation, starvation and corruption, to reinforce the idea that this is a place where nothing but misery grows out of violent cracks in the foundations of a grossly unstable society, and within a people who do not know what's good for them. The white saviour complex reinforces the view that Africans can never be the solution, that they are without agency, and that sunshine and hope only come when cradled in the warm, bright embrace of the Western world, always on time to save the day. It tells a grossly simplified story that centres the saviours over and above those whose lives they are supposedly trying to change.

It can seem an unfair charge to level at people who are just trying to 'make a difference' – but making a difference is not a neutral act. By its definition, your action will lead to a shifting of the norm, a deliberate mutation of the equilibrium. Naturally, there will be seen and unforeseen consequences – the latter often of little concern to the saviour. And as Teju Cole and others began to outline, the potential consequences of Invisible Children's prescribed actions in Uganda – none of which are mentioned in the film – were vast.

Charity appeals of this nature usually avoid getting dragged down into the tangled weeds of complexity. Practically, the easiest way to get someone to donate from a standing start is to present them with a problem followed by a solution that they can automatically accept, without the need for additional homework.

In this case, *Kony 2012* was asking to send troops into another country to affect the dynamic of a deeply entrenched local conflict.

Before any rash decisions were made to carpet-bomb Kampala in search of one man, however, voices across Uganda and experienced political experts with knowledge of the region came forward in large numbers to challenge the assertions made in *Kony 2012* and the solutions Russell and his team were promoting. The day after Cole's tweets, the Ugandan writer Rosebell Kagumire published a video blog. In it, she said:

> My major problem with this video is it simplifies the story of millions of people in northern Uganda and makes out a narrative that is often heard about Africa, about how hopeless people are in times of conflict and only people [outside] the continent can help. There have been local initiatives to end this war. The war was more than just an evil man killing children ... We need to have sound, intelligent campaigns that are geared towards real policy shifts rather than a very sensationalised story that is out to make just one person cry, and at the end of the day we forget about it. This video seems to suggest that the power lies in America and not with my government and local initiatives on the ground.

When violent intervention is on the menu, you cannot afford to leave out vital details. But it seems they were deliberately left out. In her response, Kagumire pointed out two key discrepancies in the film. First, much of the footage of Uganda was over five years old, and did not speak to how the situation had changed – some of it for the better – since the filmmakers had first met Jacob almost a decade before.

The second discrepancy is crucial to an endeavour that hinges on the Western world finding Joseph Kony in Uganda: Kony wasn't in Uganda. He had long fled to a neighbouring country.

Nobody came forward to suggest that Kony was anything other than a vile warlord who has caused unspeakable tragedy in hundreds of thousands of lives. The general agreement has always been that the quicker any sliver of power is removed from him, the better. But a desire to do good – however altruistic – should never make the 'why' the enemy of the 'how'.

MIT professor Ethan Zuckerman wrote a lengthy blog post explaining how, in these circumstances, the 'how' would just make things worse:

> Kony continues to rely on child soldiers. That means that a military assault – targeted to a satellite phone signal or some other method used to locate Kony – would likely result in the death of abducted children. This scenario means that many northern Ugandans don't support military efforts to capture or kill Kony, but advocate for approaches that offer amnesty to the LRA in exchange for an end to violence and a return of kidnapped children.

A community in northern Uganda organised a screening of the film, so locals could understand why their region had so suddenly become the focus of the Western world. Malcolm Webb, a reporter for Al Jazeera, attended the showing, and spoke to residents afterwards to gauge their reactions. They were not happy. 'For many here, the video is simply puzzling,' he reported. As the film went on, 'puzzlement turned into anger'.

That anger was shared across the country, in large part due to the imagery that was used. As Ugandan journalist Angelo Izama noted, 'good is inevitably white/western and bad is black or African'.

In an article for *The Atlantic* titled 'The Soft Bigotry of Kony 2012', Max Fisher agreed with Izama: 'It's part of a long tradition of Western advocacy that has, for centuries, adopted some form of white man's burden ... First it was with missionaries, then "civilizing" missions, and finally the ultimate end of white paternalism, which was placing Africans under the direct Western control of imperialism.'

A dam weakened by quiet humiliations had finally burst. Criticisms of *Kony 2012* appeared to build up in every major publication. The Ethiopian-American novelist Dinaw Mengestu added:

> The real star of Kony 2012 isn't Joseph Kony, it's us ... In the world of Kony 2012, Joseph Kony has evaded arrest for one dominant reason: Those of us living in the western world haven't known about him, and because we haven't known about him, no one has been able to stop him. The film is more than just an explanation of the problem; it's the answer as well. It's a beautiful equation that can only work so long as we believe that nothing in the world happens unless we know about it, and that once we do know about it, however poorly informed and ignorant we may be, every action we take is good, and more importantly, 'makes a difference'.

The continent was fighting back against the narrative that it – as UCL professor Kate Cronin-Furman and journalist Amanda Taub described it – could be reduced to evil warlords, and communities 'so helpless that they must wait around to be saved by a bunch of American college students with stickers'.

Alongside the accusations that the film represented the worst of white saviour culture came a Tumblr post by Grant Oyston – then a nineteen-year-old political science student – revealing that only 32 per cent of the donations Invisible Children received went on direct services in Uganda, 'with much of the rest going to staff salaries, travel and transport, and film production'.

Responding to the backlash, Invisible Children released a FAQ-style statement detailing everything from their aims, to how they spent their money, to a brief history of the LRA, to one section that even asked: is Joseph Kony still alive? (The answer: 'We believe so'.)

A comprehensive summary of the facts should have been the default position, not an endnote. But by the time the statement came out, the damage was largely done. *Kony 2012* had lost control of its own movement.

We can most easily understand things we've seen before, in some form – whether real or imagined, consciously or not. *Kony 2012* was open about the secret sauce it needed for success: speed. If it showed you a film you'd already watched, you could process the information as quickly as possible.

In deep dark Africa where deep dark things take place, a deep darkness has descended on young dark children and the only way to alleviate that darkness is by shining a bright white light on it.

It was a deliberate tactic. Of everything that I have rediscovered about *Kony 2012*, the most surprising is Invisible Children's post-backlash statement. Mainly how detailed and thought-through it was, and how quickly they were able to put the information together and get it out. They had the essential context all along. Which shouldn't be surprising, really. As Russell narrates in the film, the charity had been working on dismantling the LRA for almost a decade. They knew a lot more than they shared. And though explaining complicated concepts in quick, easily digestible formats can be a well-valued skill, it can also be utilised as a weapon for distortion. What you choose to include and what you decide to omit often speaks to your values, or your assumptions as to what you think society can easily comprehend.

In solving problems, we build tactics from our talents, and as experienced filmmakers with an appreciation for the power of imagery, *Kony 2012's* creators understood which images would elicit the emotional connection needed to provoke action: footage of destitute African children wandering the night. Darkness was a heavy theme throughout the film, literally and figuratively. Where light appeared, we were rarely in Uganda. Hope came when we were in the US, speaking to Russell's son, Gavin, who we were meant to relate to, encouraging us to ask ourselves, 'What if this was happening to him?'

Successfully convincing masses of viewers across the world to act instinctively required Invisible Children to lean heavily on people's existing biases about the continent. Because of those biases, people were ready to believe that the solution to a problem in Uganda could be found in Toronto or Manchester, or on a college campus in Lisbon, or maybe even in Paris. Because of preconceived notions of the continent, it was easy to accept that the filmmakers would travel to Washington, DC for a solution to Kony's rampaging cruelty, rather than to Uganda's capital, Kampala, to direct their demands towards the president who was constitutionally responsible for these lives and their welfare. It was easy to trust that a man could freely walk the lands of this chaotic jungle for twenty years, murdering young children without already being famous, because that's just the sort of thing that happens in Africa. It was easy to believe that filmmakers from California could set an arbitrary deadline of 31 December, after which efforts to capture Kony would 'expire', as if Ugandans were so helpless they had lost control of their own time.

That self-inflicted timescale, the rush to have us all end a civil war by purchasing wristbands, did not leave time for the truth. In reality, Joseph Kony was already incredibly famous, and a lot of time and local expertise had driven him away from Uganda into the thick bush of Central Africa, with only a couple of hundred men – down from thousands – to protect him.

Invisible Children did not have time to tell a new story. They needed to rework an old one that was already ingrained in far too many imaginations. And their plan would have worked, too, if Africans hadn't taken a stand. *Kony 2012* came to represent a landmark showdown with the making-a-difference industry.

In all the criticism they faced, few, if anyone, suggested that Russell and his team had anything other than a genuine desire to alleviate mass suffering. Still, in the end, Russell paid a heavy price. The video of his breakdown caught fire on the internet and *Kony 2012* became a punchline. From the most viral YouTube video in history, to being held up as the epitome of some of the worst excesses of Western condescension towards Africa.

It might seem unfair for one man to have to bear that much blame. Perhaps it is. After all, Russell and Invisible Children were simply following a script that was written and perfected decades before they had ever heard the name Joseph Kony.

*

THOSE IN THE KNOW CONSIDER the 1980s as the golden age of charity campaigns. The decade brimmed with large-scale, celebrity-driven philanthropic crusades that successfully raised vast sums of money at unprecedented rates. These campaigns became iconic pop-culture moments in their own right, divorced from their original aims and the generous intent that sparked them into being. The famous faces that fronted the initiatives became even more beloved, rising above the established order of popularity to exist on a higher plane of stardom. The dream bio now read: *celebrity and activist.*

Celebrities started travelling the world on behalf of large NGOs; they were granted audiences with presidents and prime ministers, kings and queens, and a pleasantly confused, though unfailingly polite, Nelson Mandela, whose facial expressions often betrayed uncertainty as to how the person standing in front of him had managed to secure this meeting.

These campaigns grew to become more than instruments to funnel money towards worthy causes. They were global events you couldn't turn away from, forcing attention towards something so dire the organisers demanded immediate and swift intervention. And much of this star-centred philanthropy was driven by a specific singular event in East Africa that rocked the collective consciousness of Western society.

At a point in the 1980s, it became impossible to avoid the graphic images of widespread starvation that were streaming out of Ethiopia. The country was being strangled by a once-in-a-generation famine, partly the result of a slower-than-usual grain harvest in the northern regions, where a forever-long civil war was raging. Not wanting to allow a good crisis to go to waste, the famine was then deliberately exacerbated by the military government, which saw the deepening hunger and growing desperation as an opportunity to weaken secessionist insurgents in the region, through the disruption of emergency food supplies. An estimated one million people died, while the famine created hundreds of thousands of refugees and millions of internally displaced people forced to flee their barren towns and villages.

Western governments were initially reluctant to get involved. But by 1985, donations were pouring in from around the world, inspired by an influential eight-minute BBC News segment broadcast in October 1984 and transmitted to over four hundred television stations across the globe – what we would refer to today as 'viral'.

The segment features the journalist Michael Buerk reporting directly from the northern town of Korem, where 40,000 refugees had amassed in scenes resembling a 'biblical famine' – an assessment that becomes increasingly accurate as the BBC's camera hovers over what appears to be a never-ending sea of critically famished Ethiopians, of all ages and demographics, their cavernous suffering seemingly ripped from the darkest corners of scripture. Heavy wailing makes certain there is never any silence; mothers struggle and fail to feed their severely malnourished children; bodies are gathered every morning at dawn and lined up unceremoniously along the ground to await burial; a desperate human stampede ensues as false rumours of the imminent arrival of a food shipment spread around the camp, setting off a panic of hope; armed guards stand watch over the extremely limited supplies of donated second-hand clothing that will still fail to keep the relatively fortunate recipients warm enough when temperatures dip below freezing after sundown. Here in this refugee camp in Korem, 'a child or an adult dies every twenty minutes'. Counted among the dead is an infant who we watch in the last few seconds of life. His mother, starved in body and will, looks on in silent torment at the fourth child she will lose to the famine.

Each frame is starker than its predecessor, stitched together to tell a wretched story almost impossible to watch in its entirety without engaging in some mental displacement. But the overwhelming scale of this still-unfolding tragedy was certainly very real.

What Buerk's short segment succinctly communicated – with the help of Kenyan cameraman Mohamed Amin – was the on-the-ground griefs facing the victims of a cascading crisis. The famine in Ethiopia became a glaring symbol for the world's growing disparities. And donations would certainly meet the moment, coming in from Western constituencies stunned into intercession, led by a small number of powerful, genuinely socially conscious celebrities willing to leverage the full measure of their fame to bring about immediate relief.

From here, a new tactic for extracting large donations from a traditionally reticent public was quickly perfected. Expensive TV fundraisers were created, broadcasting hours of images of impoverished, bulging-ribcaged children – flies and imminent death orbiting around their heads – as a celebrity, idling in the corner of the room, narrated their pain.

The films were solemn, intimate, and extremely effective at not only pumping the plight of the world's poorest directly into living rooms and consciences thousands of miles away, but also empowering viewers to feel that they, too, could do something about it, with a level of intervention that barely required them to move. 'For just £2,' your favourite artist whispered, conveying solemnity, 'you could be a hero.' Little else can produce the thrill of a quick-fix donation that requires almost no real engagement or effort, but leaves you, if given with genuine concern, convinced you have helped shift what Martin Luther King, Jr described as 'the arc of the moral universe'.

Of all the celebrity-backed telethons, the most revolutionary was Comic Relief.

Comic Relief broadcast its first telethon in 1988. A *Night of Comic Relief*, hosted by legendary comedian Lenny Henry live from Ethiopia, featured its now-famous mix of sketches and earnest direct-to-camera appeals. Around 150 celebrities contributed to creating original material, which ranged from brand-new episodes of classic shows such as *Blackadder* to live musical performances. The evening raised £15 million for charities in the UK and across Africa. Through comedy, the general public was connected to a reality far outside their own, and they could change that reality while being entertained. This arrangement has seen Comic Relief raise over £1 billion since its inception.

Alongside these telethons were grand, one-off showpiece events and releases, with two of the biggest starting in the same year.

In January 1985, forty-five musicians – including Bruce Springsteen, Stevie Wonder, Tina Turner, Cyndi Lauper, Ray Charles and Bob

Dylan – met in an LA recording studio to lend their vocals to 'We Are the World', an exceptionally wholesome, catchy charity single written by Lionel Ritchie and Michael Jackson, and produced by Quincy Jones.

These talents had been brought together under the banner of the United Support of Artists for Africa (USA for Africa) – a newly formed philanthropic venture that was the brainchild of the legendary activist Harry Belafonte. The initial goal of USA for Africa was to raise money for the famine, but their ambitions have since expanded to supporting causes across Africa and the United States.

'We Are the World' remains a cultural behemoth. It's heavily empowering lyrics do not focus on any one cause – rather, its writers created an umbrella anthem for an individual's ability to make a brighter day, so let's start giving.

The song contains no generic, offensive references to Africa or famine or crippling poverty – perhaps a result of the diverse team behind it. The song could encourage efforts to support survivors of a genocide as much as it could serve as a hype track for your morning run. And then there was the music video: each rotation of the camera, each jig of the lens, capturing another heavyweight musician drenched in exceptional '80s knitwear, crooning earnestly into a microphone as Quincy Jones observes like a proud father, conducting his ensemble. It's no surprise that USA for Africa has raised over $100 million for famine relief, while the song remains iconic.

Four months after the release of 'We Are the World', in July 1985, a global concert series was staged – organised by the lead singer of the Boomtown Rats, Irish musician Bob Geldof. Following the BBC's groundbreaking report on the famine, Geldof – 'outraged by what I saw' – rushed into action, using his influence and connections to speak out, quickly becoming the de facto spokesperson for this new age of celebrity-backed philanthropy.

The event was called Live Aid, and featured simultaneous concerts across nine countries, spanning sixteen hours, with the two biggest gigs taking place at Wembley Stadium in London and the John F. Kennedy Stadium in Philadelphia.

Prince Charles and Princess Diana were on hand at Wembley to officially open an event that saw 80,000 fans entertained by, among others, David Bowie, U2, Elton John, The Who, and Geldof's own Boomtown Rats. The highlight was Freddie Mercury and Queen pulling together one of the band's most iconic performances. Over in Philadelphia, Madonna, Bob Dylan, the Rolling Stones, Eric Clapton and others performed to a hundred thousand people. Some 1.5 billion viewers watched around the world. During the concert, video footage from the famine was broadcast over large screens to encourage giving. At one point, the event was raising £300 a second. In total, Live Aid helped raise £150 million to fight the famine in Ethiopia.

As iconic as they are in their own right, Comic Relief, Live Aid and 'We Are the World' only existed thanks to the success of an even earlier Geldof production that has come to define the complicated balance between making a difference and doing more harm than good.

Should a charity single educate or entertain? Be a fun, easy distraction from life's more dour entanglements, or an on-the-nose statement that means only a greedy, heartless fool would sit back and do nothing when presented with the facts? A bit of both, perhaps. After visiting Ethiopia in 1984, Geldof returned to the UK wanting to raise money fast. To achieve this, he settled on writing and releasing a song.

'I thought, it's not enough to put a pound in the charity box,' Geldof told the George W. Bush Institute in 2017. 'This requires something of the self. All I could do was write tunes, but I thought maybe we could make a record and get it out by Christmas. I thought we could make a hundred thousand pounds, give it to Oxfam or something, and be done . . . So I rang a friend in another band and said let's do this together. We gathered all the main stars of the day and recorded "Do They Know It's Christmas?"'.

'Do They Know It's Christmas?' was certainly a phenomenon; and its omnipresence every December in the UK has barely diminished in the decades since. For the recording, Geldof attracted the biggest artists of the day, including George Michael, Duran Duran, U2, Phil Collins and Spandau Ballet.

The song was a gargantuan chart success. It was the number-one single in the UK for five weeks, selling 13 million copies worldwide to date and raising over £10 million. It climbed to the top of the charts in the US too, and in several other countries around the world. From its release and positive reception, this one song birthed an entire movement of celebrity-fuelled activism that could be used to attract large sums of money from a generous public.

All this was achieved by painting a picture of a place that did not exist.

'Do They Know It's Christmas?' created a direct call-to-arms that bypassed nuance and embraced straight-to-the-veins messaging. Listening to the four-minute ballad, it is impossible not to believe there's a singular region in the world living under a fog of poverty so thick, even Christmastime – civilisation's brightest annual worldwide celebration – cannot pierce the gloom.

For a song that was crafted to help fix a very specific crisis, it never once mentions the crisis it is desperate we know about. We hear nothing of Ethiopia or famine or the tense stand-off between a military government and well-armed separatists. The fundamental question in the title is not simply asking whether the millions of people in one country – starved by what was largely a man-made devastation – can distract themselves long enough from their suffering to celebrate the birth of Baby Jesus. Instead, we are actively challenged to consider whether the entirety of Africa – a continent with more Christians than any other region in the world – is so cursed by poverty that over one billion people are incapable of knowing that Santa Claus is coming to town.

According to the lyrics, Africa is a place of 'dread and fear' where nothing ever grows. Additionally, we don't enjoy the sound of the Christmas bells; instead, doom literally chimes throughout the regions. The most outrageous line could be the one that claims that the only flowing water on the continent is the 'bitter sting of tears' that presumably flow from all our faces. Or it could be the lyric that confidently asserts outright that all anyone on the continent can hope for at Christmastime is to still be alive.

Passionately shunning nuance, 'Do They Know It's Christmas?' condensed all of the worst stereotypes of the region as one large failed state into a pleasant four-minute jingle, so easy on the ears it has lingered all these decades, fixed firmly within the annual repertoire of festive hits played in clubs and at office parties, requested during radio phone-ins, and offered as the background music for your Christmas shopping as you make your way through stores of every size and shape.

Just hearing the opening bar incites a strong urge to debunk lyrics that are patently absurd and grossly inaccurate. For the record: it does snow in parts of Africa; water runs in streams and rivers and emerges from kitchen taps as needed; crops grow, flourish and are exported to help feed the rest of the world; and people exchange gifts at Christmas that range far beyond staying alive.

But challenging the lyrics requires you to engage with the song in a way the song doesn't even pretend to engage with itself. 'Do They Know It's Christmas?' makes a calculation that, by writing a fictional story of one large dire Africa, weighed and measured by its failures rather than its strengths, the attention, revenue and action generated will justify the means.

Speaking on his approach to philanthropy, Geldof said in an interview: 'I quickly realized that politics is numbers. You can have as much money as you like, but if you really want to stop famine and other outrages of poverty from happening time and time again, the economics have to change. The way to change economics is through politics. The agents of change in our world, whether one likes it or not, are politicians. The way to get the politicians is numbers.'

This line of reasoning contains the same logic that was used by the makers of *Kony 2012*: that poverty or genocide or destitution will remain endemic in Africa unless large numbers of people outside of the region shame their governments into interceding by any means necessary. It leaves no room for interrogating what sustains these issues; just that Africa is in need, and that those who need to be convinced of this exist far outside the continent – and only when they hear about it will change come. For three decades, 'Do They Know It's Christmas?' existed largely unchallenged. Any criticism was quickly silenced, resulting in a quiet frustration shared privately throughout the African diaspora. But that silent frustration eventually found its voice when the creators of Band Aid decided to do it all again in 2014.

For the reunion, Geldof enlisted the help of Bono, One Direction, Chris Martin, Paloma Faith and fourteen other internationally acclaimed musicians to record Band Aid 30 – a charity single launched in part to celebrate the thirtieth anniversary of its favoured ancestor. This time, the song would raise money to help slow an Ebola crisis that was spreading through West Africa. But the publicity around this new version was almost entirely consumed by obsessive coverage of the predominantly white celebrities – there was even a class photo as if it was a reunion – and not so much the disease that doctors on the ground were working to contain.

Some of the original lyrics were rewritten for Band Aid 30. For example, the line about Africa being devastatingly snow-deficient was replaced with the gentler claim that there would be 'no peace and joy in West Africa' over the holiday season.

As part of the ensemble, Geldof invited Ghanaian Afrobeats star Fuse ODG to take part. However, after reading the proposed lyrics, the artist refused. 'I pointed out to Geldof the lyrics I did not agree with,' Fuse explained. 'For the past four years I have gone to Ghana at Christmas for the sole purpose of peace and joy. So for me to sing these lyrics would simply be a lie.'

What made it worse, Fuse said, was that when Geldof first approached him to take part, he had raised his concerns over the constant negative portrayal of Africa across Western media, plenty of which was present in the original Band Aid song. Geldof assured him that the new version would put the continent in a positive light.

It did not.

The music video – promoted with the hashtag #E30LA, because . . . Ebola – begins with a Black woman who appears to be near death being carried out of a room in only her underwear by two men in hazmat suits. A close-up shot of her torso follows as an ominous respiratory voiceover track plays in the background, without any commentary or explanation of who she is, where they are and why this is happening to her. These images are juxtaposed with shots of Geldof and the other assembled celebrities getting out of cars back in London, smiling and posing for a deliberately assembled bank of paparazzi. The only implication that can be interpreted from this framing is that the musicians have arrived with the cure to the previous scene tucked in their vocal cords.

Seeing the music video further confirmed to Fuse that he made the right decision not to take part:

In truth, my objection to the project goes beyond the offensive lyrics. I, like many others, am sick of the whole concept of Africa – a resource-rich continent with unbridled potential – always being seen as diseased, infested and poverty-stricken. In fact, seven out of 10 of the world's fastest-growing economies are in Africa.

Let me be clear, I'm not disregarding the fact that Ebola is happening and that people need help. Since the start of the outbreak in March, it has killed more than 5,000 people. But every human being deserves dignity in their suffering and the images flashed on our screens remove any remnants of this from Ebola sufferers, many in their dying moments when they should have it the most.

The release of the song, still titled 'Do They Know It's Christmas?', went ahead as planned, without any of the Ghanaian singer's concerns being addressed in any meaningful way.

The incident and re-release sparked a vocal response.

'The song's racism lives on in the banal way it reminds us how different they are from us, erecting an unbridgeable gulf between the "you" of the song's audience – white Britons who celebrate Christmas – and "they", who know only suffering, tears and death,' Aaron Bady wrote in an article for Al Jazeera.

Political science professor Laura Seay noted that the song 'betrays a total ignorance of the importance of Christianity in each country's culture, the sense of joy and celebration that can arise among all people even in the most dire of circumstances, and the fact that most West Africans – even in the Ebola outbreak zone – are not in fact suffering from Ebola'. In a piece for *The Guardian*, writer and radio producer Bim Adewunmi said: 'There exists a paternalistic way of thinking about Africa, likely exacerbated by the original (and the second, and the third) Band Aid singles, in which it must be "saved", and usually from itself. We say "Africa" in a way that we would never say "Europe", or "Asia". It's easy to forget, for example, that the virus made its way to Nigeria – Africa's most populous country and, for many, a potential Ebola tinderbox – and was stamped out only by the efforts of a brave team of local healthcare workers.'

Singer Emeli Sandé, who performed in Band Aid 30, later released a statement expressing her regret for taking part and called for a new version of the song to be recorded. Sandé, who is of Zambian heritage, also revealed that she and the Beninese singer Angélique Kidjo sang their own edits, but these were not included in the final version. 'I am so proud of my Zambian heritage,' Sandé said. 'No offence or disrespect to the beautiful and prosperous continent was ever intended. I apologise if the lyrics of the song have caused offence. I wish the changes had been kept but that is out of my control.'

None of this criticism fazed Geldof. In fact, he revelled in it. 'Where Band Aid is effective is that it creates all this noise,' he told the BBC. 'It creates this argument, it creates this debate. People find it very hard to understand that I love the level of criticism. I personally enjoy it.' His comments – especially about enjoying the controversy and loving the debate – are a reminder that many see 'saving Africa' like it's a new level on a video game that they are trying to crack. One day someone will accomplish it, they believe, but the joy is really in the journey, and not necessarily at the summit.

Geldof remains firm in his fundamental belief that the benefits of Band Aid were worth every second of the record. As he reiterated as recently as 2020, whatever your critique or complaint, he wants it to be known: 'I couldn't give a fuck.'

*

The two most enduring theories of ethics are consequentialism and deontology. The former proposes that the morality of an action should be judged by its consequences and not the act itself – the ends justify the means. Deontology, however, says that the morality of the action is all that matters, regardless of the outcome – without that, the theory goes, we would never be able to agree on universal principles of right and wrong to govern acts like stealing and punching colleagues.

Obviously, the best way to decide where you fall is to watch ESPN and Netflix's sensational documentary *The Last Dance*, about Michael Jordan and the era-defining, championship-winning Chicago Bulls of the '90s. There is a moment in particular about halfway through the series when, for three minutes, Jordan and his former teammate Steve Kerr take turns recollecting an infamous practice session ahead of the 1995–96 season. Up until this point, the series has skirted around the edges of addressing Jordan's infamously challenging personality and the true extent of his win-at-all-costs mentality. The consequences of his behind-closed-doors temper were more stuff of campfire tales than recorded fact. But here the documentary dives in head first.

'By the time camp started, he was in incredible shape, but he was also frothing at the mouth. That's how angry he was from losing,' Kerr recalls. 'So every day in training camp was just a war.' Jordan doesn't disagree. Instead, he explains that he felt that his new teammates were not sufficiently prepared for the battle ahead, and many of them, including Kerr, were trying to ride on past Bulls successes that they had nothing to do with.

Jordan's frustrations at the inadequacy of the men standing around him boiled over at that pre-season practice, when he punched Kerr in the face after his teammate stood up to one of his outbursts. 'I just haul off and hit him right in the fucking eye,' Jordan admits. Kerr, graciously, would later accept Jordan's apology, and would even claim that being punched would turn out to be a good thing for their relationship, as it represented him passing Jordan's test.

'From that point on our relationship dramatically improved,' Kerr says, though it's not clear what depths were left to plunge. 'Our trust in each other, everything. It was like, "All right, we got that out the way. We're going to war together."' Jordan agrees: 'He earned my respect because he wasn't willing to back down to be a pawn in this whole process.'

That season the Bulls won their fourth NBA Championship in six seasons. The scene with Kerr is framed with stirring music and shots of what was to come, as the perfect manifestation of Jordan's approach to success. As a viewer, you can either see being abusive towards your colleagues as wrong regardless of the outcome, or you can look to the end of the following season, when Kerr hit the game-winning shot from a Jordan pass to seal the 1997 NBA Championship, and believe that being punched in the face was a price well paid. That the ends justify the means.

*

As far as Bob Geldof was concerned, his means were certainly justified by the end result. A conclusion that was an easy sell to a general public used to this sort of imagery, and not well-versed in the ancient battle to see Africa depicted with grace, decency and nuance. If solely focusing on the immediate ends, Band Aid '84 directly raised millions of pounds to counter a developing tragedy, while consistently educating Western society on causes of the tragedy that they may not have otherwise been aware of. And thirty years later, it was doing the same again for Ebola, a disease with a mortality rate fifty times higher than COVID-19.

With that résumé, it's easy to dismiss 'Do They Know It's Christmas?' as just a harmless pop song – 'one of the carols', as Geldof once said – that exists to ding around your head for a month every year before retreating back into hibernation.

The reality is, however, that it never actually goes away. Not fully. Its financial and cultural success has inspired others to repurpose its basic model to create innumerable spin-offs, so we remain bombarded with these images of Africa time and again, throughout the year. On TV and in films, in adverts and newspapers.

'So what? They raise funds,' their creators argue. True. They certainly do. But are you certain that the money that is raised will fix what you intended it to fix? There is a Nigerian saying, 'Money miss road' – used when someone suddenly gets hold of a large amount of cash they were not prepared for. It's a reflection that money has a way of making its own journey, regardless of the path you may have expected it to go down.

Nowhere in the lyrics of 'Do They Know It's Christmas?' does it explain what caused the famine. For a song determined to shock people into both debate and action, it would seem appropriate for it to mention the underlying cruelty that sustained the misery.

The famine had started a year before the BBC's broadcast. But Ethiopian authorities deliberately kept it secret, not wanting reports of growing starvation to get in the way of the ten-year anniversary of the military government's rise to power.

In October 1984, once the planned celebrations were over, the government admitted to the famine and allowed NGOs access to the hardest-hit regions. They also welcomed international news organisations to cover the crisis. Instead of being embarrassed by the devastating images they knew would quickly spread around the world, the government saw them as an opportunity to exploit the West's response.

As expected, money quickly poured into the country. Some of it was certainly used to feed many thousands of people. A portion, however, was siphoned off by the government to fund a forced relocation policy that systematically rounded up innocent people off the streets, in their homes, and at food distribution centres in the rebel-controlled north, and transported them to government-controlled areas in the south. The week-long journeys were harrowing. Little food or water was provided for tens of thousands of people who were, as Doctors Without Borders described, 'transported like livestock' in trucks that were inadvertently paid for by aid agencies. The survivors were dumped in the south without the resources to build a new life, hundreds of miles from their homes. Experts estimate that around 100,000 Ethiopians died as a result of these mandatory relocations, a policy that was partly funded by donations from the Western world.

To justify the land-grab policy, all the Ethiopian government had to do was point to the viral images of malnourished infants, then claim that it was part of a humanitarian effort to resettle communities on more fertile lands, successfully hiding what experts believe was an attempt to lease the land they'd been relocated from for commercial agriculture. But it wasn't as if the international community was asking too many questions anyway. Aid appeals did not mention the government's role in the famine and the political calculations that drove it. Rather, the mass starvation was presented as if it was purely natural, a random act of wickedness from the weather gods. Just another day in the jungle of Africa.

There was now so much cash sloshing around Ethiopia that the secessionist rebels found a way of taking a little something for themselves. A BBC investigation in 2010 found that millions of dollars of Western aid – though none of it came from Band Aid and Live Aid – was intercepted by northern rebel groups, who used the money to buy weapons in an attempt to overthrow the government. The BBC spoke to one secessionist leader who estimated that his group had stolen in the region of £63 million, by posing as farmers selling grain to aid agencies. They would fill half the sacks with grain, and the other half with sand.

None of this truth and nuance found room in Western appeal films. Millions continued to make its way into the country from a generous public moved by a simple, flawed narrative. This is why the debate around the sort of images we use to collect donations should never be fun, and why it's vital there are always broad discussions about exactly how the messaging is used to get the money.

Of course, you cannot blame anyone else for the malignant actions of a military government unilaterally concerned with holding on to power. Still, the rush towards generosity was easily exploited – a reality that could have been avoided if charities had trusted the public's capacity to handle a more convoluted truth, however tangled, by taking more time to identify how best to help.

The real story of the Ethiopian famine was shocking enough. It didn't need new central characters or a corrupted plotline full of fake, lyrics-driven imagery to elicit a deep understanding that something needed to be done to save lives. The campaigns would have raised less money. But the truth could have shifted the debate towards working together to build a more sustainable solution that could bypass the evils of one government. In place of a tired answer, questions were a more fitting guiding star.

The creators of Band Aid, *Kony 2012*, Live Aid and Comic Relief care deeply about eradicating poverty and have dedicated a substantial amount of time and expertise to shaping the fortunes of those less fortunate than themselves. The same baseline intent can be found in many of the populist philanthropic initiatives that have come into existence since. These institutions are home to plenty of dedicated, conscious professionals working to develop long-term solutions to complicated problems. We should collectively welcome initiatives that are determined to push a grossly unequal world towards a more just equilibrium; a world where those who have find it hard to hoard. But we shouldn't equate making a more equal world with fundraising enormous sums of money by any means necessary.

There is an inherent instability within the concept of the end justify-ing the means. Difficult situations are often governed by multiple actors with a multitude of self-interests, leading to limitless ends and means that cannot be controlled by any one actor, no matter how noble their intent. No issue can be entirely solved by one neat campaign.

The act of giving requires considerably more than we are regularly asked to contribute: it should involve not only cash, but a dedication to understanding the crisis – something that is rarely encouraged, as it is believed to complicate impulsive donations. Without a full account of the cause and effects of weaponising images of grief, our collective ignorance can be played on by powerful forces, who are far more invested in the final outcome of any crisis than a casual viewer whose attention might not last beyond the end of a telethon. We have allowed that exploitation to occur, largely out of fear – the fear that proper due dili-gence takes time, and does not have the same emotional pull as photos of deathly sick children.

Efforts to change this dynamic are not new. Forty years ago, the author and development expert Jorgen Lissner published a seminal piece titled 'Merchants of Misery', calling out an aid industry addicted to swaddling Africa in brutalist imagery. He wrote:

> A substantial number of the advertisers will insist nothing can beat the starving child when it comes to "profitability" ... [but] the starving child image is seen as unethical, firstly because it comes dangerously close to being pornographic ... because it exposes something in human life that is as delicate and deeply personal as sexuality, that is, suffering. It puts people's bodies, their misery, their grief and their fear on display with all the details and all the indiscretion that a telescopic lens will allow.
>
> It is very telling that this type of social pornography is so prevalent in fundraising campaigns for the benefit of other races in far-away places but virtually non-existent when it comes to domestic concerns.

Lissner went on to suggest that development agencies should create professional codes of practice. There have been several attempts to do just that, and guidance is available for those who want it, including recommendations on how to allow communities to tell their own stories, how to gather proper consent, and how images should reflect a show of solidarity rather than pity.

These steps have largely been ignored, with the consequences extending way beyond inaccurate charity appeals. The golden age of campaigns normalised the perception of Africa as downtrodden and chronically in need. Not only did Western society respond to the message, it internalised it to such a degree that, decades later, when social media came along and offered a convenient platform to present perfectly crafted, idealised versions of our lives, the making-a-difference industry would find a welcoming home there too.

*

In 2019, British presenter and documentary filmmaker Stacey Dooley visited Uganda to film a donation appeal for Comic Relief. She spent two days with a community, in a small village in the eastern part of the country. While still in Uganda, Dooley documented her trip by uploading a series of photos and clips on her Instagram. First was a video of a group of women dancing. Then came two selfies of her holding a five-year-old Ugandan boy. Dooley captioned one of the photos 'OB.SESSSSSSSSSSSED' followed by the broken-heart emoji.

The photos were published without any context. Nothing about why the women were dancing or even what the boy's name was. They just existed, nameless, on her Instagram account, for us to quietly assume, based on the propensity of such images in Western culture, that these were poor Africans being helped – and, therefore, the particulars of their lives were irrelevant.

You can easily close your eyes and picture Dooley's photos without having seen them, because you have encountered several versions of them before. You may have even appeared in a few yourself, not intending to cause any harm. Africa is a mecca for thousands of young people who treat the continent as the official volunteering leg of their gap year. It's almost a rite of passage for people visiting to take photos of themselves standing in the middle of a group of smiling, ideally dancing, impoverished Africans – who often, by the nature of their circumstances, cannot give appropriate consent for their images to be used this way – before posting the evidence online as if to subtly suggest: 'Isn't it incredible that these people have found joy in a hopeless place?'

The approach we've seen for decades in expensively produced television adverts has found a new form on social media, with posts put through the social desirability filter that is more suited to the way my generation crafts our public personas: replace stark images of dire suffering with photos of you looking your best, standing next to beaming smiles from a grateful underprivileged individual. For Dooley, it may have seemed like a completely normal, non-controversial thing to do – an extremely common way to interact with Africans, modelled countless times before.

She was surprised then when the posts started to attract attention, perhaps because they were particularly jarring, even by the usual standards of this practice. The young boy didn't seem engaged at all with the photo-taking process. His gaze was fixed downwards, almost sad, while Dooley beamed brightly for the camera – an uncomfortable juxtaposition.

The first crop of comments below the posts were positive, though. Fans praised Dooley for her charity work as they joined her in cooing over the young Black boy. Slowly, however, more and more comments, almost exclusively posted by people from minority ethnic backgrounds, started to appear, asking Dooley to take down the video and images.

They were accusing her of perpetuating the 'white saviour complex' and using the women and children as props to show off her altruism. Overwhelmingly, her detractors were shocked that this was something that still had to be said in 2019.

Yet for every critical comment, there were still dozens of people championing her photos and congratulating Dooley on bringing attention to the plight of this community, despite – thanks to the lack of any discerning details – it being impossible for anyone to know from her posts which community the subjects in her images were from, or what exactly constituted their plight, proving that the Pavlovian response to seeing images of Africans framed this way is to comfortably settle into the worst assumptions.

A cultural war had broken out in her replies. Buoyed by the support, Dooley refused to take them down. The photos are still there today, years later, at the time of writing.

The controversy didn't go away. Days later, British MP David Lammy – a North Londoner of Guyanese descent – joined the chorus of critics, writing on Twitter: 'The world does not need any more white saviours. As I've said before, this just perpetuates tired and unhelpful stereotypes. Let's instead promote voices from across the continent of Africa and have serious debate.'

An understatement would be to say that not everyone appreciated Lammy's intervention. Soon after he posted his comments, he was on the receiving end of a barrage of replies declaring that he was the true racist for bringing up race. Dooley herself responded, hitting back to ask whether his problem was that she was white, and if so then maybe he 'could always go over there and try to raise awareness?'

The back-and-forth spilled into the public discourse, where for days journalists and radio presenters throughout the UK attacked Lammy and anyone else who believed you should act with the same grace in

Africa as you would anywhere else. Namely: you should avoid picking up random children you do not know for a photo that you then publish online without a clear indication of consent, for the rest of the world to see, no matter how cute or poor they are. It's unthinkable that anyone would make a habit of doing it in almost any other region of the world; that a post of you with a child you don't know personally could be celebrated.

It is clear that not enough progress has been made since the 1980s. Images are still widely understood to be harmless, as long as they have a flicker of charitable intent behind them. Too many have been unwilling to take the time to appreciate the long-term impact these demeaning depictions have had on the continent. As an experienced, compassionate documentary filmmaker who has worked on important stories including sex trafficking and domestic abuse, Dooley should appreciate the important role imagery plays in storytelling. But rather than recognising that she may have unintentionally contributed to an outdated practice and pushed harmful imagery, she responded in the same way Geldof and international charities have for decades: by claiming this as an effective way of making a difference.

It's understandably hard to imagine how a single Instagram post can break a region. Until you appreciate that it's not about a single photo, but the cumulative power of having these perceptions continually regurgitated, with multiple generations in the West growing up with the same paternalistic relationship with the continent, adding their own modern pieces to a mosaic too ingrained in the collective subconscious to easily break apart.

A few months after the Dooley row ignited, David Lammy revealed that he had asked his nine-year-old son why he should donate to Comic Relief, to test what he had learned from the campaign's messaging.

'We have to help the poor people in Africa,' his son replied. 'The poor people in Africa. At such a young age, he had ingested the singular con-cept of 'Africa' as a buzzword for pain and strife, devoid of a diverse range of people and cultures.

Preconceived perceptions breed discrimination. When Africans travel the world, we are forced to carry on our backs the same bigoted assumptions that we are coming from poverty, with relatives living in mud huts waiting for handouts from the West.

When required, quick aid can do some good in certain circumstances, and certainly there are lots of organisations that do astonishing work. But when imagery that perpetuates negative stereotypes is utilised, it regularly blocks the continent from receiving the sort of long-term investments enjoyed by the Western world, through business opportu-nities and broad sustainable tourism that empowers local populations and doesn't exploit them for quick hits.

Watching these videos might elicit some temporary empathy and have you reaching for the pennies in your pocket. But does it motivate you to go to that country on holiday? Does it make you want to start a company there or work with local businesses? Will you be moved to consider all the expertise that must exist there, in tech, medicine and the creative industries? This is what many nations need more than a charity single, however catchy it might be.

In the same spring that *Kony 2012* was released, the popular travel guide book publisher Lonely Planet declared Uganda the best country to visit that year, a recognition that was quickly drowned out by Invis-ible Children's footage of ubiquitous gloom. The Ugandan government scrambled to counter the documentary by releasing a YouTube video of its own, promoting the country and highlighting Lonely Planet's assess-ment. 'Come and see Uganda for yourself,' the then prime minister, Amama Mbabazi, said in the short film. 'You will find a very different place to that portrayed by Invisible Children.'

The damage was already done, though: 2012 was the first time in almost twenty years that Uganda would suffer a drop in tourism revenues.

Until organisations stop relying on negative imagery, Africa will remain a place widely considered to be worthy of handouts and very little else. But there are organisations working on the ground to change this. No White Saviors (NWS), for example, is a Uganda-based charity and advocacy group launched in 2018 'out of a collective frustration at the rampant abuses committed by white missionaries and development workers in Uganda and beyond'. The organisation was started by Ugandan social worker Alaso Olivia and American Kelsey Nielsen, who NWS playfully refers to as a 'white savior in recovery'. The group has amassed a strong following, with almost a million followers on Instagram alone.

NWS is the leading organisation working to identify harmful actions and imagery committed by development agencies and their staff on the continent, while offering legal support to vulnerable Ugandans. 'We are talking about historical, systematic and institutionalised power structures that span hundreds of years. White saviourism is a symptom of white supremacy and something we all have to work together to deconstruct.' Through their social media accounts, podcasts and lectures, they have worked to educate the world on the harmful effects of the rampant discrimination that often lurks beneath development narratives.

'We see it in restaurants, when a white person is served first while a black person receives crappy services,' Nielsen told *The Observer* shortly after the Dooley incident, speaking about the long-term impact this kind of imagery has on the continent. 'We see it in the way organisations pay black workers less.'

'We are trying to give our children a better education,' Alaso added.

'We are developing our countries. We need aid but it must not come with strings attached. We are saying that if you want to help, first listen to us and provide what we need – not what you think we need.'

As NWS recognises, there are serious challenges facing parts of the continent. The ramifications of colonialism are something that a majority of nations are still trying to come to terms with.

Any person or organisation of good mind and spirit can do the requisite work to understand the history of a cause, and then do their bit where specifically needed, as directed by people on the ground.

For charities, it's never too late to repent and mend your ways. In October 2020, Comic Relief announced a commitment to rethinking its approach, promising to abolish the use of stark images of starving children. 'Times have changed and society has evolved, and we must evolve too,' Lenny Henry said. 'African people don't want us to tell their stories for them, what they need is more agency, a platform and partnership.'

With agency comes a more detailed story, because those on the ground, as Teju Cole says, 'see the larger disasters behind it: militarization of poorer countries, short-sighted agricultural policies, resource extraction, the propping up of corrupt governments, and the astonishing complexity of long-running violent conflicts over a wide and varied terrain.'

Celebrities, you can take a lead from Manchester United's Marcus Rashford. Over the past few years, the footballer has mobilised his influence to advocate on behalf of Britain's poorest children, forcing the government on multiple occasions to reverse its policies on free school meals and other essential food programmes. Rashford achieved this without having to share images of half-naked white British children rummaging through the bins in Leeds or Nottingham or Cornwall, gentle piano music playing in the background, their parents huddled in the corner of the room, beaten by poverty. He didn't ask African musicians to come together to film a music video to highlight the stark realities of poverty in the UK. Rashford built a movement through facts and information. He used his platform to amplify the voices of local organisations and professionals experienced in understanding the faults in the system and how best to fix them. He went straight to the person at the top, British prime minister Boris Johnson, and not, as the makers of *Kony 2012* did, to other foreign leaders, thousands of miles away. Most importantly, the struggling families were treated with the dignity they deserved.

And if you're personally wondering how to contribute and manoeuvre around this minefield without being accused of being a 'white saviour', then go ahead and visit the continent. This shouldn't paralyse anyone wanting to contribute their time and powers. But before you do anything, first ask yourself this question: 'How would I act in a homeless shelter in London or Madrid or Sydney?' Would you ask everyone to stop what they were doing to pose for a photo with you as the centrepiece? Upon seeing a child going about their child-like business, would you stop them, pick them up and hold them aloft like a trophy? I assume not. So resist the urge when you're on the continent. And if you absolutely must take a photo of something for Instagram on your trip to Africa, try a picture of some perfectly constructed, snow-dusted Christmas decorations.

Part Four

*The Story of Democracy
in Seven Dictatorships*

My aunt repeated herself for the third time. Her flurry of words dropped like faint snowflakes confident in their once-in-a-lifetime charm. Not enough belief, however, was present in her audience for the words to settle on understanding. I looked over at my older sisters for guidance, but they were just as frozen in astonishment.

There are only so many ways you can break the news of a person's death. There are only so many times anyone would want to. Yet it was clear from my aunt's tone that for this particular task, her reservoirs of glee were bottomless, and she could go all day relaying this news, like a town crier at the peak of their game. By her fifth attempt – crackled with laughter – my sisters and I were all standing, roused by the unexpected energy that comes from surprise, our faces contorted by shock. A broken fan spluttered in the corner of the living room, losing its final battle with the wet heat of Lagos in June.

Aunty Tokunbo had called to speak to my mother. It was her she wanted to reveal the news to. They would have deciphered its implications together, a running commentary peppered with the punctuation of two Nigerians breaking the world into its component parts. *Really / Na wa oh / You don't mean it? / Chai / God dey / Ah ahn / Didn't I tell you? / You see life.*

Instead of the conversation she craved, my aunt's phone call found three teenage girls and a nine-year-old boy, home alone. It wasn't her fault that we struggled to process the information. She could not have been clearer over the phone, more obvious that she wasn't joking. Her voice carried the steady resonance of a fact rather than the hushed delicacies of gossip. She was being as definitive as any Nigerian aunty expressing a view that does not require your input. It was left to us to absorb something that for so long hadn't seemed possible.

'Are you sure?' my eldest sister asked for the final time.

'Check CNN,' my aunt replied, now bored of us.

For some reason, none of us had thought of the TV as something built for moments like this. I snatched at the remote, taking charge of the situation. Sister Number Two took it back off me. She found the right channel, and there it was.

The breaking-news caption was red with importance. I'm sure if you looked up the chosen font, it would be called Historic Implications:

Nigerian Military Leader General Sani Abacha Reported Dead

At that, the world felt lighter, as if floating was simply a matter of preference. Long-jettisoned pieces of a tainted puzzle seemed to be slowly making their way to each other. We elicited several different octaves of joyful squealing. Trey, our family dog, lifted his head by the window, his eyes wide, pleading to speak human in the way dogs do when they are concerned that the owners they rely on to remain alive are no longer capable of fulfilling that duty.

'Tell your mum to call me when she gets back,' my aunt said to silence, before hanging up.

Mum returned not long after that and we all quickly rushed outside, eager to be the one to break the news. As soon as we opened the front door, you could hear it: car horns and whistles and shouts from every direction, rising in shared celebration; the rhythms of connected relief serenading the city. Before we could reach her, her smile, piercing through the car window, reached us, betraying that she already knew. Impromptu street celebrations had broken out and surrounded her car as she drove home.

As she stepped out, she raised a single finger to her lips, silencing our excitement until we got back inside. With that gesture she was recognising another possibility – the same possibility that kept celebrations muted and the air stilted on the military base where my father was stationed hundreds of miles away, where the news of The Man In Abuja's demise was whispered in neutral tones just in case this was an elaborate ruse, a test concocted in Abacha's mind to see who remained loyal in grief.

Thankfully the reports of his death were grossly true, and the men on the base, too, could celebrate more openly. The dictator's five-year reign had ended mysteriously in the middle of the night. The accepted rumour that he was poisoned at a drug-fuelled orgy was just as likely to be true as it was to be a final attempt to humiliate him. His body was quickly buried, leaving a nation to speculate on what forces had finally relieved Nigeria from this torment and allowed the country to swing towards democracy.

Democracy is a great revealer. A country's chosen approach to the balance and distribution of power speaks to what – on its best day – the nation wants to be. How a society picks those who govern it, or what the collective does when the majority's will is rejected, is consistently seen as a way of grading how civilised that country is and how it's portrayed around the world. Nations are sanctioned based on these assessments; kicked off the adults' table, fined and banished until they repent, without much pause to understand the specific situation in question or to ask whether some of the global authorities acting as jury and executioner may have had a small role in facilitating the government they now condemn.

Africa has faced the brunt of this unbalanced treatment – looked upon like a governance-cursed monolith with a high concentration of savage warlords. One of the most common tropes in popular culture is the violent African dictator slashing through the jungle with a machete, searching for villages to pillage, children to abduct and blood diamonds to harvest. The narrative suggests there is something fundamentally ungovernable about this place and its people; something extremely uncivilised about their unhealthy relationship with power. The 'failure of African leaders' is a common phrase routinely blurted out at development conferences and high-brow lectures with patronising disdain.

As always, the reality is more intricately layered. Fifty-four countries are not governed by a singular ideology that prefers an all-conquering ruler. The continent has tangled with its fair share of authoritarians – but it's not because Africans are somehow predisposed to evil despotism. Understanding the modern dynamics of democracy across the continent is central to appreciating the specificities of each country's tussle with its identity; especially how the colonial empires, by creating countries with such mismatched geographies, played a big role in intentionally facilitating power grabs by leaving African countries with forms of democracies that did not fit the demographics the colonisers had created.

Since the independence movements of the '50s and '60s, most nations at some point have contended with a man who doesn't know when to quit. But the power dynamics at play speak to the idiosyncrasies of complex histories, rather than some binding universal voodoo that would release its grip if only Africans were not so greedy, and were as aware of the benefits of democracy as is the rest of the enlightened world.

Abacha died twenty-four years ago, a day that brought an end to Nigeria's decades-long relationship with authoritarian rule. The country would not have celebrated if Nigerians didn't know other forms of leadership than forced rule were possible. The circumstances that had brought Abacha to power and sustained him there were initially created by forces far outside of Nigeria's control. Abacha did not represent the country, nor the predilections of your average Nigerian. And his reign certainly shouldn't be used to judge the many African countries that were very much enjoying democratic government at the time.

The various whats and hows of Abacha's story exist amid dozens of tales of difficult beginnings that can help explain the continent's path towards democracy. Journeys largely propelled by seven motivating forces that do not follow a single stereotype: Cold War dealmakers; god-playing colonial masters; revolutionary heroes; opportunistic families; civil-war peacemakers; founding fathers; and, yes, the rare unhinged madman with a taste for human flesh.

I.

The Art of the Deal

I want them to move in every possible way to get Somalia to be our friend.

— Jimmy Carter

IF HOLLYWOOD WERE TO MAKE A FILM of the life and times of the late Somali dictator Major General Siad Barre, it would try to pin his car crash in 1986 – and the subsequent widespread questioning of his health and ability to continue ruling – as the seminal moment when he flipped to madness and began plotting the extermination of an entire ethnic group. But in reality, he was quite unbalanced well before then.

Political calculations made in Washington, DC and Moscow were key to his stability in office, and would leave him orphaned and power-less once he was no longer needed.

General Barre took power in a bloodless coup in 1969, nine years after Somalia gained independence. The previous president, Dr Abdirashid Ali Shermarke, had been murdered by his own bodyguard in what is believed to have been a personal attack. The military took advantage of this power vacuum, and Barre, who grew up an orphaned shepherd boy and rose to become commander-in-chief of Somalia's armed forces, was put in charge of the fledgling East African nation.

Barre quickly did what dictators do: he banned political parties, sus-pended the constitution and dismantled the judiciary. He developed a personality cult around himself, choosing to go by the moniker Victori-ous Leader.

His administration came of age during the height of the Cold War. The United States and the Soviet Union had weighed their options and decided that killing everyone on the planet in an all-out nuclear war was arguably a bad idea. Instead, the two countries searched for friendly nations around the world that they could convince (bribe) to be on their side in a pseudo war fought with influence.

Somalia's love was certainly for sale at the right price, and Washington and Moscow were ready to make a deal to help prop up Barre's dictatorship, caring very little for the person on the other side of the cheque.

Barre picked a side early, declaring in the first year of his rule that Somalia was a socialist country based on Marxist principles. He developed a state ideology that would adhere him to the Soviet Union and build a strong sense of Somali nationalism. Public events were littered with portraits of Barre superimposed next to Marx and Lenin.

Somalia and Moscow would make it official in 1974 by signing a 'Treaty of Friendship and Cooperation'. This gave the Soviet Union access to a military base in Berbera, a coastal city and major port in the northern region that would later be developed to include a missile storage facility. In exchange for this prime piece of real estate off the Indian Ocean, Moscow would help finance the strengthening of Somalia's armed forces – a necessity for any dictator trying to hold on to power in a fractured country.

Emboldened by that sweet USSR rouble fuelling their armed forces, Somalia decided in 1977 that it was time to use military action to settle a dispute over Ethiopia's Ogaden region, which Somalia claimed for its own. The desert area was largely populated by Somalis, but colonial border divisions had given it to Ethiopia.

Somali troops crossed the western border into Ethiopia, with General Barre simply claiming that his government was supporting an organic guerrilla movement that wanted to secede from Ethiopia.

The Soviet Union now had a problem. Ethiopia had a new communist military dictator of its own, who had recently ditched the country's long-standing partnership with the US, switching its allegiance to Moscow in exchange, as always, for weapons. Two of Moscow's protégés were now at war. And Somalia, the instigator, was winning.

Arming both sides was clearly a ludicrous proposition. So the USSR pushed for a peace settlement. After Barre rejected their calls for a cease-fire, the Soviet Union picked a team: choosing Ethiopia and its newer military junta, excited to partner with a nation that had been, for so long, a key US ally in the region. Along with Cuba, they cut off military support to Somalia and increased it in Ethiopia. Without Russia, Somalia was eventually forced into an embarrassing retreat out of Ogaden.

You're probably wondering: what's the point of a military dictator if he can't win a war? Well, good question.

Now left stranded by the USSR, Barre was weak and facing a coup as generals in his own military started to turn against him. He needed a new godfather to stay in power. Luckily, a recently dumped one was back on the market.

'I want them to move in every possible way to get Somalia to be our friend,' US president Jimmy Carter ordered his State Department.

Barre accepted Washington's offer of friendship, and literally sent the Carter administration a list of weapons he required to make this union official. In the meantime, in November 1977, as an act of revenge, the Somali government kicked Russian forces out of the country, giving them seven days to evacuate thousands of personnel from military bases in Berbera and Kismayu, on the southern coast. They didn't have to go far, though – just over the border into Ethiopia, to join their new partners.

The US was offered the chance to take over the bases, and just like that, in a matter of months, Moscow and Washington had unofficially traded East African authoritarian governments.

General Barre was back and as strong as ever. In 1982, he travelled to

Washington, DC to meet with President Ronald Reagan, to ensure that his understanding with the new US administration was still all good. It was. Barre was so confident, in fact, of his country's strategic value to the US in the Cold War, he even complained to journalists in Washington that the nearly $120 million in annual military, economic and refugee aid the Reagan administration was offering – a rise of about $20 million from the previous year – was not satisfactory, though when asked to characterise the vibe of the meeting, he said the 'atmospherics were excellent' and expressed confidence that 'a new chapter of closer cooperation' was ahead.

Six years later, Barre launched his attempted purge of the Isaaq ethnic group in northern Somalia. The military campaign included the almost-total destruction of the two largest cities in the region, Hargeisa and Burao. An estimated 200,000 Somali civilians were killed, while the civil war created upwards of 300,000 refugees.

Throughout this genocide, the US government under Reagan continued to help fund Barre's military regime. That support continued until the collapse of the Soviet Union in 1991. After that, Washington, no longer needing Somalia's support, started to complain about Barre's human rights record. The US government soon dropped him, pulling their aid funding.

Without the support of a foreign benefactor to lean on, Barre – like many other dictators at the time – became fragile and isolated, not helped by rumours that he had never fully recovered from his car accident years earlier. To save himself, he rushed to promise democratic elections, but it was too late. He was toppled by powerful rebels early in 1991 and fled the country, never to return, dying four years later of a heart attack in exile.

*

II.

A Very British Plot

Privatization in Nigeria is selling the Government to individuals . . . it means my country is on the market. I've never seen that before, historically. It's happening in Nigeria, Ghana, and these leaders accept this arrangement. Which makes me feel that they are agents for the Western system . . . It just shows the low mentality of my country's leaders. I thought they had developed a little bit of sense.

— Fela Kuti

CONQUERING SOMEONE'S LAND AND DESTINY is an expensive, hard business.

By the time the Europeans arrived in Africa, the continent had few centralised urban areas. Some larger kingdoms existed that governed mass populations, such as the Sokoto Caliphate, Kingdom of Ashanti, and the Kingdom of Benin in West Africa; the Zulu Kingdom in southern Africa; and the Buganda Empire in Uganda. But the vast majority of people were grouped together in smaller communities that were not dominated by a singular, all-powerful ruler. When your chosen leader is also your neighbour – easily reachable; easily dismissible – decisions need to have the general consent of the members of the community. In some cases, nomadic groups could just pick themselves up and leave if they no longer felt like their rulers were acting in their best interests.

Of course, that is not a particularly convenient arrangement for colonisers looking to conquer vast swathes of land. The aim – as with any business, and this was certainly a business – was to extract as much value from their colonies at the cheapest-possible cost to themselves. The fewer individual groups of people you have to deal with, the better: ideally, you want as many as possible to answer to one great centralised dominion.

To achieve this wider goal, the British ran the regions that they did not want to live in (because: malaria) using a system of governance known as 'indirect rule'. London would continue to make the big decisions, but on the ground they would find Africans of questionable morals – slick to a bribe, decency-deficient – and empower them with money and guns and artificial status to subjugate their own people on a day-to-day basis, placing smaller ethnic groups under the dominance of larger ones, creating new societies where they did not previously exist. At times, they completely invented leadership structures and gave out titles and clout to greedy men. Individuals who – as Fela Kuti said – were of 'low mentality'. Individuals commonly known as Big Men.

This invented system meant that the colonialists could enjoy their spoils from a cheap distance; not needing to get their hands dirty, because they had purchased souls that revelled in wrestling in the corrupt mud.

Over time, one large group was forcibly combined with another, and then another, until the British had formed an absurdly large country that was easier to manage under one banner.

To keep these disparate groups from working together to overthrow their colonial masters, the British adopted a concurrent policy of 'divide and rule' where they deliberately created tension between these ethnic groups, favouring one over the other, and placed the Big Men in their preferred clan into positions of power in government and the military.

But independence would still come, a movement that could not be resisted forever. Suddenly, these artificial countries, by British design, were filled with hundreds of demonstrably corrupt Big Men whose power and influence over their fellow citizens had been purposefully contrived. Rich, unscrupulous, uneducated, well-armed, well-positioned and often military-trained, not satisfied with having their slice of cake, they wanted to eat their country, too. And thanks to divide-and-rule, they had grown to resent the other Big Men from the other ethnic groups with whom they were now forced to share national resources and fight to be the Ultimate Big Man. But however you sliced that

national pie – and many tried to cut their own countries into pieces –
the reality was that only one of these Big Men could be president.

What this hostile whirlwind of authority created in these countries
was not so much one dangerous dictatorship, but rather a series of constant tussles for power in a winner-takes-all royal rumble that stretched
across decades, plaguing each of Britain's colonies in West and East
Africa – from Ghana and Sierra Leone to Zambia and Kenya. But none
had as much of an acute, dangerous reaction to the divide-and-rule policy as Nigeria – Britain's big, unwieldy, prized possession.

After Britain purchased the land that would eventually make modern
Nigeria from the Royal Niger Company in 1885, the northern region
formed the Protectorate of Northern Nigeria, while the south became
the Protectorate of Southern Nigeria. The two regions were then amal-
gamated in 1914 to form Nigeria. (The name comes from the Niger
River that runs through Nigeria, and was suggested by the journalist
Flora Shaw, the wife of one of Britain's most celebrated colonisers, Lord
Lugard.)

This one country now featured over 250 different ethnic groups.
Three of these ethnic groups made up 65 per cent of the population.
They would come to dominate the country: the Hausa-Fulani in the
north, the Yoruba in the south-west and the Igbo in the south-east –
three culturally rich, historically proud clans.

The British favoured the Hausa-Fulani, whose governance structure
was easier to work with. The predominantly Muslim north was run by
a relatively small number of powerful emirs in a more centralised system. To govern large northern communities, the British simply needed
to either violently overpower emirs who did not want to work with
them, or bribe those who did. Other communities were then pushed
under the governance of Britain's favoured emirs. A substantial number
of these northern leaders rejected any education outside of religious

teachings – a policy that kept significant factions of their own citizens uneducated. Wealth and knowledge were kept for a select few, and the British ensured those few received plum positions in the Nigerian military. Smaller northern communities that worried that their individual identities were being brushed over attempted to push back against the system, but they found it difficult as they were forced to fight power structures built far away from where they lived.

Nigeria's southern regions proved far more stubborn. The Yoruba and the Igbo both welcomed Western education. As a result, economic development in the south would far outpace that of the north. The Igbo in particular, who were living in smaller communities, found it easier to reject the corrupt chiefs that the British would try to install, setting up violent clashes with the colonial armies.

Very little of the colonial political arrangement worked for the Yoruba and the Igbo, so the south-west and the south-east would lead a passionate charge for independence.

In an attempt to stave off the push for self-governance, the British created tension between the three major ethnic groups to make it harder for them to work together. The country was officially split into three regions: the Northern Region, which would be dominated by the Hausa-Fulani; the Western Region, controlled by the Yoruba; and the Eastern Region, where the Igbo had the most influence. What was an unofficial geographical layering was now ingrained in the country's make-up. This arrangement encouraged people to think more of themselves as members of an ethnic group than as Nigerians. As a result, too many grew an attachment to their region rather than the collective whole.

As independence grew closer, the three dominant ethnic groups – still yet to fully develop a national identity around being 'Nigerian' – started to realise the vast possibilities of governing a cash-crop-rich independent Nigeria. They organised themselves into political parties around their identities. The Hausa-Fulanis formed the Northern People's Congress, the Action Group was for Yorubas, and The National Convention of Nigerian Citizens was led by Igbos in the Eastern Region. The British, of course, promoted these political differences in an attempt to maintain the split loyalties. They put their thumb on the election scale in favour of Hausa-Fulani leaders – who were looking to delay independence until their region caught up economically with the south's development, worried that when the British left, the new nation, with its capital hundreds of miles away, in Lagos, could leave their ethnic group floundering under the governance of others. The colonial administration supported the Northern People's Congress in regional elections in the late 1950s, and encouraged, where possible, a partnership with the Igbo, who the British saw as being more patient for independence than the Yoruba.

When freedom eventually came on 1 October 1960, all that man-made tension would almost immediately sow distrust throughout this man-made country, setting off a scramble for power well before anyone had cultivated a deep-rooted allegiance to the Federal Republic of Nigeria. The British had left, but their crafted divisions had set firmly in the country's foundations. Nobody wanted to give up their influence and be ruled by a different ethnic group.

Stripped of collegiality, 'Nigeria' as a concept would slowly unravel in the first five years of freedom, until power was the only commodity.

In January 1966, a group made up of mostly Igbo army officers executed a military coup against the Nigerian government, in the process killing the two most prominent Northerners: Prime Minister Tafawa Balewa, and the head of the Northern Region, Ahmadu Bello. Major General Johnson Aguiyi-Ironsi, an Igbo, then took power. He wanted to abolish the regions and encourage a united homeland, but that was seen in the north as an attempt to force Igbo rule on everyone else.

In retaliation, just six months later, northern officers staged a violent counter-coup; in turn murdering Aguiyi-Ironsi and replacing him with Lieutenant Colonel Yakubu Gowon. Not content with seizing back power, tens of thousands of Igbos living in the north were massacred in revenge attacks, forcing Igbos to flee for their lives back to the Eastern Region, where they commanded. Peace talks to save Nigeria failed, and in May 1967, feeling an understandable lack of patriotism and that they were only safe in their own region, the head of the Eastern delegation, the Oxford-educated Lieutenant Colonel Odumegwu Ojukwu, announced that the Igbo and the Eastern Region would secede from Nigeria to form a country of their own: the Republic of Biafra.

One problem: the Eastern Region had all the oil. There was no way the Nigerian government was going to allow them to leave. This impasse would spark an almost three-year civil war that would lead to the death of around a million people, mainly Igbos. The Nigerian government would implement an extremely effective food blockade, starving the Eastern Region – a tactic that would eventually lead to Biafra's surrender.

The Gowon administration would go on to launch a relatively successful peace and reconciliation effort. Igbos were reintegrated back into Nigeria, though they were blamed for the war and ostracised in some parts of the country. There has not been an Igbo president since.

Colonialism and the war taught Nigeria's Big Men that power was Nigeria's national language, not to be relinquished easily. The fate of your people depended on you gripping it firmly to your side and never letting it go. With the dominance of the military, the next three decades in Nigeria saw a succession of Northern generals seize power from each other. On average, Nigeria would suffer a coup every three and a half years. This would continue until the mysterious death of Sani Abacha in the middle of the night in 1998 – a seismic event that would shake the country into democracy. Enough was enough.

It was easy in those three decades for an emotionally divided nation to be ruled by whichever Big Man had the biggest gun. It was easy to convince your people that if they didn't take theirs, someone else would come along and consume it all. The British Empire had erected a house of cards, with toppling over as a key design feature. Abacha's unexpected death, a generous reprieve, presented an opportunity to pick the deck back up and build something new – that, hopefully, if caught on the right day, and glimpsed in the perfect light, could resemble something like unity.

*

III.

Vengeance

'Order your man to step aside or there will be violence.'

Cersei Lannister took in her cousin's ultimatum. Remembering the humiliations that had been visited upon her, she quickly made her decision. Never breaking eye contact, she replied:

'I choose violence.'

— D. B. Weiss, *Game of Thrones*

DYLANN ROOF CALMLY WALKED into a small basement room of the Emanuel AME Church in Charleston, South Carolina – a historic Black church whose role in fighting for racial justice for the Black community goes back to slavery.

Already in the basement were twelve Black churchgoers taking part in a weekly Bible study. A stranger to them, the twenty-one-year-old Roof was warmly welcomed and invited to take part. He accepted. For the next hour, Roof joined the group as they combed through the words of scripture, taking part in discussions and quiet meditations.

When Roof was ready to do what he was there to do, he took out a Glock handgun from his bag. The study group were deep in silent prayer: eyes closed, reflective, unaware of anything outside their reverent contemplations. Without ceremony, Roof stood up and opened fire on the three men, eight women and the five-year-old girl who had gathered there that evening, on 17 June 2015.

He didn't stop shooting for six minutes.

At a point, one of his victims, twenty-six-year-old Tywanza Sanders, tried talking Roof down. Sanders asked him why he was doing this.

'I have to do it,' Roof replied. 'You rape our women and you're taking over our country. And you have to go.'

Nine people were shot and killed that night. It was America's worst racially motivated attack in modern history. Three people survived. Felicia Sanders watched Roof shoot and kill her son Tywanza, before successfully shielding her five-year-old granddaughter. The two survived by pretending to be dead. Roof deliberately spared one person. Her job, the shooter said, was to bear witness to the slaughter and tell the world what had happened.

Roof fled the scene. A fourteen-hour manhunt would end in his capture 250 miles away from the church. He showed no remorse. 'I would like to make it crystal clear, I do not regret what I did,' Roof declared in court. 'I am not sorry.'

In the days after the shooting, investigators discovered a website belonging to Roof. On the site, the self-proclaimed white supremacist and neo-Nazi outlined his hatred of Black people and his wish that the massacre would start a race war. In several photos, Roof posed wearing a jacket stitched with a popular symbol of the white supremacist movement: the green-and-white flag of a country that no longer existed. A nation so racist it still inspires bigots the world over – even those, like Roof, who were not alive at the peak of its hatred. The name of that country was honoured in the title of his website and manifesto: 'The Last Rhodesian'.

Around thirty years before Dylann Roof was born, British colonialists had come to accept the inevitability of independence across Africa. Freedom was becoming the norm. But one colonial administration in southern Africa was refusing to budge.

Unlike much of West Africa, southern Africa and parts of East Africa had a climate that the colonialists could get comfortable with. And they did. There they implemented 'settler rule', where large populations of Europeans would come and live, establishing laws that transformed the native population into second-class citizens. They exploited natural resources and annexed all the good land for the white residents – introducing a form of white supremacism that produced a caste system that violently oppressed the Black population. It was terrorism.

In the late 1800s, this form of rule was implemented when the British colonised a sliver of southern Africa and called it Northern and Southern Rhodesia, named after Cecil Rhodes. Then came the 1960s, when Black nationalist movements in the region demanded freedom – peacefully and otherwise – from white minority rule. The authorities of Northern Rhodesia eventually agreed, granting independence in 1964. Nationalists changed the country's name to Zambia.

The whites of Southern Rhodesia, however, refused to give up power – unable to shake their fundamental belief that Black people were not capable of governing themselves; that they were better off under white rule. No longer needing to differentiate themselves from their northern neighbours, the country dropped its descriptor and adopted the name Rhodesia. The British government demanded that the Rhodesian government relinquish control to majority rule. But the whites stayed firm in their refusal. This racist movement was led by a politician called Ian Smith and his white nationalist party, the Rhodesian Front. Smith vowed that, for as long as he lived, and for hundreds of years beyond his death, Africans would never control Rhodesia.

Smith was extremely committed to this white nationalist creed. So much so that, in 1965, the Rhodesian Front declared independence from the UK, just to ensure that they could continue their racist policies without interference from London. It worked. The British government was furious at the move, but there was little they could do to stop them – these were essentially their own people. It would be the British military fighting the British military. They tried sanctions, but southern Africa was full of racist white settlers in powerful positions who came to Rhodesia's aid whenever Smith called.

With resistance from the international community largely taken care of, Smith could focus most of his attention on dampening any Black uprisings in Rhodesia. Black nationalist parties were banned, and their leaders were arrested and imprisoned for a decade. Ninety per cent of the Black population were prohibited from voting in elections. The most oppressive state-sanctioned violence came from the Selous Scouts – a regiment of the Rhodesian Army that specialised in hunting down nationalist insurgents. 'The white man is master of Rhodesia,' Smith declared. 'He has built it, and he intends to keep it.'

Smith saw the British government's attempts to intervene as a betrayal of the values he was taught by the colonial administrators who came before him. 'Within Britain itself, we were landed with a socialist government hell-bent on appeasing the cult of Marxist Leninism, at the expense of the old traditional values of the British Empire,' he would later write.

All the international community could really do was condemn the Rhodesian administration. Sanctions remained ineffective throughout the '60s, as were multiple attempts to negotiate with the regime. Meanwhile, Smith's racist defiance was winning him a growing fan base among white supremacists and neo-Nazis in the US – groups that really led the way in the racial-subjugation-of-your-fellow-citizens business. Bigots the world over marvelled at the extreme lengths Rhodesia was willing to go in order to maintain white rule. As Americans watched their own country capitulate to the civil rights movement, pro-Rhodesian movements sprang up across the US. Emblems of the Rhodesian Front came to be used in place of commonly known neo-Nazi symbols, as a safer way of signalling your bigotry to those in the know while hiding it from others.

'We think you should be able to tell the world about you without saying a word,' read a website that sold pro-Rhodesian memorabilia, including jackets and t-shirts with code words printed on them that translated to 'Shoot black people'. 'The great thing about most of our designs,' the site continued, 'is that they are essentially inside jokes and references that the general public will not understand.' The site was still live and selling in 2018, until it was discovered by journalists.

Black nationalists kept fighting for their dignity. In 1972, they launched a guerrilla war against the Rhodesian government. Two years later, to quell some of that nationalist fervour, the government agreed to release some of the political prisoners they had held captive for over a decade. The freed prisoners included the founder of the National Democratic Party, Joseph Nkomo, and the face of the revolutionary movement, a fifty-one-year-old former teacher by the name of Robert Mugabe.

Mugabe had been imprisoned in 1964 and later sentenced to twenty-one months. In the end, he spent eleven years in prison. While in jail, his three-year-old son died. Mugabe's request to attend the funeral was denied.

From prison, Mugabe and his fellow revolutionary leaders plotted their country's freedom – the eight-year guerrilla war that began in 1972. The breakthrough for Black nationalists came in 1975, when Portugal lost control of Mozambique. Freedom fighters including Mugabe were able to slip out of Rhodesia and into Mozambique to coordinate the liberation movement from there. Smith and the Rhodesian Front faced attacks from several angles, as Nkomo led the movement from Zambia and Mugabe from Mozambique.

By the mid '70s, Smith was just delaying the inevitable. Rhodesia had lost the support of many of their neighbours, especially South Africa, and the US government was starting to apply real pressure. Still, Smith wouldn't give up easily. He spent years trying to negotiate a power-sharing agreement that would leave white Rhodesians in charge of major institutions. They were willing to take a step down without actually moving their feet. Unsurprisingly, Mugabe and Nkomo rejected the deal.

Thirty thousand people had died as a result of the ongoing conflict. The British government searched for a truce by inviting all parties to a summit in London in 1975. The meeting produced the Lancaster House Agreement, which finally granted a path to independence for a new government elected by the majority, with the enfranchisement of Black voters. In exchange, whites could maintain some representation in parliament. Smith hated the deal, but he had run out of plausible options.

Four months later, the Black majority were finally freed from the oppression of minority rule. They renamed their country Zimbabwe.

Robert Mugabe was seen as a hero of the liberation movement. He had fought to bring relief to a nation that had waited so long for freedom from Smith's bigoted doctrine. At the first national election, Mugabe's party, the Zimbabwe African National Union (ZANU), won the majority of parliamentary seats. He became the country's first Black prime minister.

Things started off well. The government spent generously on public services, transforming Zimbabwe into one of the most prosperous countries on the continent. Few shed a tear when Mugabe eventually forced the Rhodesian Front from government completely in the late '80s. Mugabe was even awarded an honorary knighthood by the Queen in 1994.

However, life in Zimbabwe would turn as Mugabe gave into his two vices: hatred for the British for what they had done to him and his country, and his love of power. Not long after becoming prime minister, he wrestled all control away from his fellow nationalists, adapting the constitution to install himself as the country's first executive president. He quashed dissent and waged violence against smaller ethnic groups that were not loyal to his party, leading to thousands of deaths.

Hovering above Zimbabwe was the question of what to do with the remnants of white settler policy. Less than 2 per cent of the population owned over half of the country's arable land. British colonialism and Ian Smith had created a problem a hundred years in the making. Now it was left to Mugabe to solve it – a task difficult for anyone, and not one that was suited to Mugabe's skillset. As he stalled, resentment grew among Black farmers as the country failed to establish the comprehensive reparations programme that the president had promised to implement. A vacuum of leadership created an opportunity for those who wanted to solve the issue through violence and forced seizure. Fearing losing support, Mugabe gave them what they wanted and implemented a hastily contrived land reform programme that allowed men who claimed to be veterans of the war – though many of them were too young – to seize almost all the white-owned farms in the country. Without much planning, the farmland just ended up in the hands of government allies and farmers who did not have the means to tend to it, helping to destroy much of the economy. Still, Mugabe saw it as the revenge he and his country deserved.

The two-year-long forced evictions of white farmers made Mugabe a villain to the West. His knighthood was stripped from him, and heavy financial sanctions were placed on the country. Mugabe didn't care. It just reinforced his hatred for Britain and his mantra that all the world wanted was to re-subjugate his country. 'Zimbabwe will never be a colony again' was his rally cry.

Mugabe certainly had cause to be vengeful towards colonial Britain – but very little of that disdain did anything to help his country. Zimbabwe's economy tanked until there was very little of it at all. Its currency became meaningless, and unemployment reached 80 per cent. Professionals fled the country for better opportunities elsewhere on the continent. In the face of all this, Mugabe became more stubborn, more entrenched in his views. He had saved Zimbabwe from the white man once, he thought, and he figured that he would do it again. Ian Smith had sworn that Rhodesia would not be free for hundreds of years, yet Mugabe had achieved it in fifteen.

He slipped into violent tyranny as his nation weakened and the economic sanctions piled higher. To the disappointment of the West, there was little to nothing other African leaders were willing to do to stop him. They had all witnessed the racist brutality of Ian Smith's reign, and they still respected Mugabe as an icon of the liberation movement. At the very least, they did not want to be seen to be siding with the coloniser over the colonised.

Even with their support, Mugabe remained frustrated at the way the world was falling in love with another formerly jailed freedom fighter, who was being hailed – as he once was – as a symbol of post-colonial leadership; a name that was becoming a byword for greatness.

Sitting above the flag of Rhodesia on Dylann Roof's jacket was the symbol of another deeply racist country: apartheid South Africa.

In 1948, South Africa adopted its infamous forty-six-year-long apartheid system of institutionalised racial segregation. The movement for equality was led by the African National Congress (ANC). Their struggle for racial justice would see Nelson Mandela and other key activists of the ANC labelled as terrorists by the West, and imprisoned by the apartheid government in a penal colony. Only after his release after twenty-seven years, when Mandela rejected vengeance, was he hailed as an international icon.

Just like Mugabe, Mandela was elected president at the first election following his release from prison. But the similarities ended there, as they chose very different paths to governing their nations and relieving the stench of bigotry. Mandela chose truth and reconciliation, showing that there was another way, a peaceful way, and stood down after a single term. Mugabe chose violence. As wildly different as the two approaches were, however, neither direction could cleanly untangle the deep threads of segregation so forcibly woven into their nations' fabrics.

Though the economic and social development of the two countries is incomparable, South Africa remains painfully segregated. In 2018, South Africa was declared by the World Bank as the most unequal country in the world. Wealthy areas of Johannesburg are largely the preserve of white South Africans, while much of the Black population remains in the poor townships they were banished to during apartheid. There even exists what is essentially a white-only town. 'People who want to live in Orania buy shares in the Vluytjeskraal Aandeleblok, instead of freehold,' *The Guardian* reported in 2019. 'The screening of prospective shareholders allows for tight control. Buyers undergo extensive vetting, central to which is their fidelity to Afrikaans language and culture, a commitment to employing only white Afrikaners, and a string of conservative Christian undertakings.'

Ian Smith claimed that Black people could never run Rhodesia. But what he and other apartheid-era colonialists forgot to mention was that they would purposefully leave shards of glass scattered on the floor that would make it painful to work around, regardless of whether you chose peace or vengeance – an intention so racist that, decades later, it would still be inspiring violence against Black people, thousands of miles away, as some quietly bowed their heads in prayer.

*

IV.

The Complicated Ones

One man's terrorist is another man's freedom fighter.

— Anonymous

SIX FOOT THREE AND WIRY THIN, Rwanda's president Paul Kagame looks like he should be leaning over a bright white dentist's chair while gently explaining the merits of flossing to you. His frame is that of a person whose chances you would fear in a fight against a sudden gust of wind. Kagame exudes the energy of a band's backup tambourine player, or of a person who carefully reads the terms and conditions before purchasing a candle.

Okay, let's try this: close your eyes and imagine the most cartoonish image of an African dictator – large stomach bulging from a military uniform adorned with an absurd number of decorative medals; a gun protruding from their belt as they hold a large turkey leg in one hand and laugh maniacally while ordering the head be chopped off a local farmer. You are not picturing Paul Kagame. Now imagine the poor scientist who is sent on a kamikaze mission to explain to the dictator that the thermonuclear physics of an atom bomb means the tyrant can't fire a nuclear weapon straight from their chimney.

There you go. That's Paul Kagame.

Though he may not have the looks of a despot, his multifaceted background and audience-dependent temperament explain how he has managed to maintain an authoritarian grip over his country for more than twenty years.

Kagame was raised in a refugee camp in Uganda. His family were among the thousands of ethnic Tutsis forced to flee Rwanda in 1959 when the Hutus – who represented about 70 per cent of the country's population – violently seized power from a Tutsi monarchy that had ruled Rwanda for centuries. Tensions between the two ethnic groups had been deliberately exacerbated during the colonial period, as Germany and then Belgium favoured the minority Tutsi for positions of power, entrenching a class divide throughout the country.

It was in Uganda as a young boy that Kagame would start to plot his revenge. By his early thirties, he had risen to command the Rwandan Patriotic Front (RPF) – a Uganda-based Tutsi rebel force that planned on overthrowing Rwanda's Hutu-led government. The RPF would invade Rwanda in 1990, starting a four-year war for power.

In April 1994, shortly after a UN-backed peace settlement with the RPF was agreed, a plane carrying Rwandan president Juvénal Habyarimana, a Hutu, was shot down by a missile. Though we still don't know who launched it – both Tutsi and Hutu extremists had strong motives – Habyarimana's murder was all the excuse powerful Hutu leaders needed to do what they had long wanted to do: orchestrate the complete extermination of every living Tutsi.

And so with devastating, door-to-door, meticulous efficiency, that's exactly what they set out to achieve. In just one hundred days, around one million Tutsi men, women and children – and any Hutu that tried to stop it – were slaughtered.

The genocide only ended when Kagame's RPF, with the help of the Ugandan army, seized control of the capital, Kigali, in July of that year, forcing millions of Hutus to flee into neighbouring Zaire, now the Democratic Republic of Congo.

In the new order of power, Kagame was appointed vice president. But as the head of the military, he was effectively the most powerful man in Rwanda. It would take six years for his job title to catch up to reality.

Frustrated by his diminishing influence on the country, President Pasteur Bizimungu resigned in early 2000. Kagame was sworn in as president a month later.

Suddenly, Rwanda was being run by a former military leader shaped by an adolescence spent in an impoverished refugee camp; forced there by the same powers that would later coordinate one of history's most chilling genocides, with the sole purpose of obliterating his entire clan.

History teaches us that what should have followed was a vengeful reign of unyielding destruction that would force the Hutu to pay for their crimes – the sins of fathers visited upon sons and daughters for generations upon generations; an action that would no doubt cleave Rwanda into two and plunge the nation into a ceaseless cycle of civil war and poverty.

The reality, however, could not have been more different.

Kagame quickly dropped his military attire for the quiet and peaceful brand of an Oxford professor who seeks in life nothing more than a good book, a warm glass of milk and an expert discussion about the perfect thread count. He threw himself into the business of careful governance, poring over business reports and the latest in development theory.

As a result, few countries over the past twenty years have enjoyed as much economic and social development as Rwanda. Under Kagame, the nation's economy has grown 8 per cent on average every year, a trajectory that experts believe will only continue. His government has introduced a national health system and orchestrated significant education reforms. Dubbed the Singapore of Africa, Rwanda is currently rated in the top-forty best places in the world to do business. Its cities are some of the safest on the continent. With over 60 per cent representation, Rwanda has by far the most elected women in parliament of any government in the world. While its neighbours battle widespread corruption, Kagame forces his government officials to sign performance goals with hyper-specific targets that are assessed every year at a government retreat. And as part of its national 'Vision 2050' initiative, Rwanda – a landlocked country with fewer resources to sell – aims to become a high-income nation in the next thirty years.

Kagame's most impressive achievement is arguably how he has staunched any resurgence of the violent ethnic tensions that could easily have destroyed his country long ago. He's done this partly by implementing laws against hate speech linked to ethnicity, and rules that could be interpreted as making it illegal – or at least unadvised – to identify by ethnic group. This has ushered in an era of political peace and stability when the opposite was expected, preaching forgiveness and tolerance along the way.

Kagame's tenure has been almost universally celebrated. He is regularly invited to opine at international summits and universities; he's flushed with honorary doctorates, and he counts Bill Clinton, Bill Gates and Tony Blair among his biggest admirers. In a 2009 speech, Clinton called him one of the 'greatest leaders of our time', before praising him for the work he has done in stewarding a period of inarguable prosperity.

'I think the great victory of Rwanda was not in the economic growth, the great victory of Rwanda was not even having more than half of parliament as women,' Clinton said. 'The great victory of Rwanda was a victory of the mind and the spirit. And Paul Kagame freed the hearts and minds of his people to think about the future.'

This admiration has not only attracted glowing words but also hard cash. Almost half of Rwanda's annual budget comes from foreign aid, an arrangement that Western governments and development organisations consider to be money very well spent.

There is a reason the *New York Times* once referred to him as 'the global elite's favourite strongman'.

*

Now here we have reached the complication.

Kagame's legacy is not completely clean. He might be popular across Rwanda, but he has not left his grip on power to pure electoral chance. Kagame is technically not a dictator. Authoritarian, perhaps. Tyrant, maybe. Strongman, for sure. Just not quite a dictator. He has successfully stayed in power for more than twenty years by winning elections. But he once said of his political opponents: 'Many of them tend to die.'

And they certainly do.

Human rights organisations have spent years chronicling the dozens and dozens of his prominent and not-so-prominent political enemies – journalists, politicians, activists – who have suddenly turned up dead or facing lengthy prison sentences soon after critiquing his government. The tentacles of what is alleged to be a sophisticated government-run assassination programme are believed to have made hits on Rwandans living in exile, thousands of miles outside of the country. One of his biggest critics, Paul Rusesabagina – whose heroic actions during the 1994 genocide inspired the film *Hotel Rwanda* – was arrested and convicted on alleged terrorism charges in 2021. Among the most chilling things about his prosecution is that Rusesabagina was living in exile in the US at the time, but somehow ended up on a plane to Rwanda without realising it. 'It was actually flawless,' Kagame said of the covert operation to bring Rusesabagina to Rwanda against his will.

None of this is much of a secret to the Western world. In 2013, the US State Department noted of Rwanda: 'The most important human rights problems in the country remained the government's targeting of political opponents and human rights advocates for harassment, arrest, and abuse; disregard for the rule of law among security forces and the judiciary; [and] restrictions on civil liberties.'

Graphic tales of Kagame's harsh temper are bountiful, from reports of his ability to morph from serene professor to screaming tyrant in a matter of seconds, to stories of him personally whipping government ministers who fail to meet his standards. When asked directly in 2014 whether he had ordered a specific killing of a former spy chief living in exile in Johannesburg, Kagame denied it before adding: 'I actually wish Rwanda did it. I really wish it.'

In power for two decades, and now a youthful sixty-four years old, Kagame will be approaching eighty at the next serious test of his rule. He was meant to step down in 2017 after completing the constitutional maximum of two seven-year terms. Conveniently for him, parliament amended the constitution in his favour, meaning he can now serve until 2034.

The elections that have been held are hardly the perfect model of free and fair. Kagame often runs essentially unopposed, and accusations continue to linger that voters intending to pick other candidates are, you could say, strongly disabused of that idea by military officers standing near the polling stations. There are even suggestions that the laws against publicly speaking ill of other ethnic groups are an attempt to cover up any internal dissent at the perception that Tutsis – who make up just 14 per cent of the population – have almost complete control of the highest offices in government and society. Still, his cup – full of foreign aid, invites to speak at prestigious events, and glowing praise as an exemplar for good African leadership – continues to run over.

Kagame's reign presents a complicated conundrum about the nature of democracy, and what form of governance exactly would best suit these incredibly young, forcibly divided nations grappling with their own identities. He has brought peace and prosperity to a small country with very few natural resources, that might otherwise have imploded under the weight of ancient xenophobia. Some experts argue a strong, competent hand is what young, loyalty-divided nations require. Then again, strength is infamously hard to moderate forever. A human's pool of morality is notoriously drained by unlimited power. At any moment, the current can shift even more violently, away from economic prosperity, and an unchallenged strongman can extend his reach, unleashing a torrent of pain that leaves nobody untouched as he looks to cement what he perceives as his divine dominance. Authoritarians very rarely go down without taking their entire country with them.

The president himself might have best described the complex relationship between power and peace, despotism and progress, that signifies his complicated tenure.

In a lengthy *New Yorker* profile, Kagame tells a story of the time he spoke to a young man who had been slashed with a machete and left for dead in one of the mass graves that littered Rwanda during the genocide. Miraculously, the boy survived. Years later, as part of the country's peace and reconciliation programme, President Kagame ordered the release of some of the extremists who had orchestrated the mass killing – a few of whom were now living in that young man's village. All these years later, Kagame wanted to know how the man was coping with living just a few feet away from the people who tried to murder him and everyone he loved.

'And I asked him: "How do you manage?"' Kagame recollects in the interview. '"When you meet them, what do they tell you or what do you tell them? What is your feeling? I want you to genuinely tell me how you feel."'

The young man looked at his president and replied: 'I manage because you ask us to manage.'

*

V.

The Founding Fathers

The whole culture was to get extremely drunk and exert vandalism ... People talk about the Bullingdon Club 'trashing' places, but it was serious criminal damage ... Every piece of furniture that could have been broken was broken, every liquid sprayed around the room, the panelling was cracked, and everything was piled in a heap in the middle of the room ...

All the students who heard this late-night destruction were terrified, I remember.

[Bullingdon members] found it amusing if people were intimidated or frightened by their behaviour. I remember them walking down a street in Oxford in their tails, chanting 'Buller, Buller' and smashing bottles along the way, just to cow people ...

Boris was one of the big beasts of the club. He was up for anything. They treated certain types of people with absolute disdain, and referred to them as 'plebs' or 'grockles', and the police were always called 'plod'. Their attitude was that women were there for their entertainment ...

They had an air of entitlement and superiority . . . Many still see each other. They have long-established networks, and they think it's in their power to confer high office on anyone they choose. There is a bond of loyalty.

— A former recruitment officer for the Bullingdon Club
describing to *The Guardian* how the secret Oxford
University society – which has produced two of the
last four British prime ministers – operated

THE PRESIDENT OF ALGERIA was paralysed, that much was clear.

Abdelaziz Bouteflika could barely move. Half of his body remained stiff as he gently turned his head to hear from the two guests sitting either side of him. Bouteflika was careful not to make any sudden movements, as if worried his limbs could betray him at any moment and spill his secret – though it was obvious they already had.

It was June 2013, and the short video that his government released represented the first time the seventy-six-year-old had been seen since suffering a stroke two months earlier. The images were meant to be a show of strength – a choreographed reassurance that President Bouteflika had the required cognisance to extend his fourteen years in office and continue to govern over 43 million people. A grand performance from which Algerians were meant to come away believing that their president was still in control of his mind and body, able to fulfil his constitutional duties.

Instead he looked debilitatingly frail, unstable, and at least a decade older than he was.

The video was bad enough, but his case to remain the figurehead of this proud North African country was made worse by his decision to retreat from public life afterwards. President Bouteflika stopped appearing at events and giving public speeches. A framed picture of him – which became commonly known as The Frame – would replace him at government functions. Aside from the occasional statement released on his behalf, and periodic reassurances from government ministers promising that he was still very much alive, Abdelaziz Bouteflika became a ghost.

Then.

Without making any campaign appearances, he somehow managed to 'win' the presidential election one year later, with 81 per cent of the vote. He released a statement thanking his supporters and went back into hibernation. For six years. No public events. For six years. No public speeches. For six years. No interviews. For six years. Nothing. Who was running Algeria was as good a mystery as riddles get.

Then.

In 2019, after twenty years in office, six of them in total isolation, the eighty-two-year-old released a statement announcing that he – a critically incapacitated octogenarian who had not been seen in public for over half a decade – would be running again for president in the upcoming elections.

The country erupted in anger. Algerians of all ages and all classes spoke with the synced clarity of principle, to reject the humiliating status quo his administration had inflicted on the country. Over the next few months, tens of thousands of Algerians took to the streets in protest, demanding that President Bouteflika step down. Not at the next election, but immediately. Nothing else in the country mattered, except for Bouteflika's removal.

The ruling authoritarian elite had gone too far this time. They had played one card too many. This was the inevitable outcome of enjoying fifty-seven years of uninterrupted power.

But how had they managed to keep the hustle going for so long? How were they able to bypass shame so easily and inflict on their nation a ghost administration that existed in name only?

Hear names like George Washington, Thomas Jefferson and Alexander Hamilton and you're mentally taken back to a bygone century where people rode horses, died of the common cold, and traded slaves as easily as you swap compliments. Grand men, their nation's Founding Fathers who died more than 220 years ago, yet their words and actions still govern how their country is run. Their deeds still taught in school; hip-hop musicals dedicated to their lives. In death, their power still felt, centuries later. Now imagine if they were still alive. Imagine if Alexander Hamilton was still trying to be president.

For some African countries, independence was so recent that not only are their Founding Fathers still alive – heroic figures who fought to liberate their nation from oppression – but they have leveraged their status and never relinquished power. A by-product of a youthful nation.

After securing freedom for their countries, these men took it as their right to govern; a reward for helping birth a republic. It was a return on their investment.

If it weren't for their efforts, they argued, there wouldn't be a country at all.

Algeria today is still largely run by the veterans of its seven-year independence revolution – a battle against France that the country has taken much pride in.

After the National Liberation Front (FLN) – the country's leading nationalist political party – finally defeated France in 1962, the FLN became the governing (and only political) party. Senior officers quickly vacuumed up the highest positions in government. Authority went to the victors and the victors' younger brothers and the victors' friends and some of their business partners, too.

Bouteflika himself was a young soldier during the revolution. He fought in the military wing of the FLN under his mentor Houari Boumédiène – Algeria's second president. Bouteflika was appointed the country's first foreign minister, a reward for his work during the independence struggle.

He would have to wait years for his time in the big seat, as the powerful military backed another candidate after Boumédiène's death. Bouteflika was exiled, only to return in the '90s to help heal the country following a deadly civil war between the government and Islamists. The elite would use the devastation of the war to claim that a period of one-party stability was essential.

When Bouteflika's turn to govern came, he followed his mentor Boumédiène's lead and filled his government with comrades from the independence movement, as well as close associates and family members – also largely from that era. And with the support of his party, the FLN, Bouteflika amended the constitution twice to extend his term limits.

The old men who had run the country as their prize since the revolution just kept on running the country, with no real democratic avenue for Algerians to push back along. Elections were opaque and corruption was rampant. Political favour was based on a complex web of under-the-table connections – an elite clique that looked after each other and assured that authority remained vested in them alone.

Algerians refer to this as The System and the galaxy of shady, nameless, influential politicians, soldiers, and businessmen that populate The System are called The Powers.

Following Bouteflika's stroke in 2013, it was understood to be The Powers who were really running the government and keeping the president in office. The group included his brother and senior adviser, Saïd Bouteflika, considered by many to be the de facto president.

In the end, the announcement in 2019 that Bouteflika would run again was one insult too many. Algerians – 70 per cent of whom are under thirty years old – were fed up with the geriatrics. They did not feel a strong allegiance to these revolutionaries and were too young to remember the civil war that was often used as an excuse to not rock the boat.

Months of failed pleading from Bouteflika – or whoever wrote his statements – only delayed the inevitable. Change came after the powerful head of the army, Ahmed Gaid Salah – another remnant of the independence years – read the winds and called for Bouteflika's resignation. Without The System, he was powerless and had no choice but to step down.

Elections were held the next year. But missing a strong opposition, The Powers simply anointed one of their own, the current president, Abdelmadjid Tebboune – further locking the country in a cycle of being controlled by once-great national heroes who refuse to budge. Too arrogant to be told what to do. Too comfortable to move.

*

VI.

This Is Family Business

The president stood large. His fingers wrapped tightly around a podium. The former reality TV star adjusted his microphone before spreading his arms wide in faux shock, like a sixteen-year-old at the door of a club feigning surprise at learning their ID is fake.

'We will not stand for it,' he declared to a cheering crowd. His audience — largely made up of the family members, business associates and previously unemployable social media personalities with whom he had chosen to staff the most powerful government in the world — had stayed up into the early hours to back up his scam.

'This is a fraud on the American public. This is an embarrassment to our country. We were getting ready to win this election. Frankly, we did win this election. We did win this election. So our goal now is to ensure the integrity, for the good of this nation. This is a very big moment. This is a major fraud on our nation . . . To me, this is a very sad moment. And we will win this. As far as I'm concerned, we already have won it.'

The fraud in question was his imminent democratic removal from office.

The wealthy son of a millionaire had spent his entire life failing upwards, famous for never facing any consequences for his actions. He once proudly claimed that he could shoot someone outside of his home and get away with it. He didn't need to test out his theory before the tactic stumbled him into the highest office in the land. For four years, he and his adult children divided the duties of president and national spokesperson, while ensuring their family business was well taken care of.

To the horror of his growing list of enemies, he would often brag that he could stay on as president for the rest of his life. But first he had to win re-election. He had predicated his case for remaining in office on his supernatural ability to succeed regardless of what personal obstacles – such as a lack of intelligence, competence or decency – consistently stood in his way. But his promise that, thanks to his optimal IQ, the country would win so much it would get tired of winning, collided with reality – most specifically a deadly global pandemic, the solution for which he once suggested could involve the drinking of disinfectants.

His fellow citizens had seen enough. As the results of the presidential election trickled in during the hours before he took the podium, he had begun to panic. He and his family were being voted out.

The president did everything to remain in power. He asked a foreign government to investigate his rival; in the weeks leading up to the election he sent cheques out to Americans with his personal signature on them; the morning after the election, he ordered all vote counting to be halted – 'STOP THE COUNT,' his carefully worded statement read; he demanded the seizing of voting machines, called up state officials to pressure them to overturn their results, and asked the country's top law-enforcement official to investigate his opponent. Efforts would culminate with him and his family encouraging his followers to storm the central halls of the country's legislature in violent insurrection to block the certification of his defeat, leaving five people dead.

He refused the peaceful transfer of power for a host of reasons, not least of which were the pending investigations into his family businesses – which some reports allege profited off his tenure – that were certain to accelerate, the moment he was no longer under the invisible immunity cloak of the presidency.

MODERN MONARCHIES are more of a European thing. The right of one family to remain in place as head of state as long as they continue to reproduce is not a model that was adopted by any African country upon gaining independence. What these new countries were vulnerable to, however, were megalomaniacs willing to exploit the authority vacuum to enrich their bloodline. In place of cultivating a coherent, nurtured national identity based on common goals and beliefs, a handful of freshman leaders focused on developing a strict personality cult around themselves, preaching that the gods had granted them and their kin the keys to the country. The aim was to fashion a system whereby it became hard to distinguish where the country ended and the leader began.

Togo and Gabon, for example, have each had a father and son share power since 1967, but no single family on the continent has held their nation hostage in the dungeons of nepotism for longer than the Nguemas of Equatorial Guinea.

Obiang Nguema Mbasogo is the president of Equatorial Guinea. His oldest son, Teodorin, is the appointed vice president and defence minister; his youngest son, Gabriel, is the Minister of Mines, Petroleum and Energy; and his middle son, Ruslan Obiang Nsue, was the former minister for sport before becoming the president of the country's leading football club. President Nguema's half-brother, Antonio

Mba Nguema, was the defence minister before his death in 2019, while his other brother is the head of national security. By some estimates, up to half of President Nguema's cabinet is directly related to the president, while many more are from his hometown of Mongomo.

President Nguema has run Equatorial Guinea since 1979. The only other person to have held that office is his uncle, Macías, who was elected the country's first president following Equatorial Guinea's independence from Spain in 1968. It was from Macías that Nguema would contract his deeply held belief that he and his family have been touched by the hand of the almighty and granted providence to command their nation without challenge.

Though they were both deluded by their grandeur, theirs was not a gentle handover of power from mentor to mentee. Nguema deposed Macías in a violent coup that ended in his uncle's execution by firing squad. Just before he was killed, Macías promised that in the afterlife he would haunt everyone who had betrayed him.

Not long after Macías became Equatorial Guinea's first president, he started to spiral out of control. Some say he suffered from paranoid schizophrenia, others posit that he was scarred from watching a colonial officer beat his father to death the day before his mother died by suicide from the grief, while most think he was just a power-deranged sociopath. Whatever his chronic ailment, Macías exploited the rawness of his small country, running it as if Equatorial Guinea's only business was to service him and his relatives.

Macías established the Nguema family's grip on power by declaring himself the father of the nation – taking credit for an independence he had nothing to do with just so he could establish a powerful origin myth that would justify his gross governance. Orphaned at a young age and insecure about his lack of education, he effectively banned reading and purged the country of academics. At religious services, Equatoguineans were required to repeat the mantra 'God created Equatorial Guinea thanks to Macías – without Macías Equatorial Guinea would not exist.' That level of solipsism wasn't enough – it never is – and in the end he abolished all religious gatherings, including funerals, and demanded that only he was worshipped. He bestowed upon himself the title of Unique Miracle. Eventually, his full title would become: President for Life, Head of the Nation and Party, Commander-in-Chief of the Army, and Grand Master of Education, Science and Culture. As the supreme leader of everything, Macías decreed that he was entitled to the state's wealth. He filled his home with the nation's entire foreign reserves in cash – hundreds of millions of dollars stacked in suitcases under his bed. Anyone who challenged his omnipotence was killed. In his twisted mind, almost everyone challenged him. He had thousands executed – about a third of the population were either killed or fled the country in his eleven-year rule.

Almost every single position in his government was taken up by a close relative or a member of his ethnic Esangui clan, including his nephew, Obiang, picked to head the armed forces. They were the only people he trusted – though 'trust' is a relative term here, as his cabinet members were also executed if they were deemed not loyal enough to the 'Immaculate Apostle of Steel'.

Obiang would later write of his uncle: 'A cult of personality flourished under Macías. We endlessly sang his praises. We built statues of him in public places. His effigy figured everywhere, on our stamps, on our banknotes. The North Koreans, who have taken the art of apologetic propaganda to its farthest point, made a film about him in the 1970s, an incredible panegyric without nuance, showing that he wanted to be seen as an African Kim Il-sung, with that apparent characteristic of the Korean "Great Leader" being appreciated by his people on account of the "progress" which he had brought them.'

The Obiang-led coup in '79 wasn't an act of selflessness to rid the country of a despot. It was a move of self-preservation. Obiang – whose brother had been killed by their uncle for daring to suggest that some of the money Macías was hiding under his bed be released to pay public servants – had good reason to believe that his uncle had lost faith in his loyalty and was planning on executing him next.

After taking power, Obiang did not facilitate a new era of open democracy in Equatorial Guinea. Elections were held, but his penchant for imprisoning his opponents ensured that he often ran unopposed, winning over 90 per cent of the vote.

Like his relative before him, he saw himself as the rightful heir to a non-existent throne. An official state radio station was made to declare President Obiang 'the country's God . . . who had power over men and things'. A presidential aide then went on to declare, worryingly, that Obiang 'can decide to kill without anyone calling him to account and without going to hell because it is God himself, with whom he is in permanent contact, and who gives him this strength'.

With that, Obiang had established himself and his family as beyond reproach. What is the country's is theirs, and what is theirs is theirs. Almost immediately, he followed his uncle in filling his government with relatives and neighbours, as the political scientist Douglas Yates once outlined:

> By the end of 1980 the new government was overwhelmingly composed of members of the Mongomo clan, mostly Essangui Fang. At the top of the pyramid was Obiang Nguema, President of the Republic, President of the Supreme Military Council, Head of State, Head of Government,

Minister of Defense and Security, Minister of the Economy and Finances, and Minister of Information (He was an Essangui of the Mongomo clan). The First Vice President and Minister of Foreign Affairs was Maye Ela (also Mongomo). The Minister of Public Administration, then Minister of Health was P. Obama Ondo Eyang (Essangui of Mongomo). The Minister of the Interior was F. Mba Nchama (Mongomo), Minister of Education T. Mene Abeso (Essangui of Mongomo), Minister of Justice P. Mensuy Mba (Mongomo); Minister of Agriculture P. Obiang Enama (Mongomo); and Minister of Industry, Mines and Energy P. Nsué Obama (Esangui of Mongomo). One Mongomo cousin was ambassador to the OAU. Another one ran the UN mission in New York. One nephew served as the UN Ambassador, C. Nvono Nka Manene (Essangui of Mongomo). Another one served as the Ambassador to Nigeria, J. Micha Nsue (Esangui of Mongomo).

And another one, A. Owono Assangono (Esangui of Mongomo) was Ambassador to both Spain and Italy.

The siphoning of government resources really accelerated in the early '90s when Equatorial Guinea struck oil. Big.

In almost no time at all, this small Central African nation became one of the top-five oil exporters in Africa. The country became stupendously wealthy.

Correction: the Nguema family became stupendously wealthy.

The government makes little pretence about this; there are no efforts to publicly account for where all the nation's oil money goes. It is called a 'state secret' – an arrangement made easier by foreign banks around the world more than happy to hold the ill-gotten Nguema fortune. The US-based Riggs Bank – which was shuttered after a money-laundering scandal – was found to have housed around $500 million for the Nguemas. The family's bounty is there, in all its gold-plated wonders, for everyone to see. And of the entire bloodline, no one personifies the alleged plundering of national resources better than President Nguema's son and heir apparent, Teodorin.

Teodorin was never elected vice president. His father simply changed the constitution so he could appoint him to the post, reportedly at his mother's insistence – what have your parents done for you lately? – setting him up to take over from his seventy-nine-year-old father.

Teodorin's government salary is $5,000. But somehow he has owned multiple homes, including a $124 million villa in Paris, near the Champs-Élysées, filled with furniture and Fabergé eggs worth tens of millions of pounds. His dozens of cars were worth nearly $30 million, and he owned an expensive collection of Michael Jackson memorabilia including one of his diamond-encrusted gloves. We know all this because the French government launched an investigation into Teodorin's spending in 2017 and uncovered his expensive lifestyle. He was charged with money laundering and an international warrant for his arrest was sent out.

In reality, though, arresting the vice president (and future president) of an oil-rich country willing to ship out its oil for cheap is a complicated business that would involve spoiling a lot of powerful people's dinners. In the end, Teodorin was given a suspended fine of €30 million, which he only has to pay if he re-offends in France. Considering that he once bought a $35 million house in Malibu in cash, the fine probably won't be a big lift should he ever need to find some spare change.

Before the verdict dropped, Teodorin was asked to explain the villa and the cars and the Fabergé eggs and Michael's glove and the cash. He said that it wasn't really his but it belonged to the people of Equatorial Guinea.

That it does.

*

VII.

The Mad Kings

JERRY SEINFELD: How many world leaders, you think, are just completely out of their mind?

BARACK OBAMA: A pretty sizeable percentage.

JERRY SEINFELD: Some of these people, you must meet them, you'll just be chatting, and you look in their eyes and go: 'Oh, this guy's gone.'

BARACK OBAMA: Yeah. Part of what happens is that these guys, I think the longer they stay in office, the more likely that is to happen.

JERRY SEINFELD: Of course, they lose it.

BARACK OBAMA: At a certain point, your feet hurt, and you're having trouble peeing, and you have absolute power.

— *Comedians in Cars Getting Coffee*

'WHAT DID I DO TO YOU?' is a remarkable question for a violent dictator to ask a baying mob forty-two years into his vicious reign. The lack of self-awareness propelling each syllable as the words spill out with ease.

The only excuse for Muammar Gaddafi is that he was in a state of panic and fear when he asked it. His enemies – the kinds who at his peak he had remorselessly murdered for even thinking about harming him; those who previously would never have dreamt of looking him in the eye let alone placing their mortal hands over his supreme shell – had finally cornered him. His fate was now outsourced.

Minutes earlier, a group of Libyan rebels had hauled Gaddafi head first out of the drainage pipe their president had crawled into. Video footage shows a bloodied Gaddafi, dazed and confused, being dragged around upright before he is thrown to the ground and beaten.

It's true that a handful of leaders across the continent in the past few decades have just wanted to watch the world burn. Muammar Gaddafi was certainly one of history's greatest arsonists.

At just twenty-seven years old, Gaddafi came to power in a bloodless coup in 1969. Libya's last reigning monarch was replaced by a boy who certainly saw himself as a king. Gaddafi had captured his country by commanding a group of low-ranking officers, convincing them to rise above their stations to take it all. Before anyone could wonder how he managed to do it, he was already sitting atop the throne where he would spend the rest of his life.

*

The fundamental essence of Gaddafi's ability to hold on to power was a blend of cult, chaos and cruelty. Mainly cruelty.

He cocooned himself within a grand myth of his own mystique and higher philosophical powers. 'I am a glory that Libya cannot forgo and the Libyan people cannot forgo, nor the Arab nation, nor the Islamic nation, nor Africa, nor Latin America,' Gaddafi once proclaimed. He published his thoughts on governance in a scroll titled *The Green Book* – a play on Chairman Mao's *Little Red Book* – that was compulsory reading in schools. Gaddafi claimed his guiding philosophy was based on developing a greater theory beyond socialism and capitalism, built around 'people power'. Yet the only power source he permitted for four decades came from within himself. He burned Western books and purged the government of anyone whose power threatened to match his own. He started referring to himself using all manner of titles and nick-names. The King of Cultures. The Brother Leader. The Leader of the Revolution. The Guide to the Era of the Masses.

So confident of his all-mighty glory, he dreamt of uniting the continent under a singular authority: himself. Gaddafi, he wished, would one day lead the 'United States of Africa', desperate for the continent to bestow upon him the personal title of King of Kings of Africa.

The disjointedness of his chaos and unpredictability only helped to strengthen Gaddafi's hold on Libya. The colonel did his best work when everything around him was spinning out of control; his nation forever dizzy, he remained still in the eye of the whirlwind he blew into exist-ence. On a whim, he would close down government ministries and abolish entire industries. Political parties were, of course, banned. A Libyan population of around five million people should have luxuriated in their nation's oil wealth, but where the money went was an ongoing mystery, likely somewhere between his own pockets and extremely expensive hare-brained schemes. At the same time, he led a financial crackdown on his citizens, at one point proclaiming that there was no reason for any Libyan to have more than $3,000 in their bank account. Anything over that, he felt, should go to the government – an administration that featured little more than himself.

His eccentricities became part of his lore – a reality he encouraged as a way of maintaining uncertainty as to what he would do next, while encouraging the world to underestimate him as the 'crazy uncle' rather than a deranged despot. Gaddafi's love for flamboyant outfits and Botox in his older years kept him a peculiar sight on the world stage. Wherever he went, he travelled with a giant Bedouin tent, where he would entertain guests and sometimes sleep. In a speech to the UN in 2009, he rambled well past his fifteen minutes' allotted time, incoherently ranting for over an hour and a half about his real and imagined enemies. For much of his tenure, Gaddafi kept a revolving phalanx of female bodyguards, and publicly professed his love for former US Secretary of State Condoleezza Rice. 'I support my darling black African woman,' he said on the network Al Jazeera, adding: 'I admire and am very proud of the way she leans back and gives orders to the Arab leaders. Yes, Leezza, Leezza, Leezza – I love her very much.' When his palace was stormed following his death, intruders found a photo album that featured nothing but photos of Ambassador Rice.

Odd peculiarities do not keep you in power for four decades. What really sealed it for Gaddafi was his unrelenting campaign of wanton cruelty and violent repression – unleashed, upon his own people and any other nation that caught his malevolent attention, with a personal joy that relatively few historical dictators, anywhere in the world, would have taken. By his design, Libyans never knew where his wrath would descend – a swirling bedlam that helped snuff out organised opposition.

Gaddafi commanded a secret police force to weed out not only actual dissenters but potential ones, too. His eyes and ears were everywhere. Televised public hangings were common in the 1970s; bodies were left in the streets to remind those who dared organise against him that he had chosen violence. 'Execution is the fate of anyone who forms a political party,' Gaddafi said in 1974.

Hundreds of people – journalists, politicians, lawyers, academics – were routinely tortured and disappeared, as the crackdown grew more widespread. The many failed coup attempts kept him paranoid. Gaddafi routinely purged the military of powerful officers, killing any soldiers accused of plotting to oust him. Around 1,200 inmates of the Abu Salim prison – many of them political prisoners – were summarily executed in 1996. He may not have had a penchant for eating human flesh like Idi Amin, but he wasn't averse to depraved gore. A former hired assassin told the BBC in 2014 that he was expected to bring back the severed heads of Gaddafi's rivals, because he liked to store them in a deep freezer in his palace which he could visit when the mood took him.

Gaddafi's wrath extended well beyond Libya's borders. Throughout the 1980s, his government became one of the world's leading state sponsors of terrorism. He funded guerrilla groups across the continent, picking up debts as his cash ushered in coups throughout Africa. Gaddafi's largesse also found its way into the pockets of the IRA. The worst of his sponsored atrocities was the Lockerbie bombing in 1988, when a bomb was detonated mid-air on Pan Am Flight 103, killing 270 people from twenty-one countries.

Ostracised for a decade, he found his way back into the good graces of the West when he promised in the '90s to stop giving money to terrorists.

Gaddafi's renewed diplomatic relations couldn't save him when the Arab Spring revolutions started toppling dictators. As the uprisings, which in Libya began in February 2011, started to entangle the region's old elite, Gaddafi chose not to go quietly into the night. Instead, as the rebellion grew apace, he thrust himself in front of cameras, threatening to crush the dissenting 'cockroaches' leading the anti-government protests in Benghazi. He promised to do this 'house by house'. His rhetoric gave Western alliances all the excuse they needed to pierce Libyan airspace and take out his convoy as he attempted to find safe harbour from the growing mob.

In the end, he died in the vengeful arms of the people whose hearts he had once claimed to live in. But even imminent death could not bring him the gracious clarity of sanity that had eluded him his adult life.

'What did I do to you?' he asked.

Perhaps, in the end, Colonel Muammar Gaddafi was fortunate his executioners did not answer his query. If the mob had taken the time to count his wicked deeds one by one, they may have chosen to prolong his suffering rather than allow him the swift death Gaddafi had rarely granted his enemies.

*

Democracy is meant to illuminate where despotism darkens. We've certainly been encouraged to believe an untruth: that Africa in its entirety is withering away under the darkness of dictatorships – eternally damned by revolving caricatures of evil men shutting down radio stations and suspending constitutions, while their spendthrift wives travel the world in gold-plated jets. In reality, less than 10 per cent of the continent is under authoritarian rule.

If we are who we allow to govern us, then it's easy to see the region as overrun with unscrupulous megalomaniacs unable to recognise how easy life would be under the basic tenet of one-person-one-vote. This view has pushed intervention as key to our salvation, and policies that believe punishment will straighten our spines. It was intervention, however, that kept dictators in Somalia and Ethiopia in office, and that divided Nigeria into disparate factions chasing the one thing that seemed permanent: power. It was outside forces that waged a racist war across southern Africa, and have helped hide the ill-gotten wealth of families that have forced monarchy on their own nations. It was fighting off these interventionist forces that made heroes of men better suited to the battlefield than the presidency.

And, most consistently, it is punishing interventionism that keeps blameless citizens suffering under the weight of sanctions that the international community impose to force countries to define democracy as the West demands it. Efforts to reverse this course very rarely work. The day after Trump supporters staged a violent insurrection at the US Capitol in an attempt to overturn the results of the 2020 presidential election, President Emmerson Mnangagwa of Zimbabwe accused the United States of losing its moral right to condemn other nations for their democratic processes. For the last decade, the US government has imposed a series of strict economic and political sanctions against Zimbabwe. Multiple southern African countries, as well as the UN Commission on Human Rights, have long called for the lifting of these sanctions, to help Zimbabwe's severely crippled economy. 'Sanctions have been in place since the early part of this century, and have led only to the suffering of ordinary people rather than bringing about political change,' the UN has pleaded.

The sanctions were initially intended to put pressure on then president Robert Mugabe to implement democratic reforms. However, despite Mugabe's removal in 2017, the US government has on several occasions extended the sanctions, most recently in March 2020, accusing Mnangagwa's government of not adhering to the basic principles of democracy. 'Last year, President Trump extended painful economic sanctions placed on Zimbabwe, citing concerns about Zimbabwe's democracy,' Mnangagwa wrote on Twitter. 'Yesterday's events showed that the US has no moral right to punish another nation under the guise of upholding democracy. These sanctions must end.'

Mnangagwa was speaking to an obvious hypocrisy, an approach that has taken many patronising forms. On the day of the insurrection itself, many US politicians and political pundits across the country kept claiming, incredibly, that America was not being America, and instead compared the violent scenes happening in Washington, DC to 'something you would see in a third world country', despite the fact that everyone could see it was very much happening in America. Senator Marco Rubio – who just two days before the November election had celebrated a group of Trump voters trying to run a Biden–Harris campaign bus off the road – wrote on Twitter: 'There is nothing patriotic about what is occurring on Capitol Hill. This is 3rd world style anti-American anarchy.'

The lack of precision and the laziness of thought, language and solutions regarding despotism in Africa stops us from getting to the various root causes and coming up with sustainable fixes to ensure that the dynamics that maintain them are removed as nations continue to establish themselves. Of course, the blame cannot be separated from the actions of the continent's worst, who have taken advantage of the disarray and the early turmoil of half-baked nations – but the more efficient we are in removing the opportunities to exploit, the more chances there will be for ordinary people on the continent to have a voice in terms of how their destinies are governed. It's the only way to ensure fewer nine-year-olds in the future, high off the binary of good and bad, will celebrate the sudden death of a despot.

Part Five

There Is No Such Thing as an African Accent

and

Binyavanga Wainaina Is Still Right

So you want to make a Hollywood film about Africa?

There is no need to try anything new.

Pitch one of five concepts only: I: Generic, exotic African savannah as the background to young colonial love that somehow inspires a young village boy to learn to read. (Suggested title: *Soul of Africa* or *Rebirth*.) II: A rich New Yorker with 'no time for love' is forced to leave her high-powered job. She is convinced to Get Away From It All by going on safari in Africa, where the lavish city lifestyle to which she has become accustomed is replaced by the rudiments of basic village life. There she meets and eventually falls for the only other white person there – a fellow American who has been living among Africans for decades, and has thus earned the respect of the locals. Adjusting to African life is a struggle at first, but with the help of an entire village that has nothing better to do, the New Yorker discovers a part of herself she never knew existed. She gives back by teaching a young village boy how to read or by saving a tiger cub from poachers. (Suggested title: *Wild Love* or *My African Adventure*.) III: A young village child, against the odds, learns to read to save his impoverished village. The young boy learns at night, using a makeshift light fashioned out of wire and tenacity. (Suggested title: *African Dream* or *The Servant Boy*.) IV: A coming-of-age story about a young man trying to balance his ambitions with what his ancestors expect of him. His ability to read is up in the air. (Suggested title: *Spirits of Africa* or *Destiny*.) **V:** A thriller about an unfolding genocide that threatens to destroy multiple villages until a white man intercedes. Sadly the situation is too grave for anyone to learn to read, but that all changes when the white man agrees to adopt a former child soldier orphaned by the war, and they return together to Cleveland, where the child learns to read so he can address the United Nations about the plight of his country. (Suggested title: *Death in Africa* or *Savages*.)

Regardless of plot: you must start your film with the camera high in the sky, surveying vast rolling grasslands that stretch until they simply cannot stretch any more. Let the camera hang still over the title sequence as our eyes settle on Real Africa. No signs of a modern, technologically advanced civilisation should visually block the view of these rolling plains: no tall buildings, paved roads, or illuminated billboards advertising expensive fragrances.

Land. We should just see land.

The sun should ideally be rising, signifying a new day in this magnificent jungle. A sunset will work, too. Just make sure the sun is moving in one direction or the other. A Real African's Day is not governed by alarm clocks or the timetable for commuter trains. It is unbothered by traffic or light pollution. Africans have a preternatural connection to the Earth's elements, especially soil. If you've selected the sunrise option, you want to project the sense that the very carbons and atoms that make up our planet are rising along with it. The ground should rustle. A stream should flow. A large, majestic baobab tree must stand majestically, just off-centre. It is majestic.

The first sound we hear can only be from a lone deep voice chanting slowly in a nondescript African-sounding language. Swahili is the traditional go-to dialect, but you can easily get away with a soft, melodic incantation of 'Zulu' repeated over and over again. Do not let the location of your film influence the specific language you choose. And whatever you do: absolutely no subtitles. The meaning is irrelevant. Your audience will automatically accept the words as profound, the intonation poetic. Fold in some sharp clapping and low thumping drums to give the chanting additional weight in the authenticity department. Remember: music in Africa has not changed for centuries.

It's time for the animals to gather in their various collective nouns. Close-up on a flock of birds gracing the sky in perfect unison; wide shot on a dazzle of zebras drinking from a watering hole as a tower of giraffes pick at tall trees behind them. Let's follow a herd of antelopes galloping resplendently as they start their nine-to-five jobs being a herd of antelopes that gallop resplendently.

Now for the Africans. Turn the soundtrack up as we montage through regular African life. Cut to: a tribe of warriors just standing around in full Zulu regalia. If they're not standing, they should be jumping. Again, it doesn't matter why. What matters is that they must never be seen sitting, unless your Western protagonist insists they relax, to which they will look confused before acquiescing. Do not give them a storyline of their own. They are stoic ancient figures that must always look stoic and ancient. Cut to: an African village in the middle of the desert; a sea of brown corrugated roofs crowning homes, packed tightly together, that could all collapse at any moment. Cut to: a matriarch stirring a giant iron pot over an open fire. Cut to: a goat tied to something. Cut to: smiling children, despite it all, running through fields, smiling. Cut to: children running through narrow, poorly drained streets. Cut to: children running.

Your impending-genocide-civil-war epic should now smash-cut to the jungle, where merciless African militants are riding in a convoy of all-terrain, open-air 4x4 jeeps, carrying AK-47s over their heads and heading towards the village you've just pleasantly set up.

Your romantic colonial drama, however, should find our Kind British Colonialist in a bright white home in the middle of a poor township, surrounded by African servants with broad smiles and no personal ambitions. Write in everyone's favourite African servant boy whose humour betrays an intelligence stymied by his sad upbringing. For reasons never fully explored, your servants should grow to greatly admire the Kind British Colonialist they work for, to the point where the Kind British Colonialist is rewarded with an honorary title that loosely translates to 'You Are Officially an African Just Like Us Now'. Take your time letting this dynamic play out. A key turning point will be when the Kind British Colonialist reprimands a Mean British Colonialist for not being kind enough to their African servant. Later in the evening, the Kind British Colonialist should comfort this servant before the servant continues their servant duties.

Your rich New Yorker should be overdressed, struggling with the heat and insects of the wild African jungle. Avoid subtlety. Include a joke in which, out of frustration, they ask a confused local where the nearest Starbucks is. The African should certainly appear confused – the juxtaposition of consumerism and poverty will set things up for a very important life lesson later in the film. On their first day, the New Yorker should come face to face with a wild animal, as regularly happens each day across Africa. They will be instructed to remain perfectly still, beginning a series of vital discoveries that, in time, will lead to your protagonist returning to New York having learned that the real problem wasn't that they were living in the jungle, but that the jungle was living in them. Think about it.

Your film will need an elephant. Somewhere, at some point, you will certainly require one, maybe three. Uses for an elephant include, but are not limited to: I: A visual aid to demonstrate the grand natural splendour of Africa. Instruct your elephant to walk in and out of shot behind two characters as they speak. II: A young African child's best friend. The animal will understand him when nobody else does. III: For comedic effect, have your elephant wrap its trunk around and lift up the rich

American early in their 'I hate Africa' phase. As they scream for help, pan to a couple of Zulu warriors smiling. Your audience will chuckle intuitively because they had not previously imagined that tribespeople knew how to smirk discreetly. The perfect set-up for when the elephant later appears out of nowhere to save your protagonist in a moment of distress, from which they will suddenly think: 'I get it. I get Africa'. A completed journey of understanding must include an evening scene where the entire village has gathered for traditional African dancing around a crackling fire. A gaggle of small children should appear out of nowhere to whisk your protagonist to their feet and, for the first time, they will join in the dancing. Smiling, they catch the eye of The Other White Person – a look that says, 'I told you Africa is wonderful.'

A moment will arise in your coming-of-age narrative when the twenty-something looking to chart their own path will face a life-defining obstacle. No earthly being can help them. Obviously. Have your actor stand in the middle of a field and confer with their ancestors at twilight. Should your budget not extend to a convincing reanimation of a long-since-dead ancestor, you may substitute in an elderly village seer who could be anything between 80 and 370 years old. Ideally the wise man should be blind, but this might be too heavy-handed. A walking stick is not.

Mark their eventual ascent into adulthood with an ancient ritual like a tussle with a lion, or a requirement to interpret a prophecy. A simple twenty-first birthday party is not authentic enough.

A coming-of-age story about a young African woman can only involve her attempts to avoid a prearranged marriage.

Frequently asked questions:

Classrooms: African classrooms are singular, rundown concrete buildings with no lighting and large black chalkboards, where students in tattered uniforms sit in rows behind splintered tables.

Travel: Jeeps and two-seater propeller planes only. Applies to anything from a period drama to a genocidal thriller. Flying should be kept to scenic tours over grasslands and lakes. If your main characters find themselves accidentally navigating over a bustling metropolis with large shopping centres, you have gone too far and must immediately turn back to Real Africa.

Clothes: White and brown khakis, wide-brimmed safari hats for your white characters. Rich Africans dress decadently in a mix of animal print and kente cloth. Designate the person with the highest status by draping a lion-hide sash over their shoulder.

Promotional poster: A wide shot of a savannah, a large sun teetering over the horizon, partially obscured by a single baobab tree. Pick one item to appear alongside the tree: I: A large mammal. II: A boy sitting in the tree. III: Images of the protagonist hanging in the clouds. IV: A scary militant hanging in the clouds.

Now, perhaps your film isn't set in Africa but features African characters. Do not feel obliged to cast anyone from the continent. Instead, your actor can just adopt the classic Hollywood African accent: let them drop their voice an octave deeper, sit heavier on each syllable, overpronouncing each word while speaking painfully slowly. It should sound like African tongues are allergic to English, worried that an errant word might catch and release a blood-curdling poison. It should sound like your character is naive, vulnerable, yet overly eager to impress. They should say 'back in my country . . .' a lot to demonstrate the cultural chasm between the excesses of the West and the rudimentary nature of African society.

African refugees living abroad need to be domesticated. But first, let them marvel at running water or drive-through fast-food sites or how big malls are. A recent critically acclaimed film had one refugee ask if there were any dangerous animals such as lions living in the American city they had just moved to. Feel free to have one of your characters do the same.

An African student in an American high school drama should be smart or visibly hardworking, forever concerned that the protagonist has not studied for tomorrow's big test. Your African student should be sweet, culturally unthreatening and dispense sage advice on a whim. 'In Africa, we have a saying . . .' marks the beginning to the end of anyone's problem.

They must not join the high school football team until the coach absentmindedly spots them running in another context. When queried, let your African student explain that, growing up in Africa, they had to chase after gazelles every morning for breakfast or else their family didn't eat. After a poor start in their first match, the student will be asked to imagine the opposition are gazelles, which will transform them into the best player on the team.

In college, your African student should be forced against their best objections to leave their dorm to attend the big frat party. On arrival, they should appear allergic to the debauchery. Later, after they've innocently drunk from the punch not knowing what was in it, the camera should find them standing on a roof, drunk, happier than they have ever been in their life. 'America is wonderful!' they will scream, before cannon-balling into the pool to wild cheers.

Ultimately, whether in college or high school, your African student should be motivated by one thing: fear of their ultra-religious, super-conservative parents, who are always stern and serious, imparting wisdom in parables and long-winded speeches about the village they grew up in and the sacrifices they made.

Your African Parents Living Abroad must never be deliberately funny or nonchalantly cool like the parents of the other children at school. They should hate the idea of their child joining the football team right up until NFL draft day. Only film your African parents wearing

'African colours', and in one of two locations: church, or on their door-step waiting to ask their child 'Where! Have! You! Been?'

These late arrivals will continue, until, as punishment, the African Student Living Abroad is sent back to Africa to learn some humility and manners by reconnecting with their roots. When they land, the sun will be rising or setting. Because: Africa.

*

Binyavanga wainaina knew there was a difference between a country and a continent.

The late Kenyan author and activist knew there was a difference between how countries and continents are portrayed in the media depending on who inhabits them. He understood the lasting impact of a simple story, and he made it a key tenet of his life's work to erase reductive tales wherever he found them. Wainaina's gift was to seek out every lazy stereotype of Africa and defend the region, on a forensic, itemised level – a constant battle, for which he was always on guard. His chosen weapons were his disarming wit, a biting satire, and his willingness to use his status as one of the greatest writers of his or any generation to empower storytellers from across the continent to tell and retell their own stories, using their cleaner brushes to paint a more exhaustive portrait.

The continent, he wanted it to be known, is more than what some want to see it as, and he used whatever form he needed to proselytise that message – whether it be essays, articles, a memoir, talks, open letters. Whatever.

In 2013, for example, Wainaina addressed one of his open letters to Madonna, after the singer was accused of being angry about a recent visit to Malawi, where the government had not given her the VIP treatment she felt she deserved as someone who had built schools in the country and adopted multiple Malawian orphans. The accusation was made by the then president of Malawi, Joyce Banda, who released a statement, her frustration clear in every syllable: 'Granted, Madonna has adopted two children from Malawi,' she said. 'According to the record, this gesture was humanitarian and of her accord. It, therefore, comes across as strange and depressing that for a humanitarian act, prompted only by her, Madonna wants Malawi to be forever chained to the obligation of gratitude. Kindness, as far as its ordinary meaning is concerned, is free and anonymous. If it can't be free and silent, it is not kindness; it is something else. Blackmail is the closest it becomes.'

Wainaina jumped in, thanking Madonna for 'choosing' Africa in her search for somewhere to make a difference. 'I wish to thank you for being a caring mother to all the children of Malawi, to all the children of Africa,' Wainaina wrote in his pointedly sarcastic open letter. 'If Malawi has been ungrateful and treated you badly, you must know my country Kenya has orphans too. Kenya specialises in making tourists feel very happy and at home, dancing around an African fire, drinking gin and making happy sounds in the middle of herds of animals and on beaches.'

He continued: 'As a civil society activist working on the African girl child I would love to talk with you about coming to Kenya where the girl child needs you very much. She is surrounded by wild animals! And corruption!'

Arguably, Wainaina's most celebrated work started as an angry email sent to the editors of the literary magazine *Granta*, which had published an 'Africa Issue' that forgot to feature writers from the continent. In his 'incredibly long and very funny email . . . [that] went on and on for thousands of words,' as one editor at *Granta* would later describe it, Wainaina denounced the magazine for publishing 'every literary bogey-man that any African has ever known'.

'It wasn't the grimness that got to me, it was the stupidity,' Wainaina remembered of the 'Africa Issue'. 'There was nothing new, no insight, but lots of "reportage" – Oh, gosh, wow, look, golly ooo – as if Africa and

Africans were not part of the conversation, were not indeed living in England across the road from the Granta office. No, we were "over there", where brave people in khaki could come and bear witness. Fuck that.'

Wainaina's email arrived many years after the issue was published. The *Granta* editors on the receiving end were not actually responsible for the issue's content. Still, they didn't respond with defensive anger. They didn't try to gaslight him or explain how Africans should be grateful for any coverage at all, or make a veiled reference to reverse racism. What they did instead was exactly what you would hope anyone in their position would do: they listened, took his points into consideration and set out to do better.

Better would come in the shape of a reimagined issue, titled 'The View from Africa,' where writers from across the continent, including and especially Wainaina, were commissioned to set the narrative.

Wainaina's contribution would eventually morph into a reworking of his email, a joyful satire that succinctly hits at the stereotypes of Africa that are often present in literature; the same style I have attempted to adopt – though I could never do it full justice – for the Hollywood films in the opening of this chapter. It was titled 'How to Write About Africa'. His advice includes:

Always use the word 'Africa' or 'Darkness' or 'Safari' in your title. Subtitles may include the words 'Zanzibar', 'Masai', 'Zulu', 'Zambezi', 'Congo', 'Nile', 'Big', 'Sky', 'Shadow', 'Drum', 'Sun' or 'Bygone'. Also useful are words such as 'Guerrillas', 'Timeless', 'Primordial' and 'Tribal'. Note that 'People' means Africans who are not black, while 'The People' means black Africans.

Never have a picture of a well-adjusted African on the cover of your book, or in it, unless that African has won the Nobel Prize. An AK-47, prominent ribs, naked breasts: use these. If you must include an African, make sure you get one in Masai or Zulu or Dogon dress . . .

Remember, any work you submit in which people look filthy and miserable will be referred to as the 'real Africa', and you want that on your dust jacket. Do not feel queasy about this: you are trying to help them to get aid from the West . . .

You'll also need a nightclub called Tropicana, where mercenaries, evil nouveau riche Africans and prostitutes and guerrillas and expats hang out.

Always end your book with Nelson Mandela saying something about rainbows or renaissances. Because you care.

'How to Write About Africa' was a triumph, and is still much loved and referenced today across the continent and diaspora. It became the most shared essay in *Granta*'s history, perfectly capturing the tropes that literature has circled its stories around: the comically evil politician, the overly romantic description of vast savannahs, the galloping antelopes, and the 'book cover with a heroic-looking conservationist'.

It was word perfect and should have been enough to push every writer, journalist and creative away from these tropes.

But literature just continued down the same degrading slope.

'How to Write About Africa' was written almost twenty years ago. The original *Granta* issue that Wainaina had protested was published a decade before that. Yet despite the many years that have passed since, every word Wainaina wrote still rings true today. So little has changed in the way Africa is portrayed in popular culture.

Charities, however misguided, have the excuse that their science says the use of generic, stark, reaction-tested imagery is a way to elicit that special blend of sentiments that precedes a donation. But pop culture has no such need to stick with the same characters, plots, and framings that are projected in films, TV, books and magazines. No evidence exists that readers and audiences demand to consume content where Africa is a savannah-only scenescape full of characters with no back story, and whose happiness is graded by their proximity to a kind foreigner on a journey to find themselves and inevitably save the hapless local villagers.

Popular culture is meant to transport us to a world outside of our own. If people can go out of their way to learn Klingon or get emotionally lost in meet-cutes in countrysides thousands of miles from where they live, then they could stretch their imaginations far enough to envisage a story of a rich family in Djibouti who try to teach their social-media-addicted kids the value of family time by taking them on a long road trip, with hilarious consequences. Or a teen drama about two sisters from Botswana whose only Christmas wish is to reunite their divorced parents.

If anything, things have got worse in the decades since Wainaina first spoke up. Coupled with literature, Hollywood seems committed to the outdated models that the industry has leaned on for generations, despite desperate calls to showcase something different. There's a frustration that is clearly still far from going away.

*

Few things unite the continent more in frustration than the comically inaccurate way Africa and its people are portrayed in popular culture. It's at times deliberately dismissive, often nonsensical, and occasionally inadvertently hilarious. Almost never is there an honest attempt to do the work of recognising the cadences of the lives and livelihoods of over a billion people.

Hollywood is the ringleader – the culprit most responsible for cleanly packaging stereotypes of Africa and delivering them as high-budget entertainment that the rest of the world has come to accept as fact. But literature paved the way; the industry has worked incredibly hard since at least the 1800s to fill as many pages as possible with tales of noble Western conservationists trekking through dark African wildernesses to save small people from their big problems. Always by a river.

Literature comes a very close second. But: Hollywood. Its screens are simply too big and too highly defined. Its content too mass-marketable. The go-to formulas have proven frustratingly lucrative, and a magnet for critical acclaim.

Since 1912, there have been over fifty remakes of *Tarzan* – a film that is essentially about a white man who is raised by apes yet is still smarter than the savage locals he swings from tree to tree to govern. Meanwhile, Academy Awards have been generously handed out to box-office hits that use Africa as a backdrop for relatively unrelated plots (*The African Queen*, 1951); stories that romanticise the colonial era (*Out of Africa*, 1985); and films in which a brave Westerner is parachuted in to save Africa from nefarious forces (*Gorillas in the Mist*, 1988; *The Constant Gardener*, 2005). Each one of these films features Africans as bit-part players in their own countries, having to be convinced by outside forces either to take an action in their own best interests or watch someone else take care of it for them.

Fashionable in the early 2000s were historical and semi-historical thrillers about savagery, genocide and conflict. *Hotel Rwanda* (2004) told the true story of a hotel manager in Kigali who saved thousands of Hutus and Tutsis during the Rwandan civil war. *Blood Diamond* (2006) stars Leonardo DiCaprio as an Afrikaans mercenary who uses a former slave labourer (Djimon Hounsou) to hunt for a rare conflict diamond in the middle of the Sierra Leone civil war. And *The Last King of Scotland* (2006) features Forest Whitaker in an Oscar-winning turn as the (allegedly) human-flesh-eating dictator Idi Amin. This Academy Award–winning triumvirate certainly contain stories worth telling, with themes and characters that have played a part in the continent's history. But their successes produced a template for an ever-expanding genre of crazed cigar-smoking African warlords in dirty fatigues and red berets giving long drunken speeches as their mercenaries chase poor Africans through the jungle and recruit children to their armies. The BAFTA-nominated *Beasts of No Nation* (2015), starring Idris Elba and adapted for the screen by Cary Fukunaga from Uzodinma Iweala's novel, was a deservedly well-received attempt at a nuanced portrayal of the life of child soldiers. Less nuanced, however, was the entirely fictional *Tears of the Sun* (2003), which packed multiple tropes into what was essentially a white saviour narrative: a US Navy SEAL Team is sent into the jungle of a brink-of-civil-war Nigeria to rescue Monica Bellucci as a nurse who refuses to leave her 'helpless patients to be slaughtered by rebels'. Bruce Willis, the SEAL Team leader, agrees, and together Bellucci and Willis save the Nigerians from a wholly invented conflict. In 2020's *Rogue*, Megan Fox also leads a team of mercenaries and American soldiers through the African wilderness to save hostages, battling miscellaneous local rebels and wandering lions on their way to safety.

Recent family-friendly fare has featured *The Good Lie* (2014), in which a group of Sudanese refugees receive asylum in the US. In America, they are shocked to learn that their female host somehow functions as a human despite the fact she is not married ('Your survival skills are very impressive,' one refugee says) and that there are no wild lions roaming around Kansas City. The same year produced *Blended*, starring Adam Sandler and Drew Barrymore as a pair of American divorcees who the writers send to a holiday resort in Africa to fall in love. The portrayal of Africa and Africans in the film is so retrograde that the *New Yorker* film critic Richard Brody called it 'grotesquely offensive', with *New York Times* critic A. O. Scott noting its 'quasi-zoological depiction of Africans as servile, dancing, drum-playing simpletons'.

Holiday in the Wild (2019) is a Christmas film that trudges far safer ground, avoiding the more overt stereotyping of *Blended*, though it still includes many of Real Africa's greatest hits: slow-mos of giraffes galloping in wide fields, mischievous elephants, and Africans colluding to help the two white protagonists fall in love.

Finally, alongside *Out of Africa* and *The African Queen* are the films that saw it necessary to just throw 'Africa' in their titles, in a way they would never say 'Europe' and even though their characters rarely venture much further than a single game reserve or township, let alone country: *Africa Screams* (1949), *Ernest Goes to Africa* (1997), *I Dreamed of Africa* (2000), *A Good Man in Africa* (1994), *Lost in Africa* (2010), *Nowhere in Africa* (2001), *My African Adventure* (2013), *Father Africa* (2017).

To name a few.

It can be exceptionally hard to shift images and beliefs from our consciousness when they are built around entertaining storylines that we all enjoy. These limited narratives unwittingly bleed into completely unrelated stories that end up broadcasting, even for the briefest of moments, some representation of the continent, whether it's a throwaway piece of dialogue or more visual elements.

My personal favourite in this genre lasts no longer than a minute and appears near the end of a film that is impossible not to adore: *Independence Day*. Following the US government's discovery of the secret sauce for defeating the invading aliens, the military relay that information to troops across the world, letting them know exactly how the counteroffensive will work once Will Smith and Jeff Goldblum destroy the mothership. A stirring montage of global cooperation follows, as tactics are distributed from Area 51 in the Nevada desert to their intelligence counterparts on each continent. Each continent, that is, except for one: nobody bothers to inform anyone in Africa – a region, I can only assume, that is presumed to be unequipped with sophisticated planes brandishing sophisticated weaponry. A strange oversight, considering the continent is supposedly overrun with warlords and cold-blooded military dictators. You would think with our apparent penchant for genocide, Africa would top the list of places you would call when the aim is to eradicate an entire civilisation.

You're right in thinking this is a tiny detail, an easy oversight to make. And normally I'd be all for letting it slide. That is, if Africa didn't make a quick appearance a few moments later, when the aliens have been defeated and it's time for the traditional Hollywood worldwide-celebration sequence where we cut across the globe to see snapshots of the delighted masses. We eventually land on what is meant to be Africa. Representing the continent are five topless young boys dressed as native warriors, coated in red tribal paint, running through bushy grasslands as they literally carry spears that they thrust into the air in jubilation. It's now obvious that we couldn't help the military operation – we don't even have roads or electricity, let alone fighter jets.

The absurdity of it makes me laugh each time. I'm just saying: if an otherwise excellent movie could go through all that effort to create a complex identity and backstory for far-off aliens, the least the producers could have done was stretch their imaginations to give Africans a pair of jeans to throw on. Maybe even one fighter plane between us, with 'Africa' emblazoned on the side as if we all cobbled together to pay for it. That's all I'm asking.

These small slights are served everywhere. And once you start to notice them, they become impossible to avoid. You see it in the way characters recite generic African proverbs they claim to have learned on their travels in Africa; and how dressing like an African routinely means wearing a dashiki drowned in tie-dye. It's in the ubiquitous use of suns, savannahs and large trees in film posters; and how drums are made to feature at every celebration, regardless of culture. It's in how Africa is promoted as steeped in ancient mystique and primitive rituals passed down from generation to generation, without leaving space for stories of the creators shaping society in new ways every single day. It's in how older Africans are presented as rigid and incompatible with the modern world, when many of our forebears were liberators, culturally and technologically progressive. Not all of us can summon the spirits of our ancestors at a moment's notice when a complex problem needs solving. Not everyone is a member of a deeply traditional and spiritual community.

It's how little is expected of Africa that can be hardest to swallow, and the way entire cultures are flattened to feed a handful of storylines deemed worthy of the continent.

Not much better are the documentaries that purport to explore Africa's cultures, yet demonstrate very little curiosity for the breadth of experiences across the continent. At any given time along the Earth's circumference, a ponderance of producers are brainstorming a new 'ground-breaking experimental series' where we marvel at a secluded tribe living somewhere in the bush. For contrast, the exploration is normally conducted by a Western presenter sent to live among them, tasked with surviving without their usual luxuries. They are sent to learn about the tribe and their funny traditions, such as how they arrange marriages or their lack of interest in starting wars with other nations.

Inevitably, what the documentary is really about is the journey towards personal discovery the presenter goes on, where they learn: i) not to take their own lives and luxuries for granted; and/or, ii) 'That these people are just like us.'

A recent version of this was Channel 4's *The British Tribe Next Door*, broadcast in the UK in 2019. Presenter Scarlett Moffatt and her family were dropped in the Namibian desert to live alongside the nomadic Himba tribe. The twist: the show built a replica of the Moffatt family home, complete with all their personal belongings, right next to the Himba's cluster of huts. With their expansive home standing right there, the Moffatts could introduce the Africans to indulgences such as electricity, shoe collections, washing machines and a staircase, while the Brits sampled the traditional Himba lifestyle the show chose to high-light, of goat herding, trekking miles to fetch water, and walking around semi-naked.

The Moffatts were exceedingly polite throughout the experiment and did well to treat their Namibian counterparts with respect, engaging with the process in good faith, not gawking at their new neighbours in wonder or seeing them and their lives as beneath their own. But the four-episode series could not escape the stark imagery: Westerners rep-resented advancements in modern technology, science and culture, while the Africans embodied a bygone, underdeveloped civilisation stumped by the intricacies of an oven.

The Himba way of life is certainly of considerable value, and no less worthy than any other. But these juxtapositions of the West and Africa, whatever the intention, only fuel the same harmful stereotypes that colonialists utilised – that Africa is full of uncivilised people and their uncivilised ways – to justify their actions. To that we've added charity campaigns, making it easier to believe that the only solution to opening their eyes comes from outside the continent.

This portrayal could have been avoided. You can find the exact same amenities in the homes that fill the Namibian towns and cities that exist only a few miles away from where the Himba live. Perhaps a less harm-ful, more informative programme could have brought a contemporary, working-class Namibian family from the capital, Windhoek, to live alongside their Himba compatriots, and together they could have explored – for each other and the rest of the world – what it means to be Namibian in the world today. They could have had a discussion about culture, traditions, and the effects of climate change on nomadic communities and cities. They could have engaged in a revealing discussion on the government's policies of building more towns and cities over Himba land to cater for the forever-growing urban population. In this version, Africa would have been represented on both sides, and it would have avoided the promotional material that featured images of a British family playing with gadgets as Africans peered over their shoulders in bewilderment.

Instead, the imagery that was used solidified that long-standing divide between how people in the West picture their own lives and the lives of Africans, and it's always easier to dehumanise those you're unable to relate to.

This is part of the ramifications of what author Chimamanda Ngozi Adichie described in her 2009 TED talk as the 'danger of a single story'. When the same narratives are repeatedly regurgitated, we internalise them, make assumptions and pass judgements based on the thinnest shreds of evidence, which would dissolve if only we subjected them to the lightest of truths.

During that talk, Adichie recounted her experience of arriving at university in the US from Nigeria, and shocking her American roommate because Adichie wasn't the sort of African she had expected to meet:

> She asked where I had learned to speak English so well, and was confused when I said that Nigeria happened to have English as its official language. She asked if she could listen to what she called my 'tribal music', and was consequently very disappointed when I produced my tape of Mariah Carey . . . She assumed that I did not know how to use a stove.
>
> What struck me was this: she had felt sorry for me even before she saw me. Her default position toward me, as an African, was a kind of patronising, well-meaning pity. My roommate had a single story of Africa, a single story of catastrophe. In this single story, there was no

possibility of Africans being similar to her in any way, no possibility of feelings more complex than pity, no possibility of a connection as human equals.

More affronts would follow Adichie, including the lecturer who claimed that the characters in her novel were not 'authentically African' because they were too much like him, 'an educated, middle-class man' who drove cars and was not starving. Only a few years ago, the internationally bestselling author was asked by a French journalist whether Nigeria had any bookshops.

Reshaping the narrative requires those in the Western media – journalists, producers, actors, writers, that podcast you do with your mates – to commit to telling broader stories of fuller histories, with multilayered characters that exist to do more than ward off cholera or fight the burning of their farms by a comically evil militant.

Still, hope swims in this sea of generalisations – a few beacons of light that will hopefully show the cultural tastemakers and gatekeepers of popular culture that not only is nuance possible and the right thing to do, it's incredibly lucrative.

*

CHADWICK BOSEMAN HAD TO FIGHT for his voice. The actor had been cast in a role that would represent a transcendent moment in cinematic history that both continental Africans and the Black diaspora would celebrate together.

But first: he had to fight.

Boseman had been hired to play the titular role of T'Challa in Marvel Studios' first major Black-led superhero film, *Black Panther*, based on the comic-book character of the same name who was created in 1966 by

Stan Lee and Jack Kirby in the middle of America's civil rights movement. The creation of a Black superhero at that time was a deliberate political statement.

Keeping true to that same intent, the 2018 *Black Panther* film was a radical reimagining of Hollywood's cinematic portrayal of Africa. Central to this magical counter-vision is Wakanda: a fictional African nation that is untouched by the curse of colonization. Boasting a history devoid of foreign occupiers draining it of its wealth and self, the landlocked kingdom is one of the most prosperous, technologically advanced civilisations the world has ever known.

In order to keep it that way, Wakanda operates a policy of isolationism – closing itself off from the rest of the world as protection from the galaxy of global vultures that history has proven would most certainly descend should the world discover Wakanda's greatest secret: the country is home to Earth's only source of vibranium, the strongest metal on the planet, used to power Wakandan life – from flying spaceships and Black Panther's suit to their highly sophisticated levitating train network.

Wakanda's wealth extends beyond its riches. It runs on a system of egalitarian principles that ensure women are valued equally to men – the Dora Milaje are the country's all-women militia, while T'Challa's younger sister, Shuri (Letitia Wright), is responsible for maintaining the nation's technological advances.

The only voice that is consistently silenced in the film is that of Everett Ross – an American CIA agent played by Martin Freeman – whenever he speaks or moves out of turn in Wakanda. In one scene he is admonished by Shuri ('Don't scare me like that, coloniser!') for skulking around her laboratory. Later, Ross is literally barked into silence when he tries to interject in a discussion about Wakanda's internal politics.

Here is a story of a free and glowing nation – not just valuable for a scenic backdrop, but humanised and endowed with a central authority.

A rare cinematic vision from Hollywood of a prosperous African coun-try and its innovative people as the dominant narrative, setting their own destiny through their ingenuity and not only existing to display pain, suffering and naivety, or to clear the pathway for a foreigner's jour-ney. Wakandans are not made to wait for a Western character to teach them how to figuratively read; they are the main characters. The savages in this telling are not the Africans, but those who would look to exploit their superior way of life.

This should not be extraordinary. 'Wakanda is no more or less imaginary than the Africa conjured by Hume or Trevor-Roper, or the one canonized in such Hollywood offerings as *Tarzan*,' writes the author and historian Jelani Cobb. 'It is a redemptive counter-mythology. Most filmmakers start by asking their audiences to suspend their disbelief. But, with Africa, [director Ryan] Coogler begins with a subject about which the world had suspended its disbelief four centuries before he was born.'

None of this reimagining was created by accident. Everything was on purpose and with purpose, buttressed by strong intent. It was a vision worth fighting for. And, at times, that's exactly what its Black creators, cast and crew had to do, especially when it came to preserving their characters' identities.

Take T'Challa. He is the king of a big proud East African nation. It would only follow that he should sound like one. Yet Marvel originally wanted T'Challa to have a British accent when Boseman first played the role as a cameo in *Captain America: Civil War*, the dialect of Africa's most prodigious coloniser. The studio was worried that audiences would not be able to relate to him otherwise, or understand what he was saying. But Wakanda had never been colonised by the British, so where would this mysterious accent have come from? Marvel planned to explain this away by claiming T'Challa picked it up while studying in the UK.

Boseman refused.

'It felt to me like a deal-breaker,' the actor told the *Hollywood Reporter*. 'I was like, "No, this is such an important factor that if we lose this right now, what else are we gonna throw away for the sake of making people feel comfortable?"'

What message would diluting T'Challa have sent? Perhaps that the king of Africa's most successful nation wasn't so Wakandan after all. By adhering to Hollywood's orthodox strategy of disregarding the nuances of African cultures, Marvel would have undermined the central goal of the character.

To their credit, Boseman added, Marvel Studios eventually agreed.

Later, the predominantly Black creative team behind *Black Panther* were just as determined to maintain the authenticity of the vision. The film's director and co-writer Ryan Coogler – whose debut film, *Fruitvale Station*, chronicled the murder of twenty-two-year-old Oscar Grant, shot in the back by a police officer as he lay face down on the platform of an Oakland train station on New Year's Day 2009, unarmed and handcuffed – revealed that he decided to sign on to direct the film when he first saw Boseman's T'Challa speak in deeply accented Wakandan to his father, T'Chaka (John Kani), after watching an unfinished cut of *Civil War*.

There was more to protecting the watering-down of the characters' identities than ensuring they didn't sound British. The creative team for *Black Panther* didn't fall into the trap of thinking their characters should sound 'African' either. They worked deliberately to avoid Hollywood's dreaded obsession with the generic African accent – the deep, slow bellowing noise that has haunted the continent for as long as moving pictures have existed, drowning out the thousands of distinct sounds of a region until they dissolve into nothing.

The language of Wakanda is actually Xhosa, one of South Africa's official languages. A dialect coach was on hand to help Boseman and the other actors match their accents to the language. Some actors, many of whom are from the continent, based their accents on their own heritage, a decision the creatives made to recognise that, even within African countries, there is no universal sound due to the multitude of ethnic groups they contain. Africa would need over two thousand countries for each nation to be represented by a singular dialect.

As with any skill, however, the end results varied: Winston Duke's M'Baku in voice and mannerisms was as exquisitely Igbo as a kola nut, while some accents never quite arrived at their destination, though it wasn't for a lack of trying – an effort that bled into every artistic consideration, from Ruth E. Carter's costumes to the soundtrack. What matters was their relative intent compared to what they could have got away with if they had lazily leaned into the accepted orthodoxy.

Recognising that there is no such thing as an African accent was pivotal. Identity requires specificity; no more so than when humans communicate. The generic accent is one of the ways cultures are pillaged. It starts with the terrible accent but then grows into a more harmful stench that lingers: a representation that devalues the unique sounds and traditions of each region.

There are real consequences to this.

Marvel Studios may not have realised it when they made their original request to strip T'Challa of his accent, but a cornerstone of colonisation was aggressive assimilation policies that forced these artificial nations to consider the language of their colonisers as superior and more civilised than their own.

Colonialists were not able to completely wipe out native languages. But too much of the continent internalised the idea that their mother tongues were inferior, and embraced government policies that institutionalised this idea, including punishing students for speaking in their native language or what is often dismissively referred to as 'the vernacular'.

This thinking slipped from institutions into general society, and for many cultures it remains normal for us to consider our own accents to be suboptimal compared to British and American ones. You pick up this way of thinking at a young age, and it becomes normal when you travel or live abroad to soften your sound and hide your accent until you can barely recognise your own voice – and, eventually, your accent is completely gone. Worst of all, for the same reasons Marvel worried others wouldn't be able to relate, you start pronouncing your own name wrong, to appease those who pop culture has raised to have very little curiosity for the depth of traditions across the continent.

It's certainly a dynamic that impacted my thinking when I moved from Lagos to the UK at ten years old – and that of many of my friends and family members who moved abroad when they were young. With the excitement came a certain understanding that, for the first time in my life, I was about to be fundamentally different from everyone else around me. I would look different and sound different, and have a name that reminded people, on sight, that I was different. Even at such a young age I understood that people might see me and immediately make assumptions because I was coming from this great expanse they only knew as 'Africa', with their visions of an unknowable landscape and wild dangers hiding in every bush. It was this pressure that had me immediately thinking about what I might need to change, what corners and edges I could sand down.

What I settled on first was my name. I've always loved it, so it wasn't something that I actively wanted to give up. But as those in minority communities know too well, you become conditioned to see your full self as negotiable, if it means peace. I knew my name to be an inconvenience to others not well-versed in Nigerian monikers. My thinking was also made easier by having a middle name that's far more universal: Emmanuel. With my mind made up, I decided to run the decision by my parents.

'I think it would be easier if I went by Emmanuel at school,' I said, more as an announcement than a request.

'You can, if you want,' they replied.'But I think one day you will learn to value being different.'

There was a serenity to their delivery that immediately put me at ease, happy to rest in their assuredness. Relieved, I let this one go and decided to keep my name.

I'm fairly certain that if *Black Panther* the film had existed then, I never would have even considered it. Nor would I have quickly found ways of softening my accent.

In the end, Ryan Coogler's *Black Panther* entered the world not as some arthouse, experimental indulgence that only catered for a tiny clique of initiated Black intellectuals. *Black Panther* and its reverence for language, *Black Panther* and its celebration of natural hair, *Black Panther* and its detailed costumes, *Black Panther* and its political reimagining was a colossal global success that is embedded firmly within the consciousness of multiple communities entwined by a shared goal. And, as a result, it made money: $1.2 billion. A month after its release, it became the highest-grossing superhero film of all time in the US. Today, *Black Panther* is the twelfth-highest-grossing movie of any genre in filmmaking history.

But just like vibranium-rich Wakanda, the depth of its relevance goes far beyond its financial pull. The movie proved that a gigantic audience had been starved of a narrative outside of a handful of tropes. This was an expansive African-nation-with-value story that jumped out from the screen and shaped itself into wings, transporting people from their homes and turning Black Panther's debut into less a release and more a collective worldwide experience – inspiring the kind of detailed, minute-by-minute planning with friends and family normally reserved for New Year's Eve or the World Cup Final.

Viewing parties were held from Johannesburg, Montego Bay, Addis Ababa and Dodoma to Peckham, Paris and Harlem. Across Africa, cinemagoers turned up to viewings in their finest Ankaras, Bògòlanfinis, Panos, Kanzus, Kofias and Kaftans. Meanwhile, the stock price of Kente cloth soared as all the fabric in all of the diasporan land was bought up to be royally adorned on the heads and shoulders of millions of Black people living out their African fantasies. Videos spread across social media of young children moved to tears the first time they came face to face with the promotional poster showing Black superheroes in full pomp. Not a baobab tree or sunset in sight.

Black Panther's vision of an African nation was not only important for white audiences who had consumed a very narrow representation of the continent. Popular culture's reductive treatment has had a prolonged negative impact on Africa's complicated relationship with the Black diaspora – most acutely with African Americans still tangling with the trauma of a stolen ancestry transported in slavery to a country that has developed new ways of levying oppression each calendar month since. There remains a curiosity within much of the community to reseed those destructively uprooted roots on the continent, and reengage in a space where being Black is not exceptional. *Black Panther* transcended cultures and brought together Africa's present occupants and its far-flung descendants, in a collective appreciation of its imaginative and meticulous storytelling.

The film worked to occupy a broad space that African-American writer Adam Serwer of *The Atlantic* calls 'The Void', which he defines as 'the psychic and cultural wound caused by the Trans-Atlantic slave trade, the loss of life, culture, language, and history that could never be restored'.

He writes: 'It is the attempt to penetrate The Void that brought us Alex Haley's *Roots*, that draws thousands of African Americans across the ocean to visit West Africa every year, that left me crumpled on the rocks outside the Door of No Return at Gorée Island's slave house as I stared out over a horizon that my ancestors might have traversed once and forever. Because all they have was lost to The Void, I can never know who they were, and neither can anyone else.'

It's arduous enough to form a deep bond within the abyss when there is no realistic way of knowing precisely where your forebears were taken from on Africa's vast plains. But it is a journey made more vexing by the flattening of Africa's cultures and histories, leaving nothing specific to grab on to and making room for blame to be apportioned and misunderstandings to flourish, such as the lingering concerns that African countries – who have spent most of their modern history trying to establish their own independence – have not done enough to assist the Black diaspora in their fights for equality, or thrown enough rope into The Void so that individuals can better find their way home, whatever that might mean to an individual. Africa just remains this vague notion of whatever you can conjure in your own mind.

This gaping chasm is embodied in *Black Panther*'s main adversary, Erik Killmonger, played by Michael B. Jordan. Killmonger grew up in Oakland, California, perilously sculpted by America's historically poor treatment of its Black citizens, his father's civil rights ideals and his own hardened military training.

Killmonger is not impressed by Wakanda's wealth; he is unmoved by its spaceships and futuristic town centres and automated sneakers. Frustration flourishes in place of awe, resentment that Wakanda has gone to such lengths to shield itself in a high-tech gilded cage while Black people the world over suffer under racial and colonial oppression. From his vantage point, Wakandans have chosen to hoard long-term security and prosperity over their duty to offer aid and comfort to their ancestral brethren in The Good Fight.

'Y'all sitting up here comfortable. Must feel good,' Killmonger says in his first showdown with T'Challa and the Wakandan Constitutional

Council.'It's about two billion people all over the world that looks like us. But their lives are a lot harder. Wakanda has the tools to liberate 'em all.'

The liberation Killmonger seeks is not cultural. His pitch is for Wakanda to use its reserve of vibranium weapons to lead a violent, Black-led global revolution against white governments and their international systems of racial oppression – a war that would crush white supremacism and herald an age of total Black domination. By arming insurgents spread around the world, Wakanda would be the harbinger of vengeance for the entire Black race, bringing winter to those who have made a policy of subjugating Black populations.

Killmonger's violent Black supremacist utopia is obviously far from the actual, day-to-day desires of the diaspora. After all, it represents an imperialism that would replace one colonialist mindset for another – this time, we later learn, with Killmonger, not 'Africa', forever on the throne.

But his character gives voice to a fit of under-spoken anger that perhaps the Black diaspora has been abandoned by Africa. Killmonger speaks to a dream of an Africa that serves as a sanctuary for a community that is too often made to feel untethered from the white-dominated countries they exist in, or from ideals that regularly seem to want nothing to do with them. It speaks to a Pan-Africanism that connects the struggle of every Black person, and places responsibilities to alleviate racial suffering within each other's grasp.

The fulfilment of this dream has been partially stunted by Africa's very limited treatment in popular culture. It remains a dark, unknowable place for too many who are desperate to read between the lines. As the African-American author Carvell Wallace writes:

> From Paul Cuffee's attempts in 1811 to repatriate blacks to Sierra Leone and Marcus Garvey's back-to-Africa Black Star shipping line to the Afrocentric movements of the '60s and '70s, black people have populated

the Africa of our imagination with our most yearning attempts at self-realization. In my earliest memories, the Africa of my family was a warm fever dream, seen on the record covers I stared at alone, the sun setting over glowing, haloed Afros, the smell of incense and oils at the homes of my father's friends – a beauty so pure as to make the world outside, one of car commercials and blond sitcom families, feel empty and perverse in comparison . . .

Never mind that most of us had never been to Africa. The point was not verisimilitude or a precise accounting of Africa's reality. It was the envisioning of a free self. Nina Simone once described freedom as the absence of fear, and as with all humans, the attempt of black Americans to picture a homeland, whether real or mythical, was an attempt to picture a place where there was no fear.

The reach of a richly depicted Africa extends beyond the continent's borders and into the desires of those searching for something vital that has eluded generations of families, right back to slavery. 'You know, you got to have the race conversation,' Ryan Coogler explained to the *New York Times* about the conversations Black parents have with their children about racism. 'And you can't have that without having the slavery conversation. And with the slavery conversation comes a question of, OK, so what about before that? And then when you ask that question, they got to tell you about a place that nine times out of 10 they've never been to before. So you end up hearing about Africa, but it's a skewed version of it. It's not a tactile version.'

Wakanda and its wholly invented reality offer a tactile dreamscape. Something you can hold and see and build a connection with, that can exist on your skin and feel like solid hope under the soles of your feet.

You have to go back a long way for the last major Hollywood attempt at a non-stereotypical portrayal of Africa. Exactly thirty years before *Black*

Panther, Eddie Murphy starred as Prince Akeem Joffer in the iconic rom-com *Coming to America*.

We meet Prince Akeem on his twenty-first birthday. He is the heir to the throne of Zamunda, a wealthy African nation equal in standing to any other. As a member of the royal family, Akeem enjoys a life of unimaginable, joyously fanciful privileges: his official alarm clock is a live singer, while rose petals are thrown at his feet wherever he walks. Akeem does not so much as brush his own teeth.

Knowing only privilege, Akeem becomes restless and bored of a life in which every minuscule and meaningful task is taken care of for him. Life in Africa is simply too good.

Included in the responsibilities handled on his behalf is that of finding a wife. After meeting his arranged bride at his lavish birthday party, Prince Akeem, who has never left Zamunda, convinces his father, King Jaffe, to allow him to travel the world with his best friend, Semmi, so as to return more mature and worldly from his experience. His father is understanding and gives him forty days to 'sow his royal oats' before he is to return to Zamunda to fulfil his duties.

Prince Akeem's actual plan is to use that time to fall in love, and where better to find a suitable partner for a prince, he decides, than in a place called Queens. It's in New York where the majority of the film is set. Here, the two Africans, Akeem and Semmi, are not confused simpletons from a backward world. Quite the opposite: Akeem has come to America in the hope of experiencing an ordinary existence. As a result, it's the US that bears the brunt of *Coming to America*'s jokes. (Of course, an even depiction of Africa or Africans does not have to involve another group being maligned in its place. But as the director, writer, star and almost all of the cast are American, the humour is achieved with a healthy dose of self-awareness.)

Akeem takes plenty of glee in the world opening up to him. 'What part of Queens do you want?' a taxi driver asks as they pull out of JFK

Airport. 'Take us to the most common part,' Prince Akeem smiles. 'That's easy,' the driver returns. 'If there's one thing Queens has got a lot of, it's common parts.'

Akeem and Semmi barely have time to move into a rat-infested apartment that was also the site of a recent murder before their luggage is stolen. Semmi, unsure as to why they can't move into accommodation befitting their status, struggles to adjust to their new life of frugality and goes behind his friend's back to write to King Jaffe asking for an extra $500,000 to survive their New York turmoil. Akeem, meanwhile, thrives while cosplaying poor – working his entry-level job as a cleaner at a McDonald's rip-off called McDowell's, and seeing the world through the eyes of regular, hard-working blue-collar workers, something he knows nothing about back in Zamunda. The only person that directs bigoted comments their way is the film's main antagonist, Darryl, the wealthy scion of an Afro Sheen-esque products empire who is presented as ignorant and obnoxious. 'Wearing clothes must be a new experience for you,' Darryl scoffs at Akeem at one point. 'What kind of games do you play in Africa? Chase the monkey?'

A few scenes later, Prince Akeem will steal his girlfriend.

Coming to America was only made because Murphy had the power and clout to insist the African characters were always projected on equal standing. Just as with *Black Panther*, its wide shunning of stereotypes was supported with big audiences and financial success, making $250 million worldwide to date and floating in that magical ether of cult-classic status.

*

It's worth remembering that Wakanda and Zamunda do not exist. And that there are dozens of real African countries that do live and breathe.

It's worth remembering that to depict Africa with graceful intent is not only to portray wealthy royal families soaked in sovereign opulence. Not everything good about the continent needs to be wrapped in a royal robe and elevated to the exemplary. What these films at their best signify, however, are broad, creative, forward-thinking propositions to how Hollywood and the world can think beyond what they think about Africa. Ideally, with time, when the course is fully corrected, we will see them and their astral protégés as pieces of a multilayered jigsaw, alongside both expansive and earthly stories of regular, everyday life.

Next to them should sit big-budget productions and indie endeavours that depict contemporary Africa – a region where well over 50 per cent of people live in cities or are heavily reliant on urban areas. 'Real Africa', as with any continent, unquestionably encompasses small, rural towns and villages that share land with magnificent wildlife grazing on green and pleasant lands. But they, too, are underserved by reductive narratives that cast them as background characters or in a roiling, devastating struggle, ready to be picked off at any time by forces beyond their control.

What is lost in all this are extraordinary stories of the remarkably ordinary. From the world's second-largest region, with thousands of languages and individual ethnicities and histories, you can only imagine how many tales there are still to tell of misguided love, old sacrifice and comedic entanglements; of office politics and politics politics; of teenage dramas, and hospitals with a surprising number of non-medical-related happenings going on. All set in specific, existing places. Without them, we limit the opportunity for people to build unique connections with countries in ways that humanise them and push back against the one-size-fits-all vision of the continent.

In *Black Is King*, Beyoncé's visual album to support the 2019 remake of *The Lion King*, she enlisted the visions of creatives from across the continent to strengthen her own imagination. Following the premise of the film, there were the expected themes of royalty and the burden of sudden responsibility passed down to a young sovereign displaced from his own, searching for an identity. But it didn't feel like it was set on a distant, galactic plane, in an Africa thousands of miles above reality. The specificity of representation brought by the army of African creatives that Beyoncé had the foresight and modesty to allow to flourish created a bridge between various Black experiences, on the continent and beyond.

It's not that Africans need the validation of popular culture knowing that they exist. Industries such as Nollywood have long done a remarkable job at telling vast stories of the particular, at our speed and in our accents – and, with more investment, will continue to grow, because there is so much to share, so much more to see. Seeing yourself accurately represented, however, is a reminder that you and yours are not a side plot to a grander narrative. You *are* the narrative, the main characters for whom the sun rises.

But, twenty years ago, Binyavanga Wainaina could have told you that.

Part Six

The Case of the Stolen Artefacts

If the British Museum were to return even half of the looted objects they have, it will become a small museum in every sense.

— Professor Chika Okeke-Agulu

I.

The Looting

THEY TOLD A SPECTACULAR LIE then walked away with hundreds of treasures.

But before that: giant walls snaked through the Kingdom of Benin. The mammoth structures – in total believed to be four times the length of the Great Wall of China – encased and divided one of the most culturally rich, technologically advanced pre-colonial empires. Believed to have once been the largest manmade structure on Earth, the walls were described by *The Guinness Book of Records* as 'the world's largest earthworks carried out prior to the mechanical era', featuring moats and guardhouses for protection, ditches, and a complex drainage network to ward off flooding. A Dutch traveller noted that the walls were 'as shiny and smooth by washing and rubbing as any wall in Holland . . . they are like mirrors'. The kingdom was cherished.

For centuries, the Kingdom of Benin was one of the most powerful in the region. Its capital, Benin City, was home to thousands, ruled by a single familial lineage of obas whose bloodline can be traced to today – a family continuing to govern descendants of an ancient kingdom that would never fully recover from the destruction and the spectacular lie that was to come.

But before that destruction: there was 1691, and the Portuguese sea captain Lourenço Pinto's observation that 'Great Benin, where the king resides, is larger than Lisbon; all the streets run straight and as far as the eye can see. The houses are large, especially that of the king, which is

richly decorated and has fine columns. The city is wealthy and industri-
ous. It is so well governed that theft is unknown and the people live in
such security that they have no doors to their houses.'

The walls split the city into hundreds of neighbourhoods, and at its
peak in the 1600s it stretched across hundreds of miles of West Africa.
In a multitude of ways, the Kingdom of Benin defied the colonial trope
of backwards Dark Africa – figuratively and literally. There was order,
built with mathematical precision. 'The city and its surrounding villages
were purposely laid out to form perfect fractals, with similar shapes
repeated in the rooms of each house, and the house itself, and the clus-
ters of houses in the village in mathematically predictable patterns,' the
writer Mawuna Koutonin notes. This meant that the main streets 'ran
at right angles to each other' and 'many narrower side and intersecting
streets extended off them'.

'Many of the court's daily operations were formalized and delegated
to specialized guilds,' the art historian Benjamin Sutton writes. 'These
included a guild that managed the oba's wives and regalia; another solely
concerned with the transmission of oral histories; and craft guilds that
oversaw the production of all the court's art, such as the brass casters
guild, the ivory and wood carvers guild, and the bead makers guild.'

This entire scene was illuminated by a complex network of street
lamps way ahead of their time, fuelled by the palm oil Benin would
trade with the Portuguese, alongside beads, carved ivory and materials.
It was this relationship, along with an indulgence in the slave trade, that
made the kingdom exceptionally wealthy. It was a partnership they
would come to rely on – so much so that obas were known to teach
their families to speak passable Portuguese to ensure the relationship
continued past their deaths. With this prosperity, it was understood
that all residents would be looked after, and there would be no need for
crime or for anyone to covet thy neighbour's stuff.

At the centre of the main city was the oba's court – a phalanx of palaces and administrative buildings bordered by its own vast wall. Adorning this barricade were thousands of the kingdom's greatest works, and so exquisite were these objects that they would inspire one of history's greatest thefts. But before that: these artefacts were made by 'artisans [who] have their places carefully allocated in the squares which are divided up in such a manner that in one square [I] counted altogether one hundred and twenty goldsmith's workshops, all working continuously,' as Pinto wrote.

As with many communities of that time, Benin implemented a powerful oral tradition, where histories were passed down through storytelling, across consciousnesses and through generations and villages. These stories – though they could sometimes contradict; such is the way of whispered tales – offer a broad understanding of centuries of history.

The Kingdom of Benin had another trick, however. Not only did they whisper their history, but they also hung it up for all to see – decorating the walls of the great palaces at the centre of their empire. What Pinto referred to as 'goldsmith's workshops' were actually the sites of hundreds of people working on the kingdom's finest treasures: stunning, intricate brass plaques, figurines and sculptures; ivory tusks and brass commemorative heads; figurative tableaux and wooden ornaments that were displayed throughout the city and worn by members of the royal court at important events. On the plaques, which were produced over the space of five hundred years, were engraved the history of the kingdom and the narratives that characterised its present, while the commemorative heads were used to honour great women and conquering obas. Such was the kingdom's crucial economic relationship with Portugal, many of the bronze plaques depicted Portuguese soldiers.

These priceless artefacts, known collectively today as the Benin

Bronzes, belonged to those who made them; they were created by the memories and the skills of the artisans, and the vision of a self-sufficient West African empire that was forced to struggle against an external force knocking hard on its famous walls. But these treasures are no longer in the Kingdom of Benin, which exists today as parts of southern Nigeria. They are no longer there because those external forces kept knocking until they forced their way in.

James Phillips died in January 1897. He died in the British Niger Coast Protectorate, or as the residents called it: the Kingdom of Benin. He died, the British story goes, on a peaceful mission to speak to the oba about how the two great societies could better work together. Yet despite his noble intentions, the tale continues, Phillips and nine other British officers were ambushed by savages and massacred as they approached Benin City.

Revenge, then, was appropriate, they said. The British government could not simply watch while these untamed Africans murdered its people in what an 1897 issue of the *New York Times* referred to as the 'City of Blood'. A proportional response was required. And it was decided – with a heavy heart, of course – that it should be the complete and total destruction of the Kingdom of Benin.

James Phillips died in January 1897, and some have questioned Phillips's intentions in attempting to travel to Benin City. They say it wasn't peaceful at all, and that Phillips and his team were the instigators, there to wage war on the oba and depose him unless the kingdom agreed to stop thwarting the British government's efforts to trade freely through the region and eventually own it all outright. Unfortunately, we may never know the truth. The only evidence we have of Phillips's mysterious intentions is a letter he wrote in which he explained his intentions in great detail:

The King of Benin has continued to do everything in his power to stop the people from trading and prevent the Government from opening up the country. By means of his Fetish he has succeeded to a marked degree. He has permanently placed a Juju on (Palm) Kernels, the most profitable product of the country, and the penalty for trading in this produce is death. He has closed the markets and has only occasionally consented to open them in certain places on receipt of presents from the Jakri chiefs. Only however to close them again when he desires more blackmail ... I feel so convinced that every means has been successfully tried that I have advised the Jakri chiefs to discontinue their presents ...

To sum up, the situation is this: the King of Benin whose country is within a British Protectorate and whose City lies within fifty miles of a Protectorate Customs Station and who has signed a treaty with Her Majesty's representative, has deliberately stopped all trade and effectually blocked the way to all progress in that part of the Protectorate ...

The Revenues of the Protectorate are suffering. I am certain that there is only one remedy, that is to depose the King of Benin from his Stool. I am convinced from information, which leaves no room for doubt, as well as from experience of native character, that pacific measures are now quite useless, and that the time has come to remove their obstruction.

I therefore ask for [the prime minister's] permission to visit Benin City in February next, to depose and remove the King of Benin and to establish a native council in his place and to take such further steps for the opening up of the country as the occasion may require. I do not anticipate any serious resistance from the people of the country – there is every reason to believe that they would be glad to get rid of their King – but in order to obviate any danger I wish to take up a sufficient armed Force, consisting of 250 troops, two seven-pounder guns, 1 Maxim, and 1 Rocket apparatus of the Niger Coast Protectorate Force (NCPF) and a detachment of Lagos Hausas 150 strong, if his Lordship and the Secretary of State for the Colonies will sanction the use of the

Colonial Forces to this extent . . . I would add that I have reason to hope that sufficient Ivory may be found in the King's house to pay the expenses in removing the King from his Stool.

The idea was for Phillips and a small contingent to head to Benin City first and make the oba an offer he could only refuse, creating the grounds for all-out war. The British party also arrived in the middle of a sacred festival, at a time when they knew their presence would not be welcomed. The people of Benin were not naive; they knew what the British wanted, and knew of the many local villages British forces had ransacked across Africa, including the villages of the Ashanti kings in what is now Ghana, who they had forcibly deposed in recent months. But they were not willing to suffer the same colonising fate. When Phillips and his entourage arrived at the edge of the city, they were immediately told to turn back or they would be shot for invading. They carried on anyway. Only two of his party escaped with their lives.

To justify what was to come next, the British immediately made efforts to reframe Phillips's entire exercise as a peaceful, honest trading mission that innocently ran into a blood-thirsty native population – the spectacular lie.

James Phillips died in January 1897, and a month later – which is like the equivalent of a day in modern travelling time – the British managed to put together an army of five thousand men and ten naval ships in what they claimed was a wholly spontaneous siege of the Kingdom of Benin. The great walls were destroyed and the oba fled into exile as the entire region was razed to the ground by heavily armed British troops instructed to burn down every town. Thousands of people were killed as the British faced down a local population who did not have access to Maxim guns – weapons that in their totality could fire 380 bullets a minute. Nor did the local population have war rockets or bolt-action rifles. For what was sold as a spontaneous mission, the colonisers were curiously well-armed and organised.

A diary entry by a British soldier outlines the casualness of the destruction:

20 April. I brought the rocket tube into action, and sent five 24-lb war rockets into Okemue, setting the houses on fire. Under the covering fire of the 7-pr and two Maxim machine guns ... I thoroughly destroyed the town of Okemue.

28 April. I made a reconnaissance in force to a village one hour's march from Ekpon, owned by Abohun, encountered a few of the enemy, burnt and destroyed the village.

1 May. Sent Captain Heneker and company to destroy town of Udo; burnt and completely destroyed the large town of Ugiami, including the king's house.

The invasion didn't end with the massacre. 'After dispersing the natives with Maxims and volley firing, Benin City was ours,' a doctor who accompanied the troops later testified.

There were prized artefacts to be had. Thousands of them. The ones that adorned the walls and told the stories. 'All the stuff of any value found in the King's palace and surrounding houses has been collected,' one soldier documented in his diary. 'A large quantity of brass castings & carved tusks have been found. Two tusks & two ivory leopards have been reserved for the Queen. The Admiral & his staff have been very busy "safeguarding" the remainder, so I doubt if there will be much left for smaller fry ... The whole camp is strewn with loot, chiefly cloths, beads etc, and all the carriers are decked out in the most extraordinary garments ... [they] are at present engaged in celebrating the occasion with a war dance, chanting their deeds of valour.'

The story of the death of James Phillips in 1897 featured a savage massacre. But it wasn't by the people of Benin. The story was later repurposed as an unfortunate conflict rather than a planned destruction and pillage, because of the treasures the British troops stole from the Kingdom of Benin and later sold – and, crucially, where those treasures are today.

*

THEIR SIGNATURE MOVE was to slice their enemies' heads clean off. As they walked, an assistant would ring a bell behind them – the sound a reminder for all men to 'get out of their path, retire a certain distance and look the other way'.

They were the Mino – 'Our Mothers' in the local Fon language – modern history's only recorded all-women militia. European explorers nicknamed them the Dahomey Amazons. The Mino were a killing force whose role was to protect the citizens of the Kingdom of Dahomey and its ruling monarch. For two centuries, they conducted their duties impeccably.

At their peak, there were six thousand soldiers, trained to be fearless and merciless. Jean Bayol, a French naval officer who visited the kingdom's capital, Abomey, in December 1889, later recalled how he'd watched a teenage recruit walk 'jauntily up to [a prisoner of war], swung her sword three times with both hands, then calmly cut the last flesh that attached the head to the trunk'.

A priest in 1861 claimed to have witnessed a training exercise that involved thousands of women climbing 120-metre-high thorny acacia bushes.

As Father Borghero fans himself, 3,000 heavily armed soldiers march into the square and begin a mock assault on a series of defenses designed to represent an enemy capital. The Dahomean troops are a fearsome sight, barefoot and bristling with clubs and knives. A few, known as Reapers, are armed with gleaming three-foot-long straight razors, each wielded two-handed and capable, the priest is told, of slicing a man clean in two.

The soldiers advance in silence, reconnoitring. Their first obstacle is a wall – huge piles of acacia branches bristling with needle-sharp thorns, forming a barricade that stretches nearly 440 yards. The troops rush it furiously, ignoring the wounds that the two-inch-long thorns inflict . . . The bravest are presented with belts made from acacia thorns. Proud to show themselves impervious to pain, the warriors strap their trophies around their waists.

Dahomey was extremely proud of its warriors. The vast majority of the Dahomey Amazons were volunteers; many joined as teenagers. A few, however, were forcibly enrolled when their fathers or husbands reported them to the king for being too strong-headed and independent to live with any more.

Multiple theories exist for how they were formed. By some accounts, they started off as specialist elephant hunters who were told after a particularly successful shoot that 'a nice man hunt would suit them better'.

An alternate origin myth suggests they were created by Queen Hangbe – an eighteenth-century monarch deposed by her younger brother soon after taking the throne – to serve as specialist bodyguards for the palace. The Mino's value eventually extended way beyond the monarch's personal protection when they were formally integrated into the military. The Dahomey Amazons made up about a third of Dahomey's fighting force, but were widely considered by foreign armies to be warriors stronger and braver than their male counterparts.

The Mino's courage didn't go unrewarded; they were granted considerable status in Dahomey. Alongside a bell to herald their movements, they were adorned with considerable wealth, lived in the royal palace and were members of the kingdom's Grand Council, the body that determined laws and policy for the region.

The Mino's final battle started in 1890. When the French arrived.

Dahomey had fought hard to remain free of colonisation. The kingdom had managed to resist the attempts of the British, who were sweeping up much of West Africa. 'The personal courtesies of the King,' a British colonial explorer wrote, 'compared badly with his stubborn resolve to ignore, even in the smallest matters, the wishes of Her Majesty's Government.'

It was France, however, who would wage full-on war on the kingdom to secure the region – now the country of Benin – for its empire. Two major battles ensued as the Dahomey forces, now led by King Béhanzin, tried to go on the offensive, using their greatest weapons: the Mino.

Still, they were no match for France's advanced weaponry. The Dahomey suffered heavy defeats before retreating back to Abomey. They would try and rearm. But so would the French, who marched on the palaces at Abomey in 1892, led by General Alfred-Amédée Dodds.

On the front lines of the battle, the Dahomey Amazons killed dozens of French soldiers but lost hundreds of their own. The two-year war finally ended when King Béhanzin, refusing to surrender, set fire to his palace before fleeing, in the hope that none of Dahomey's prized artefacts – royal figurines, carved palace doors patterned with intricate designs, regal thrones, large statues – would end up in French possession.

But they did.

As the French transported these artefacts back to France, the Mino didn't give up. The Amazons that survived simply took off their uniforms and ran covert operations, seducing French soldiers then slitting their throats as they slept. That wasn't enough, however, to save the treasures that the Dahomey would rather have burned to a crisp than see in the hands of their colonisers.

*

IT WAS JUST A MILITARY OPERATION to free multiple hostages – so, naturally, the army brought with them a curator from the British Museum.

The entourage featured 13,000 soldiers; 26,000 auxiliary personnel; 40,000 animals, 44 of which were elephants trained to pull big artillery guns; and a curator from the British Museum.

The target of the military operation was Maqdala – a secure mountaintop fortress, haven and the seat of power of Emperor Tewodros II, the ruler of Abyssinia, an ancient monarchy that stretched over what is modern-day Ethiopia and Eritrea.

In an effort to maintain his stronghold, Tewodros sent a letter to Queen Victoria in 1863, requesting that the monarch provide military and logistical support to help the emperor ward off his many challengers. As a Christian, Tewodros assumed the British would jump at the opportunity to help strengthen his power base over the Muslims in the region who wanted him out. Disappointed to find no help coming from Queen Victoria – not even a response – Tewodros made the rash decision of taking multiple British diplomats hostage, including the British ambassador to the region. The British sent more diplomats to negotiate their release. Tewodros took them hostage, too.

The standoff continued until 1868, when the British government, under pressure from an angry public, launched one of the most expensive and expansive expeditions ever – which they claimed was needed to free a handful of hostages guarded by just a few thousand men.

Just to get to Tewodros's Maqdala fortress, the British contingent built roads, laid twenty miles of railway lines, created harbours complete with warehouses and piers to store equipment, and constructed desalination plants to produce drinking water. To ensure they could pass through northern Ethiopia without encountering trouble, the expedition bribed many of Tewodros's sworn enemies, rewarding them with weapons and other gifts in exchange for free passage. The operation cost the British government £1.3 billion in today's money, a curious amount to spend on a mission whose stated aim was to free a handful of poorly guarded hostages. It's almost as if the tens of thousands of military personnel, dozens of elephants and the curator from the British Museum were there to secure and transport something else.

Tewodros was cornered, helpless and dazed, as he faced down one of the best-equipped expeditions in history, ironically buoyed by the rivals he had asked the British to help him defeat. Desperate and increasingly isolated, the emperor launched an ill-advised counteroffensive against the encroaching British military in an attempt to catch them unaware. The subsequent battle – if you can call it that – lasted just ninety minutes. Hundreds of Ethiopian soldiers were killed, thousands more injured. There wasn't a single British casualty.

Tewodros started to release hostages, but the British forces and the museum curator just kept on coming. As a final act of defiance, Tewodros took his own life rather than be taken as a prisoner. Leaderless, the few remaining Maqdala troops quickly laid down their weapons.

With the hostages freed, the real expedition could begin.

Throughout his reign, Emperor Tewodros II had aimed to establish Abyssinia as a centre of scholarship and higher learning, amassing a large quantity of cultural and natural relics that were displayed throughout Maqdala. The British troops pillaged it all – a collection that included: a gold crown, jewellery, textiles, hundreds of manuscripts, solid gold chalices, and processional crosses.

The ransacking was not only limited to the emperor's fortress; local churches were raided and robbed of sacred religious items, such as a dozen tabots representing the Ark of the Covenant – the Old Testament shrine that is believed to hold the original Ten Commandments. So sacred were these artefacts to the Ethiopian Orthodox Church, the belief was that only priests should ever even set eyes on the tabots.

One eyewitness account noted that Tewodros's corpse was stripped clean by a 'mob, indiscriminate of officers and men, rudely jostling each other in the endeavour to get possession of a small piece of Theodore's blood-stained shirt'. Pieces of the emperor's hair were cut and taken as souvenirs, while his seven-year-old son, Alemayehu, was carried off by British soldiers, later to be given as a gift to Queen Victoria.

The company ransacked so many items, they needed fifteen elephants and two hundred mules to transport the treasures away from Maqdala. Incredibly, they just so happened to have brought with them enough elephants and mules. Emptied, the Maqdala fortress and surrounding churches were burned to the ground. The famed Anglo-American explorer Henry Morten Stanley observed of the destruction at the time:

> The easterly wind gradually grew stronger, fanning incipient tongues of flame visible on the roofs of houses until they grew larger . . . and finally sprang aloft in crimson jets, darting upward and then circling round on their centres as the breeze played with them. A steady puff of wind levelled the flaming tongues in a wave . . .
>
> The heat became more and more intense; loaded pistols and guns, and shells thrown in by the British batteries, but which had not been discharged, exploded with deafening reports . . . Three thousand houses and a million combustible things were burning. Not one house would have escaped destruction in the mighty ebb and flow of that deluge of fire.

Just days after the invasion, pillage and destruction of Maqdala, and before they had even left Ethiopia, the expedition held a two-day auction of the looted items, giving the officers and assembled dignitaries an opportunity to pick up anything they hadn't already managed to stow away. Fortunately for the British Museum, one of their own curators was on hand. The museum curator, Stanley noted, was 'armed with ample funds', outbidding everyone on the best treasures. Good thing they came prepared.

*

THE EXTERMINATION ORDER WAS CLEAR. Its intent deliberately precise. 'Any Herero found inside the German frontier, with or without a gun or cattle, will be executed. I shall spare neither women nor children. I shall give the order to drive them away and fire on them. Such are my words to the Herero people.'

With vigour, what was promised was enacted.

Germany's colonial presence in Africa may not have been as expansive as France's or Britain's, but their pit stop on the continent before they lost it all in World War I was devastating for the millions of people who fell into their grip.

A key post of their limited empire was called German South West Africa – a large semi-arid territory in southern Africa, known today as part of Namibia. Controlled from 1884, Namibia only gained independence in 1990.

Thanks to its agreeable climate, around 30,000 Germans settled in the colony, occupying land through confiscation and a series of disingenuous treaties. The land seizures partly destroyed the livelihoods of traditional cattle herders in the region, particularly those of the Herero and Nama ethnic groups, whose way of life largely depended on the grazing and trading of cattle.

Frustrated by the theft of their land and property, and the destruction of their way of life, the Herero and Nama revolted in an attempt to try to regain some control of their property and stop further German incursions onto their land. A conflict erupted in 1904, in which dozens of German settlers were killed.

As punishment for the uprising, the German government appointed Lothar von Trotha – an experienced colonial general with an unflinching reputation for violence – to repress the Herero and Nama uprising. Trotha's solution was to bypass compromise and declare the systematic extermination of the local population. 'My intimate knowledge of many central African nations (Bantu and others) has everywhere convinced me of the necessity that the Negro does not respect treaties but only brute force,' he declared.

There was some opposition from his colonial colleagues to the impending extermination, but not for humanitarian reasons. 'I do not concur with those fanatics who want to see the Herero destroyed altogether,' said Theodor Leutwein, the regional governor of German South West Africa, who Trotha replaced for not being ruthless enough. 'I would consider such a move a grave mistake from an economic point of view – we need the Herero as cattle breeders ... and especially as labourers.'

Trotha disregarded this touching protest and charged ahead with what would become the first genocide of the twentieth century, and what the UN would describe in 1985 as one of the worst massacres in history. Eighty per cent of the Herero population and 50 per cent of the Nama people were murdered by the German colonial army. Estimates put the death toll in the range of 100,000. Thousands died of dehydration when the Herero – women and children included – were forced to flee into the desert, while the Germans poisoned watering wells to ensure any survivors could not possibly make their way back to their ancestral lands alive.

Others were taken as prisoners and sent to concentration camps –
effectively death camps – where 75 per cent of the Herero and Nama
sent there, died there. While they were still alive, the prisoners were
subjected to racist scientific experiments and barely fed, and many were
forced into slave labour and worked to death.

Herero women were required to collect the skulls of hundreds of
victims, then boil, clean, and finally shave them using shards of glass.
The skulls were subsequently sent to Germany as part of experiments
that aimed to prove Black people were part of a biologically inferior
race. Historians believe these experiments on the remains of the Herero
and Nama acted as a precursor to the Nazi ideology of race purity.

German South West Africa did not suffer alone. The remains of victims of oppressive policies throughout Germany's colonies were stolen
away and used to further phrenological research – a now-discredited
pseudoscience that proposed you could determine the extent of a person's mental faculties by measuring the shape of their skull.

At the same time, Germany's colonial army was using similar tactics to
quell another anti-colonial uprising in Tanzania. Thousands there were
killed, as the governor of then German East Africa, Gustav Adolf von
Götzen, explained: 'As its last option, the [colonial army] had to use the
cooperation of hunger. Burning down villages, fields and food supplies
might seem barbaric to the distant observer. This method of warfare
was not just the most promising one, but also the only practical one.
According to me, military actions alone will be fruitless, only hunger
and hardship will be able to force people into final submission.' The
leaders of the uprisings in East Africa were publicly hung and decapitated, and their remains transported to Germany.

Skeletons and skulls were collected like trophies throughout German colonies such as Rwanda, Burundi and Togo. Collecting the bones
wasn't an option, but an order. 'Any occasion to rescue a large number

of skulls from being destroyed in the ground or in a fire should be zeal-
ously used,' the anthropologist Felix von Luschan demanded of colonial
officers.

Aside from justifying their beliefs in European racial superiority, the
stolen remains of the victims of colonial rule served further purposes.
Firstly, to humiliate local populations into submission by showing them
that even in death they could not escape. But also to make money, as
they were sold to institutions willing then, as they are now, to put them
on display.

*

THE SCALE OF THE DESTRUCTION was seen as something to be
proud of. 'The town burnt furiously,' a colonial official described in his
diary, adding: 'The thick thatched roofs of the houses, dry as timber
except just on the outside, blazed as though they had been ready prepared for the bonfire . . . Slowly huge dense columns of smoke curled
up to the sky, and lighted fragments of thatch drifting far and wide
upon the wind showed to the King of Ashanti, and to all his subjects
who had fled from the capital, that the white man never failed to keep
his word.'

The promised word was that total violence would be inflicted on
Kumasi, the capital of the Kingdom of Ashanti of the Gold Coast. Their
crime was resisting a colonial army that had periodically waged war on
them in the hope of gaining hold of the gold that had given the Gold
Coast its name. The Asante king, Kofi Karikari, had proven resilient in
defending his nation from a determined force desperate to seize control
of a prized patch of Africa. The reputation of the country for its gold
was such that almost all Europeans sought a foothold in the country:

Portuguese, Dutch, British, French, Germans (Brandenburg), Danes, Dutch, and Swedes all built forts and castles of varying qualities along the coast of some 500 kilometres,' historian Dr Kwame Opoku writes.

The British took their lack of success in penetrating the Gold Coast as a personal insult. In 1872 they decided to deal with, as one high-ranking colonial officer described it, 'the continued menace' of the Asante. Without serious provocation, the British commander in the region, General Wolseley, declared British troops would 'march victorious on the Ashantee capital' for no other reason than to 'show, not only to the King, but to those chiefs ... that the arm of Her Majesty is powerful to punish, and can reach even to the very heart of their kingdom. By no means short of this can lasting peace be insured.'

The Asante didn't want war and tried to negotiate a peace agreement. The other side of the table wanted war and wasn't afraid to admit it by levying all kinds of absurd demands on the king. In exchange for just negotiating peace, Britain demanded the king hand over his son and mother, and the heirs to four other kingdoms. King Karikari obviously refused. Meanwhile, he tried appealing directly to London, asking they ignore the 'false information' being passed to the government claiming brutality on the part of the Asante.

The British came anyway in February 1874 and burned it all down. But before they set the fire, they ransacked the treasures, as explained by an aide to General Wolseley:

> The first room visited was one which during the day had been seen to be full of boxes, some of which, at all events, contained articles of much value. Here were found those gold masks, whose object it is so difficult to divine, made of pure gold hammered into shape. One of these, weighing more than forty-one ounces, represented a ram's head, and the others the faces of savage men, about half the size of life.

Box after box was opened and its contents hastily examined, the more valuable ones being kept, and the others left. Necklaces and bracelets of gold, Aggery beads, and coral ornaments of various descriptions, were heaped together in boxes and calabashes. Silver plate was carried off . . . Swords, gorgeous ammunition-belts, caps mounted in solid gold, knives set in gold and silver, bags of gold-dust and nuggets; carved stools mounted in silver, calabashes worked in silver and in gold, silks embroidered and woven, were all passed in review.

Several more insults were to come. First, the British left the Asante with a bill of '50,000 ounces of approved gold' to cover the cost of burning down and pillaging their capital city. Next, they waged war on Kumasi again twenty years later, under the pretence that the Gold Coast still owed the British money from the first war. They ransacked more of the treasures that remained, as the Gold Coast officially became a British colony.

The final humiliation endures. Though the Gold Coast, now Ghana, no longer falls under British control, almost all of the treasures they looted do.

*

THE LIST OF LOOTINGS ARE ENDLESS.

A tooth taken from a Congolese independence hero; the skull of a Tanzanian revolutionary warrior prised from his shoulders and taken abroad to be experimented on. A South African woman taken to Europe in 1810 to perform as a carnival freak attraction in life and have her remains publicly displayed in death. There are the nearly eight thousand Cameroonian artefacts that found their way out of the country between 1885 and independence; and the hundreds of treasures looted in the 1890 invasion of the Ségou palace in what is now Mali. There were the coordinated French 'scientific missions' of the 1920s and 1930s where ethnographic explorers were sent to scout and collect artefacts – the most famous sojourn a two-year mission spanning Dakar in West Africa to Djibouti in East, in which hundreds of priceless items were unjustly acquired. These treasures and all the others taken from countries across Africa – from Benin to Ethiopia, the Gold Coast to Namibia, Chad to South Africa – are the spoils of a one-sided war, transported to be held where they remain today.

*

II.

The Spoils

Let us be clear on this point: the arrival of loot into the hands of western curators, its continued display in our museums and its hiding-away in private collections, is not some art historical incident of 'reception', but an enduring brutality.

— Dan Hicks, curator at the Pitt Rivers Museum in Oxford

THREE THOUSAND MILES AWAY and across a square. Down a deceptively wide road and through the tall iron black gates and below gold security spikes. Wait in line, then proceed past security and forty-three imposing columns and up the eleven steps guarding the entrance.

Three thousand miles away and you're standing in a famous atrium illuminated by an immense glass ceiling, awning two acres of exclusively indoor space and a conspiratorial number of cafés selling warm drinks at roasting prices. Move across this cavernous court and along past the gift shop, unsure as to where the gallery room is until you spot the sweeping vertical banner with an arrow pointing down two flights of simple stairs. Just above the arrow, the banner is marked in dramatically large letters: 'AFRICA'.

Suddenly, more than ever, feel every inch of the three thousand miles away.

Descend into 'Room 25' and be greeted by walls lined with glass cabinets so impeccably cleaned at first it appears there is nothing between you and the spot-lit spoils. Avoid the instinct to reach out and touch the treasures unless you wish to face a deservedly patronising stare from a small child or a security guard pondering if this is your first time in a museum.

Clockwise past dozens of displays of contemporary artworks and regular references to the 'traditional ways of African culture', and you will come to *the* room and you will see *them*.

In this compact room within the colossal British Museum are almost a hundred Benin Bronzes and other assorted treasures, each accompanying description written by winners who routinely adopt a historically generous interpretation of 'gifted'. Here are the ivory lions and carved doors; brass worship heads and leopard-shaped hip masks that denoted your rank in the royal court; grand weapons and exquisite jewellery, artefacts that once belonged to the people they belong to.

Against the far wall is the main attraction: fifty-six Benin Bronze brass plaques, suspended in the air in eight columns of seven rows; their shadows patterning the bare white wall behind them, gaps in the silhouette appearing where the plaques have been damaged.

Three thousand miles away from their source, and a small wooden bench has been placed in front of the plaques for you to sit and ponder whatever it is you are personally moved to sit and ponder. I sit. And ponder. These priceless plaques are the only treasures here not lodged behind a see-through glass fortress. The room falls silent for several moments. I look around to find that I suddenly have the space to myself on a late summer evening. In that quiet solitude, the ghosts of my ancestors appear, three thousand miles from where they are buried, and whisper to me: 'Steal them back.'

Or at least I think that's what they said. I can't be sure they whispered at all. It's even possible there were no ghosts. This room, you see, inspires a certain narrative freedom. Everywhere, an expensively constructed fable to justify why *they* are *here*. Where they have been for 125 years. Three thousand miles away.

Meanwhile, the same scene is playing out in rooms adjacent to vast atriums and under spectacular ceilings across Europe and North America. The same scene is playing out seven thousand miles from Namibia, in New York City; four thousand miles from the Democratic Republic of Congo, in Brussels; two thousand miles from Senegal, in Paris; three thousand miles from Ghana, in London; six thousand miles from Rwanda, in Germany. The same scene is playing out thousands of miles from Chad and Cameroon and Ethiopia and Kenya and Benin and Eritrea and Guinea and the Ivory Coast and Gabon and Mali and Madagascar and Angola.

Thousands of miles from where they belong.

*

III.

An Ongoing War

IT CAN BE HARD TO FOLLOW, if you allow it to be.

In reality, however, it is all very simple.

Let's start where there is broad agreement: 90 per cent of Africa's material cultural legacy is being kept outside of the continent. The vast majority of these artefacts – numbering into the hundreds of thousands, possibly more – were violently looted as a result of colonial plundering. Soon after they were stolen, sometimes that very same day, the treasures were sold by whichever invading force had carried out the pillage. Some of these artefacts ended up in private collections, but most of the goods quickly found their way into museums. They are still in those same museums. The objects you can see in galleries only account for a small percentage of the total number of artefacts in the general possession of museums. The main bulk of this precious loot has been stockpiled, hidden and locked away within the bowels of the Western world's most illustrious institutions; well away from the grasp of visitors and certainly kept out of the reach of the African countries they were stolen from – nations forced to beg for their treasures for over half a century.

Understanding this can only lead to one logical moral question: how have museums justified the continued hoarding of treasures that were stolen through a deliberate campaign of systematic violence, and whose owners have pleaded continually for their return ever since they were taken?

Here's how: museums have come together in a collective performance that frames the discussion of restitution as some impenetrable
riddle. All confusion is by design. The reality, again, is very simple: 90
per cent of Africa's material cultural legacy is being kept outside of the
continent. It was stolen through a campaign of mass violence.

This tactic of misdirection and showmanship was put on paper in
2002 when eighteen of the self-described 'world's great museums and
galleries' published a statement on the website of the British Museum
explaining their reasoning for rejecting suggestions that they should
return the loot. The museums – including the Louvre, Metropolitan
Museum of Modern Art in New York, the Guggenheim, Berlin's State
Museums and the Art Institute of Chicago – called their shared belief
system the 'Declaration on the Importance and Value of Universal
Museums'. The declaration opens by condemning theft, in theory: 'The
international museum community shares the conviction that illegal
traffic in archaeological, artistic, and ethnic objects must be firmly
discouraged.'

That out of the way, the statement veers into rationalising the idea
that it's wrong to steal items but it's okay to keep stolen items, because
times have changed and they cannot be held responsible for the circumstances through which the items were originally accumulated. 'We
should, however, recognize that objects acquired in earlier times must
be viewed in the light of different sensitivities and values, reflective of
that earlier era,' the declaration continues. 'The objects and monumental
works that were installed decades and even centuries ago in museums
throughout Europe and America were acquired under conditions that
are not comparable with current ones.'

But this can't possibly be true, because it was considered theft then,
making the conditions very much comparable to now. In a speech to
Parliament, British prime minister William Gladstone expressed shame
and 'deep regret' that the Maqdala treasures from Ethiopia had been

looted and 'were thought fit to be brought away by a British army'. Gladstone 'could not conceive' why it was deemed acceptable to take items that to Britain, he said, were largely 'insignificant', but to the people of Abyssinia were 'sacred and imposing symbols'.

In response, Robert Napier, who led the invasion and subsequent pillage, tried to assure Parliament that, at the very least, the most sacred items in the loot would be returned as soon as possible. 'The best way of treating the crown and the chalice would be for the State to purchase them and deposit them in the British Museum until an opportunity offered for restoring them [to Ethiopia],' he said. 'And that opportunity would arise when a Government was established [in Ethiopia] with some prospect of stability. Their selection of the party to whom they [the British] should give the crown and chalice would be an indication that they regarded them as the rightful rulers of the Empire.'

Prime Minister Gladstone was hardly impressed by this weak concession. He shot back: 'Lord Napier said these articles . . . ought to be held in deposit till they could be returned to Abyssinia. It was rather a painful confession, because, if they ought to be returned, it seemed to follow that they ought not to have been brought from Abyssinia.'

This was in 1871. The Maqdala treasures were never returned. The crown and chalice never even left London. Today, they are still in the possession of the V&A Museum in south-west London, which promoted the objects on its website at a recent limited exhibition before they were put back in storage – with the crown described as a 'work of exquisite craftsmanship and an important symbol of the Ethiopian Orthodox Church'. If these exquisite items carry such important symbolism, then Gladstone's suggestion in 1871 would still ring true today: they belong with those for whom that symbolism actually matters, for them to decide in what way the objects should interact with the rest of the world.

It may have been easier to get away with. But by the standards of the

1870s, the forced excavation of vast quantities of a nation's prized heir-looms was still considered shameful. Times, clearly, haven't changed that much.

Without explaining the exact degrees by which moral codes have shifted, the declaration moves on to its next point: that ownership is simply a matter of holding on to something for long enough; that some-how, in the preceding years, these inanimate objects have flipped allegiances. 'Over time, objects so acquired – whether by purchase, gift, or partage – have become part of the museums that have cared for them, and by extension part of the heritage of the nations which house them.' Just imagine what they mean to the countries that crafted them.

The declaration then arrives at the core justification used by the museums. That, as the title of the document alludes to, museums based in North America and Europe serve a higher purpose; they are not regu-lar galleries as you would find elsewhere. Instead, they should be considered 'universal museums' – spaces that, due to their prized loca-tion, serve the entirety of humanity – and as such, the objects in their possession traverse regular boundaries of ownership. Returning these artefacts to be displayed in clearly less desirable countries that attract less tourism, they argue, would deprive the rest of the world: 'The universal admiration for ancient civilizations would not be so deeply established today were it not for the influence exercised by the artefacts of these cultures, widely available to an international public in major museums.'

Believing the artificial construct of the 'universal museum' rests solely on accepting that the word 'universal' means North America and Europe. It means believing that the 'people of every nation' can easily travel to London, New York, Paris, Berlin, Brussels and Amsterdam. And that it wouldn't serve countries considered less desirable to have ownership of their own treasures so they too can possess some token of desirability.

Believing it requires you not to question how universal these spaces are when they exist in countries that in recent years have implemented stricter immigration policies that specifically target the people living in the regions where these artefacts originated. And for you not to wonder why a great number of these items aren't available for public view if the desire is to ensure easy access to these works of art. The British Museum, for example, holds nine hundred Benin Bronze treasures, yet only around a hundred of them are on display. The remaining eight hundred are kept permanently locked away, presumably somewhere near the dozen sacred religious tabots from East Africa believed to represent the biblical Ark of the Covenant. Today, the tabots – which the Ethiopian culture minister described as 'a fundamental part of the existential fabric of Ethiopia and its people' – are housed in a locked room in the basement of a museum three thousand miles from Ethiopia, serving no purpose at all.

Among all this, museums have chosen to adopt a significant degree of wilful ignorance when it comes to the treasures in their possession. Very little effort has traditionally been made to carry out a full inventory of their stockpile, a total contradiction of the argument that they are safer in Western hands. 'Museums know so little about what they hold, and they share just a fraction of what they could know,' Dan Hicks, professor of contemporary archaeology at the University of Oxford and a curator at the Pitt Rivers Museum, writes in his book *Brutish Museums.*

'The sheer haphazard nature of the supposed western curation of universal heritage is shocking,' Hicks continues. 'Even the British Museum remains unable to publish any comprehensive account of what is in their collections and unwilling to publish what it knows for now . . . As some institutions begin to open up their archives, and while others batten down the hatches, concerned too much would be revealed about how poorly loot is cared for, how much might be mislaid.'

These are not the actions you take if your primary concern is to ensure these objects are enjoyed as widely as possible by the greatest number of people. Western museums have been criticised by pro-restitution groups for focusing their energies on developing mythical belief systems to anoint themselves the legal guardians of treasures that were never orphaned. Of the Maqdala artefacts, the V&A describes itself as 'custodians of these Ethiopian treasures.'

All of this feels like an effort to deliberately obfuscate; to avoid talking about what we're meant to be talking about. Take this quote from the director of the V&A, Tristram Hunt, summarising his position on why his museum is reluctant to support handing back ownership of the arte-facts in their possession: 'There remains something essentially valuable about the ability of museums to position objects beyond particular cul-tural or ethnic identities, curate them within a broader intellectual or aesthetic lineage, and situate them within a wider, richer framework of relationships while allowing free and open access, physically and digitally.'

The V&A, in fact, seems eager to celebrate colonialism: 'For a museum like the V&A, to decolonise is to decontextualise,' Hunt writes. 'The history of empire is embedded in its meaning and collections, and the question is how that is interpreted. A more nuanced understanding of empire is needed than the politically driven pathways of Good or Bad. For alongside colonial violence, empire was also a story of cosmo-politanism and hybridity.'

The declaration attempted a similar ruse: 'Museums are agents in the development of culture, whose mission is to foster knowledge by a con-tinuous process of reinterpretation. Each object contributes to that process. To narrow the focus of museums whose collections are diverse and multifaceted would therefore be a disservice to all visitors.'

This shallow wordplay deflects to where there is already broad agree-ment: museums should not be limited only to curating exhibitions that educate on the history of the country they are situated in. And that showcasing interconnected stories can be a partial remedy to the rise in far-right nationalism sweeping the world. But none of this speaks to why objects cannot fall under the legal ownership of those they were long stolen from – especially when we know they were stolen. Without addressing this gross imbalance, the simplest of painful realities endures: 90 per cent of Africa's cultural legacy was shipped out of the continent during the colonial era for the same reason that it is currently being kept on display. The objects are magnificent and of exceptional value, and their presence in any country makes that country richer.

That would be so much simpler to admit.

*

IV.

Restitution

IN MAY 2021, the Belgian government announced plans to repatriate around two thousand artefacts looted from the Democratic Republic of Congo. The decision to return these items came after Belgium's science minister, Thomas Dermine, declared that any items that can be proven to have been plundered 'don't belong to us'.

'Instead of a piecemeal approach by artwork, we said let's adopt a more radical and holistic approach,' Dermine said in a statement. 'Everything that has been acquired through force and violence under illegitimate conditions must in principle be returned. Objects that have been acquired in an illegitimate fashion by our ancestors, by our grandparents, great-grandparents, do not belong to us. They belong to the Congolese people. Full stop. Cultural heritage is one of the riches exploited by the colonial powers, and taking thousands of objects from colonies deprives the citizens of the former colony access to their own history, culture, creativity and spirituality of their ancestors.'

Much of this progress, the thirty-five-year-old Dermine said in an interview with the *Art Newspaper*, has been driven by changing attitudes across the country. 'There has clearly been a generational shift in Belgium and the new generation has a different relationship with Africa.'

That generational shift found its voice in the summer of 2020, as tens of thousands of predominantly young people took to the streets of cities across Belgium to demand their government take responsibility for their colonial legacy. The demonstrations – the largest of which attracted 15,000 people to Brussels – were sparked by the Black Lives

Matter movement that forced a racial reckoning in countries around the world following the murder of George Floyd. Statues of King Leopold II – the Bored King whose violent policies led to the deaths of 10 million people in the short-lived Congo Free State – were taken down across the country, while large swathes of Belgian infrastructure that was dedicated to Leopold was renamed.

The decision to return two thousand plundered artworks counts as progress. But only just. That number represents less than 2 per cent of the country's total collection of artefacts that originate from Africa. Just outside of Brussels sits Belgium's Royal Museum for Central Africa, home to around 120,000 items, the majority of which come from the DRC.

The DRC is used to the slow-trickle return of its own possessions. After making their first request to have their own artefacts back in 1960, the Central African country was sent 144 items. Fifteen years later.

It's not exactly clear how many items in total Belgium will return in the future as a result of this new awakening. The government believes that at least 60 per cent of the artefacts in the Royal Museum for Central Africa were acquired through legitimate purchases, though the steps they took to make that assessment have not been made public. That leaves the provenance of tens of thousands of treasures still to be assessed by those with a vested interest in keeping them.

The piecemeal approach of returning a minuscule fraction of looted goods has been the go-to tactic for European and North American museums. Tiny amounts ladled into begging bowls to give the impression what they are serving is in any way filling.

As with Belgium, much of the recent movement across Europe to repatriate items, however small, was forced by the Black Lives Matter movement. It's impossible to reckon with histories of systemic racism without reassessing the horrors of colonialism and how nations continue to benefit from it today. King Leopold II's statue wasn't the only one to fall. He was joined by others, including monuments to the southern African imperialist Cecil Rhodes and the slave trader Edward Colston, whose involuntary plunge into a river in Bristol went viral. The reckoning was not an attempt to rewrite history, as critics wrongly claimed, but, for the first time, to widely acknowledge its foundations, and work towards making amends in order to recognise where history threatens to repeat itself.

Museums were not immune. They were forced to be central to this conversation, but not in the idyllic, low-stakes way they wanted to engage. The British Museum faced heavy criticism after it joined other institutions in releasing generic, perfunctory statements supporting the cause of racial equality, without addressing the bigotry that exists at the core of keeping plundered goods from across the Black diaspora hostage. 'We are aligned with the spirit and soul of Black Lives Matter everywhere,' Hartwig Fischer, the director of the British Museum, said. 'The death of George Floyd and of many others must sharpen our awareness of how much more we as a major public cultural institution need to do in the fight against inequality and discrimination.' However, in an interview shortly after the release of the statement, Fischer strongly denied accusations that looted artefacts were central to the museum's collections.

A handful of other museums in the UK and Ireland did move to address a limited number of artworks in their possession. The Horniman Museum in London pledged to work towards returning a dozen items in its collection that were collected through 'colonial violence'. In a statement, the museum recognised that 'the wealth that enabled Frederick [Horniman, the museum's founder] to make his collection, build his museum, and campaign as a social reformer, was reliant on . . . a trade built on the exploitation of people living in the British Empire'.

The National Museum of Ireland said it would return twenty-one items; the National Museum of Scotland, which houses eighty items from Benin, told the Museum Association that they are 'committed to sharing information and knowledge and working towards a major reunion' of their artefacts. The Church of England promised to give back two Benin Bronzes, while the University of Aberdeen set out plans to return one Bronze after admitting it was 'acquired in such reprehensible circumstances'.

Still, these identified treasures amount to a paltry slice of the UK's full stock. A considerable bulk of the hoard remains in the British Museum, the V&A and the other national museums. These institutions have all lined up behind the government's philosophy that museums should 'retain and explain' – the view that those small plaques next to plundered objects which detail the story behind their theft are enough of a concession. But the harm of these plaques is that they push a false narrative, framing the theft as an incident that occurred in a bygone era rather than something that never ended and will forever continue, as long as the items remain under the legal ownership of the museums. For accuracy, these panels should describe how these items are still being held against the will of their owners. There has been no shift in museum morality. The timeline is unbroken. They were taken, they were kept.

Regardless of philosophical positions, these national museums claim that a British law, written in 1963, blocks them from permanently returning any stolen loot, though the text of the code doesn't appear to do that at all. As well as allowing museums to give back artworks that are duplicates or damaged to the point they become 'useless for the purposes of The Museum', the British Museum Act permits them to return any object they consider 'unfit to be retained in the collections of the Museum'.

A basic, humane reading of the law should get you to a place where you consider items obtained through the deliberate destruction of communities and the murder of tens of millions of innocent people 'unfit to be retained'.

Instead, these major institutions have deemed it sufficient to offer temporary loans back to the continent – an arrangement African countries are reluctant to accept as it would amount to an admission that the artefacts no longer belong to them.

Over in the US, where the highest number of artefacts are housed outside of Europe, the conversation around restitution is somehow managing to occur at an even slower pace. New York's Metropolitan Museum of Art (MET), home to around 160 artefacts from Benin, has committed to facilitating the return of three Benin sculptures as an act that shows the museum 'is committed to transparency and the responsible collecting of cultural property'. At the same time, the museum has said that other, more renowned items, such as the Queen Idia masks, are not being considered for repatriation.

With less of a direct role in Africa's colonisation, American museums have managed to dodge the brunt of the restitution conversation by claiming that the items in their collections were obtained through more traditional means, decades after the pillaging occurred. Their collection of artefacts, the MET have said, 'were largely given to the institution in the 1970s and 1990s by individuals who acquired them on the art market'. Research by Dan Hicks estimates that around forty museums in the US – including the Smithsonian, the Philadelphia Museum of Art, the Brooklyn Museum, the Art Institute of Chicago, Boston's Museum of Fine Arts, Harvard University's Peabody Museum and Yale University's Art Gallery – are in possession of looted artefacts from West Africa. By contrast, only ten museums in the whole of Africa are home to a Benin Bronze.

France, meanwhile, has chosen to embark on a different journey – or, at least, has signalled a willingness to find their keys.

In 2017, President Emmanuel Macron addressed a crowd of students at the University of Ouagadougou in Burkina Faso. Macron decided that it was time to acknowledge history. 'I am from a generation of the French people for whom the crimes of European colonialism are undeniable and make up part of our history,' he said. 'I cannot accept that a large part of cultural heritage from several African countries is in France. There are historical explanations for that, but there are no valid justifications that are durable and unconditional. African heritage can't just be in European private collections and museums. African heritage must be highlighted in Paris, but also in Dakar, in Lagos, in Cotonou.'

Palates cleansed, he arrived at the main course: 'In the next five years, I want the conditions to be met for the temporary or permanent resti- tution of African heritage to Africa.'

It was an unambiguous pledge that the leaders of Western countries had tried every which way to circumvent. It acknowledged the theft, but instead of making excuses, Macron took the logic to its natural moral conclusion: return stolen artefacts plundered in a bloody siege.

What has had the most impact on the art world since, however, is not Macron's speech, but the report he commissioned next. Tradition- ally, commissioning broad studies is what governments do when they want to abandon a public pledge, or at least delay it until it is no longer feasible.

But in this case, he turned to two well-respected experts on the issue of restitution: art historian Bénédicte Savoy, who had described Macron's declaration as fuelling a 'heated debate about colonial amnesia'; and Senegalese economist Felwine Sarr.

The report came out a year later, in November 2018. Its findings were devastating for large museums such as the Quai Branly in Paris, which alone holds around 70,000 of the 90,000 artefacts from sub- Saharan Africa that are in France.

Savoy and Sarr concluded that 'any objects taken by force or pre- sumed to be acquired through inequitable conditions' should be returned to their country of origin, with a broad definition of what constitutes force and inequity: all objects should be returned that were acquired through 'military aggression'; or from the descendants of 'military personnel or active administrators on the continent during the colonial period'; or 'through scientific expeditions'; or items that were temporarily loaned but were never returned; or artefacts that were gifted to the museum after the independence era but were clearly taken before 1960; or items that were gifted by any former heads of state convicted of corruption.

Critically, the report moves the emphasis away from having to prove that artefacts were violently pillaged, requiring institutions to show that artworks were acquired on equal terms – a strict criterion that museums know they would struggle to pass. The Savoy-Sarr report goes on to reject long-term loans or setting up temporary exhibitions in origin countries as a substitute for full restitution, because of the psychological impact that would have on societies having to deal with the loss of their artefacts for a second time.

Savoy and Sarr denied that, if adopted widely, their recommendations would completely empty out French or European museums. Instead, they aimed for a 'rebalancing of the geography of African heritage in the world, which is currently extremely imbalanced, as European museums have almost everything, and African museums have almost nothing'. There is no reason to assume that African countries would not happily loan items to Western museums if given the chance. Unless, of course, you are concerned that they will treat the West the way they have been treated.

Unsurprisingly, museum curators were not thrilled with the report's conclusions. Prior to its release, Stéphane Martin, then director of the Quai Branly, praised Macron's speech, saying that 'nowadays we cannot have an entire continent deprived of its history and artistic genius'. But when the reality set in, Martin felt very different. He called the Savoy-Sarr report a form of 'self-flagellation and repentance' and argued that it tainted 'everything that was collected and bought during the colonial period with the impurity of the colonial crime.' Similarly unaware or unbothered by what colonialism actually involved, one of the director's main concerns was that items 'linked to colonisation (administrators, doctors and soldiers), or items gathered during scientific expeditions' would suddenly become vulnerable to being returned, which was kind of the point.

The director of the Quai Branly didn't see all bad news. He predicted that, in the end, Macron and the French government wouldn't go through with it, and would opt for the increased 'circulation' of these artworks – a vague term that likely translates to the temporary loaning of these items in strict conditions back to African countries who will again have to forfeit them in the future.

So far, Martin's instinct for sensing government inaction is proving to be well attuned. Very little has come from the report. Three years after it was published, Macron's government has approved the return of just twenty-seven artefacts from Senegal and Benin. Culture minister Roselyne Bachelot described the decision to return these objects as an 'act of friendship and trust', making efforts to make it clear it was not an 'act of repentance.'

By now, the report had called for museums in France to work on the return of items to Benin, Senegal, Ethiopia, Cameroon, Nigeria and Mali, for starters, while creating a universally accessible, comprehensive inventory of how each artefact came to be housed in a French museum, giving the sort of clarity on theft that would make it harder to avoid the right moral conclusion. The government seemed to be shifting back towards a position of making restitution policy based on convenience. 'France will examine all requests presented by African nations', as one minister outlined, calling for people not to focus on the sole issue of returns.

Despite the deliberate slow-walking of the process, Sarr sees promise in how the report has galvanised others to take up the issue of

Africa's lost legacy more seriously. 'The question of restitution is being increasingly debated in Europe, Africa, and the United States by intellectuals, artists, civil society, researchers,' he told the *New York Times*. 'It's become a central question, and real progress has been made.' He admitted, however, that 'things are not moving as fast as we would have liked' and that 'the French government is striving for a middle way that would be a mix of restitution and circulation. From a historical standpoint, that's a retreat.'

Just as in Britain, France also has its own archaic law to consider. This time it's from the sixteenth century, and it considers anything within their museums to be 'inalienable', making it essential that the government follows through on its promise and takes it out of the hands of museums who patently do not want to see change come at their expense.

There is one country that appears truly ready to wash off the stain of their stolen artefacts. In 2019, Germany's sixteen regions came together to sign a joint declaration that promised to cast off their loot. Key to this effort was the creation of a public database of each treasure – where it came from and under what conditions it was taken – a level of transparency that other Western countries have refused to undertake. Two years later, in April 2021, the German government, in an attempt to 'face up to our historic and moral responsibility to shine a light and work on Germany's historic past', set out concrete plans to return what could be up to 7,000 pillaged artefacts within the year; effectively anything that was collected by force. The governments on the receiving end of these objects have already publicly declared that they are happy to loan some of these items back to Germany should they request them.

Germany is working to return more than pieces of art. Part of their restitution efforts include the physical remains of thousands of people taken to Europe during the colonial era for racist scientific experiments and the exhibiting of their skeletons in museums. Research by

Christian Kopp – the co-founder of Berlin Postkolonial, which works to see the return of African remains – estimates that two German scientists alone amassed a collection that featured the remains of 15,000 people. Some of these bones were sold to other organisations, including a haul of four thousand skeletons and skulls from the Herero genocide that went to the American Museum of Natural History, where they remain still and where recent research has been carried out on them.

The work to repatriate these remains will require extensive investigation. Two dozen skulls were repatriated to Namibia in 2018, while thousands more remain in Germany, primarily from Rwanda, Tanzania and Burundi.

This work is not unique to Germany, however. After the BLM protests, Belgium took steps to return the last remains of the former Congolese colonial hero Patrice Lumumba.

Lumumba lead his nation's independence movement before becoming the DRC's first prime minister at just thirty-four years old. He lasted three months. Lumumba was arrested in a coup and assassinated, his body dissolved in acid. A single tooth, however, was kept and sent back to Belgium.

In 2020, a court in Belgium ordered the restitution of Lumumba's tooth to his family. 'My first reaction is, of course, that this is a great victory,' his daughter, Juliana Lumumba, said shortly after the restitution order was made. 'At last, sixty years after his death, the mortal remains of my father, who died for his country and its independence and for the dignity of Black people, will return to the land of his ancestors.'

If only more treasures could take a similar journey. Because when they do, they are always greeted by grateful masses relieved at the opportunity to staunch an open wound.

*

The line stretched out the door. Then down the street, and wrapped itself around the Zinsou Foundation in the city of Cotonou, the capital of Benin. The photograph shows dozens of Beninese schoolchildren, workbooks in hand, waiting to see a small selection of their country's greatest treasures back on home soil for the first time since they were forcibly taken. The students were just some of the 275,000 people who rushed to visit the exhibition in 2006 before the items were returned to France as a condition of the one-year loan deal from the Quai Branly museum to mark the centenary of the pillage of the Abomey palaces.

That so many people turned up to the exhibition demonstrated how deeply communities most affected by the continued stockpiling of their artefacts thousands of miles away want access to their physical cultural heritage. Yet despite that profound desire, there is very little African countries can do to force the Western world to abandon this colonial mindset and give up their sacred treasures.

For over a hundred years, they have tried asking and collaborating and deliberating, to no great success – a stalemate that, unsurprisingly, has led to a few believing that more drastic action is necessary.

Mwazulu Diyabanza has been nicknamed the 'Robin Hood of Restitution'. He's been called the 'Real Life Killmonger' after the villain of *Black Panther* who steals back a prized Wakandan artefact from the fictional Museum of Great Britain. 'How do you think your ancestors got these?' Killmonger asks a British curator before the theft. 'You think they paid a fair price? Or did they take it, like they took everything else?'

During the BLM summer, Diyabanza vowed to personally ensure the return of looted artefacts to the continent. 'Wherever the riches of our heritage and culture have been stolen, we will intervene,' he told *The Guardian*.

His methods are as simple as his intentions. The Congolese activist walks into European museums, grabs a pillaged item and calmly walks out. Or, at least, he suggests he is going to walk out, but instead gives the police every opportunity to arrest him. There is no struggle once he is caught; he has never reverted to violence. Diyabanza often gives a speech setting out his motives and intentions, right there on the gallery floor, informing nearby security staff of what he is about to do. A quick denouncement of colonialism, and it's time to grab. He doesn't succumb to subtlety. In September 2020, he snatched a Congolese funerary statue housed in the Afrika Museum in Berg en Dal, south-eastern Netherlands. The entire thing was broadcast live on Facebook.

His actions, which he has called 'active diplomacy', have also seen him try to take a statue from the Quai Branly that was stolen from Chad, and lift a ceremonial ivory spear from the Museum of African, Oceanic and Native American Art in Marseille. Diyabanza was arrested and charged, but a court in the southern French city recognised the political nature of his actions and found him not guilty of theft. He hasn't always been so lucky – in the past he has been fined hundreds of euros and is currently serving out a suspended prison sentence.

As far as he is concerned, with or without the approval of the court, he has nothing to be ashamed of. 'You do not ask thieves if you can reclaim your stolen property,' Diyabanza has said many times. For him, he's just avenging the loss of not only his country and continent's legacies, but also of his immediate family. Diyabanza's grandfather was the governor of a province in DRC when Europeans came and plundered the region, taking dozens of precious heirlooms – ceremonial garments, canes, jewellery – that he is trying to locate and take back to the DRC. He believes one of his grandfather's engraved bracelets is at the Afrika Museum. Similar artefacts taken from the DRC, known as Lemba bracelets, have been located at the Brooklyn Museum and the World Museum in Liverpool.

'Being there, and seeing the bracelet [at the Afrika Museum] was extremely moving,' he told VICE. 'I was emotional to see the wealth that belongs to me in other people's hands, that was taken through violence and brutality and then put on display.'

When it comes to storming European and North American museums, Diyabanza is spinning on a dance floor all by himself. The rest of the fight for restitution is being carried out now, as it has been for decades, through tedious, painful deliberations with museums that would rather release statements about working in 'close dialogue with African partners' than make serious strides towards redressing the gross imbalance.

Regardless, it has taken an immense demonstration of discipline and determination from individuals and groups across the continent to even get to this point. Some on the front lines, like Diyabanza, trace their lineage back to those who were directly stolen from. The grandson of the legendary Tanzanian freedom fighter Mangi Meli – hung and decapitated by Germany for resisting colonial forces – has led the hunt for Meli's skull, which was among those taken to Europe to be experimented on. The Benin Dialogue Group is a working consortium from the region that has for the past fifteen years engaged in dialogue with representatives from Europe's largest museums, including the British Museum. The current focus of the group is to secure enough artefacts for the eventual opening in 2025 of a new $100 million museum in Benin City designed by the renowned Ghanaian architect David Adjaye, which will be known as the Edo Museum of West African Art. A common trope pushed by Western museums is that African countries do not have the capabilities to look after their artefacts, and so they are better off in the hands of the Western world – a theory that has its origins in a form of white supremacy, similar to the arguments that were made by the original colonialists who considered Africa full of savages incapable of governing themselves.

In another effort, the organisation Digital Benin is working to create a digital archive of all the stolen loot and where items currently reside, a project that will hopefully provide much-needed clarity and transparency, showing the depth of the ongoing plunder by bringing 'together photographs, oral histories, and rich documentation material from collections worldwide to provide a long-requested overview of the royal artworks looted in the nineteenth century'. A lot of history was lost when the items were looted. The project will attempt to stitch much of this back together.

'Part of what happened to Africa as part of the colonial encounter is the diminishment of the cultural wealth of Africans by the symbolic violences done to them,' Chika Okeke-Agulu, a professor of African art at Princeton University, told VICE. 'The question of repatriation has everything to do with the possibility of reconstructing Africa's cultural heritages because that is necessary and important to the psychic progress and psychological progress of African peoples.'

Taking into consideration everything that has been returned and promised to be returned in the near future, 80 per cent of Africa's material cultural legacy would still remain outside of the continent – in universities and national museums and homes and adorning the walls of art galleries, great and small.

The battles waged in the late 1800s never ended. The spoils remain the spoils – a theft that took away from African countries the sort of treasures that they could use to help tell their own stories. This enduring one-sided war is a reminder that, when fully committed – as the colonial General Wolseley declared as his army approached the Gold Coast in 1882 – the power and might of the Western world 'can reach even to the very heart of their kingdom', for as long as it wants.

Part Seven

Jollof Wars: A Love Story

A party without Jollof rice is just a meeting.

— Many, many people

Author's note

I am not neutral.

To truly understand where we're going, you will need, at the very least: some rice, tomatoes, onions, a red pepper, my mother's supervision, Maggi, one Scotch bonnet chilli or two or perhaps three, and an over-exaggerated belief in your own abilities.

JAMIE OLIVER genuinely had no intention of offending anyone. 'There was no intention to offend anyone,' he said in a statement.

The renowned chef did not know of the war he had inadvertently stepped into. Unarmed, unprotected. Naive to the critical dangers around him. It was just a recipe, after all. For rice. Just rice.

If, like he was, you are among the uninitiated, then it is understandable that upon learning of the reaction of the African diaspora, you would think Jamie Oliver had stormed into every kitchen in West Africa and personally slapped each onion-dicing grandmother and tomato-blending grandfather in sight.

Oliver's actual actions were less premeditated, of course. But a (hilarious) violation nonetheless. The acclaimed chef published his own bizarre recipe for Jollof rice – a dish that is considered nothing less than a treasured heirloom throughout the region, that should, at all times, be handled with care. And though it's been almost a decade since he published his formula, it is still spoken of with disdain in homes, barber shops, and on food blogs across West Africa. The blurb of That Recipe – now scrubbed from the internet – spoke of Jollof as a vague concept rather than a true reality. Believing that, the British chef felt he had the licence to somewhat experiment, which for many in the region is comparable to a passer-by suggesting they attempt brain surgery for the first time using your grandmother as a guinea pig. Jamie Oliver's rice included lemons, for reasons never explained. Parsley and ground coriander abruptly appeared from nowhere. The inclusion of cherry tomatoes was baffling enough – but keeping them whole? Heartbreaking.

Tens of thousands of people raged online after it hit the internet. #JollofGate trended for three days, with prominent food bloggers and bestselling authors weighing in.

Jamie's perceived sin was to try to create a hybrid version that he thought would please everyone, when in practice it upset everyone because it stripped a dish that is fundamentally rooted in the familial into something devoid of a home to call its own – the opposite of what this dish represents in terms of the identities and history of millions of people.

*

Open the window and let the warm air carry in the sounds of the DJ you've hired for your rent-a-canopy party. If he's not warming the microphone by repeating 'one . . . one . . . two . . . two . . . one . . . one . . .' for twenty-five minutes straight, you have hired the wrong person. Chop the vegetables in half and pour them, with the tomatoes, into a blender, then pulverise until smooth. Though other countries may disagree, try not to be swayed by complex aromatics. Keep it simple: the secret ingredient is always confidence and never fennel.

A HEALTHY, WELL-BALANCED RIVALRY that doesn't serve as a mask for subtle bigotry is a delightful thing. It requires time and investment, and with that, patience; it can bind people who otherwise would never find common ground, and motivate you to maintain your standards or else suffer the public shame of enduring the German word for others taking a coordinated pleasure in your misfortune. A delightful little thing.

Then there is food, which is a perfect way to access the cultural anatomy of a people. It's a great resource for learning about a community's rituals and rhythms. What we choose to gather around at the most important milestones of our lives acts as a lighthouse for our core identities. We are grounded by the foods we reach for whenever we seek easy comfort or a modicum of control; when we require something to anchor us to our community and remind us that we are lifetime characters in a broader story that stretches beyond the edges of our imagination. When we are at our hungriest, we are left with no other option than to fully reveal our true selves and bare for all to see the madness we normally do so well at hiding.

Combine these two things at their best – rivalry and food; competition and culture; identity and a faultlessly packed plate – and you get the battle Jamie Oliver accidentally stumbled into: the Jollof Wars.

Jollof rice, you could say, is just a rice dish. A sweet, spicy, triumphantly orange and irrationally delicious rice dish that you will find in Burkina

Faso, Sierra Leone, Benin and Ghana; in Senegal, Niger, Nigeria, Guinea Bissau, Liberia, Togo and everywhere in between. And yet, like snowflakes or New York bodegas, no two plates are the same.

Without needing to seek too hard, you will find Jollof at birthday parties, funerals and night clubs; being secretly sourced from the back of a fridge for breakfast, and the motivation for a thorough investigation whenever a newly arrived VIP at a Lagos wedding reception that started six hours ago is forced to ask a petrified waiter, 'What exactly do you mean by it has finished?'

You will find it steaming in red coolers, mountains of it dousing flimsy paper plates, and wherever two or more family members are gathered with the intention of counting their blessings, if not one by one, then at least in bulk.

You could say Jollof rice is just a rice dish. Yet that wouldn't explain the mythos and mystique, the reverence each grain of goodness is given. It wouldn't explain the way it has been used by the individual members of an entire region as a show of strength: every West African country claims Jollof as their own; each one fervently believes that their specific variation is the region's best. And though they are all wrong except for Nigeria, their continued insistence has fuelled the long-standing rivalry of the fabled Jollof Wars. It's key to the joy of this ongoing stalemate that a feud which is essentially over the optimal combination of a handful of vegetables and rice has given African countries not used to being recognised for their individual gifts and cultural seasonings an opportunity to platform their individual efforts.

Jollof rice is just a rice dish that has become a proxy for national identity and regional status. The three loudest armies in the war are Ghana, Senegal and Nigeria. Liberians are not shy, either. Neither are the Gambia or Sierra Leone. Ghanaians are certain that their more complex version – utilising a far wider array of ingredients – has created the perfect sauce for their choice of fragrant rice to stew in. Nigerians prefer a simpler, more disciplined, smoky dish, blessed by firewood and the nation's addiction to enjoyment – though our argument for superiority, as in all things, primarily revolves around the immovable confidence that governs the country.

Senegal's case is frustratingly rather rigid. They point to heritage: Jollof, locally known as Thieboudienne, was invented sometime in the fourteenth century in Jolof – a state that was part of the Wolof Empire in what is now modern-day Senegal, though parts of it stretched into the Gambia. Jolof was home to the Dyula travelling traders, believed to have carried their delicacy throughout West Africa. As they did, it was adapted and adopted to fit specific regional tastes.

Seven hundred years later, and Jamie Oliver is being inundated with messages questioning his sanity over the improper use of a lemon wedge. The Dyula could not have known that their travels would one day lead to internationally renowned musicians recording Jollof diss tracks with accompanying music videos; or that the internet would become a stream of revolving memes and hashtags taking sly shots at other countries' versions of the dish.

Seven hundred years later, and 'Jollof' is used as an adjective to describe the intense bounciful sensation of a party that is so well balanced your only requirement is to have a good time. There are entire food festivals in multiple major cities on the continent and throughout the diaspora (Toronto, London, New York and elsewhere) exclusively dedicated to gathering dozens of chefs in blind-tasting competitions where they must defend the honour of their nations or have their citizenships revoked (in spirit). Government ministers are being asked to resign for suggesting another country's Jollof could possibly be better.

There is considerable unity in this light-hearted, deliberate demonstration of culinary lunacy; region-wide pride in being able to collectively share in the history and the present of a treasured antique that cannot be pillaged – one that additionally serves as the entry point into discovering all the incredible cuisines around the region. Jollof is likely the first thing a local would recommend you try before you graduate to the delicate soft starches dipped into heavy stews, thickened to draw from bowl to tongue.

Through a common experience of migration, the differences in recipes are slight, thoughtful and nuanced, allowing for specific variations to bloom, flavoured by the history of the continent.

It is just a rice dish. But be grateful that African communities are so particular when it comes to the particulars of food. Jollof is part of a wider culinary tradition that has impacted the tastes and traditions and economies of billions of people, thousands of miles away, who can trace the connective tissue of their societies back to the foodways of the continent. Across Europe, Latin America and the Caribbean.

But none have felt the impact of this more than the United States.

Enslaved Africans carried within themselves, and on their persons, the foods and techniques that dazzled the new world of the American South and the Caribbean. Southern plantation owners particularly delighted in the foodways of their slaves. 'The Negro is a born cook,' slave owner Charles Gayarré wrote in an 1880 issue of *Harper's Magazine*. 'He could neither read nor write, and therefore he could not learn from books. He was simply inspired; the god of the spit and the saucepan had breathed into him; that was enough.'

Elizabeth Swanson, the wife of a Virginia governor, agreed: 'It takes a big fat Negro mammy with a round shiny face to cook a ham, and the secret she can never impart. It is a sort of magic . . . and when you get some of that kind of dainty, you are eating indeed.'

From Africa came the staples of now-established Southern and African-American cooking: okra, yam, black-eyed peas, hot peppers, and watermelon. From Africa came rice, including red rice dishes similar to Jollof, which the South served with a side of economic revo-lution. This rice, expertly tended to by African slaves brought over for the express purpose of cultivating it, made the Southern states the wealthiest in all the land – a yield of millions of bags a year sold, a figure that dropped by nearly 80 per cent when slavery was abolished.

'Those from the rice crucible were among some of the earliest trans-ported by the Transatlantic Slave Trade to what would become the United States,' writes food historian Dr Jessica B. Harris in her Netflix-adapted book *High on the Hog.* 'Those from the yam crucible arrived later, as the voracious slave trade made its way down the West African coast from Senegal to the Gold Coast, then south to the Bight of Benin and beyond.'

New flavours and produce married with the traditions of Native Americans, and European influences facilitated a fresh assortment of dishes – from jambalayas to gumbos (the creolization of the French word for okra), black bean stews to crispy fried meats with seasoned green vegetables, pepper pots to sweet soft pies and Hoppin' John. Their talents and ingenuity – barbarically forced from them – revolutionised the foodways of the United States. The endurance of the enslaved Afri-cans and their descendants birthed a Black culture that is now foundational to modern America.

Away from the direct heat, the involuntary labour of African-American cooks – their specific origins stripped from them by slavery – propa-gated a new, lucrative mythology of gracious Southern hospitality that endures today. Word spread through the US of how you could arrive in a Southern home, whether in the early morning or deep into the night, and expect a spectacular feast of soups, seasoned stews and steaming desserts prepared fresh and with a smile.

'Up every day before dawn, they baked bread for the mornings, cooked soups for the afternoons, and created divine feasts for the evenings,' says historian Kelley Fanto Deetz. 'They roasted meats, made jellies, cooked puddings, and crafted desserts, preparing several meals a day for the white family. They also had to feed every free person who passed through the plantation. If a traveler showed up, day or night, bells would ring for the enslaved cook to prepare food. For a guest, this must have been delightful: biscuits, ham, and some brandy, all made on site, ready to eat at 2:30 a.m. or whenever you pleased.'

Those squeamish about the slavery that served up their comforts developed a concurrent mythos of the happy Black cook or nanny, delighted by servitude and working in gracious harmony with her white masters, whether enslaved or newly freed in a deeply segregated America – a trope that is still pushed in films and popular culture today.

Beyond the US, the transatlantic slave trade created cultures across Latin America – especially in Brazil, where foods like Akarajé can find their twin on the continent, and where cultural landmarks such as carnival and the samba were developed by the country's African demographic. Africa and its descendants are rarely acknowledged for this seismic influence, this transformation of identity, this shaping of billions over time, enabled by the communion that comes with feeding, preserving and protecting.

*

Pour the vegetable mixture into a high-sided pan already warmed with an inch of oil and fragranced by diced onions and tomato puree. Your home should be buzzing, plantain frying, and small chops – puff puff, spring rolls, gizzard, samosa – flying. The oil should sizzle loud enough to compete with the sound of your uncle in the other room arguing with nobody about the state of politics in the region. Cook the vegetables down, and when your eyes tell you the time is right, add the rice. Long grain for maximum absorption power. Ghanaians lean towards basmati rice, which is their right to do as an independent sovereign nation, but it doesn't make it correct. Either way, should you unconsciously find yourself smiling at the sound of the rice gliding into the tomato mixture, just run with the emotion, allow it to overwhelm you. Seasoning is more culture than instruction, so just do your best. The rice will be done when it's done. You can only leave it to plump and absorb its bright red elixir. All that's left to do is sit back and wait for the largest socio-economic demographic on the continent to arrive: aunties. They run large companies, maintain the social order and mind your business. From the moment they step into the room, you will be overrun, so nod politely and be agreeable where possible, without committing to setting a specific date for your own wedding.

WELL BEYOND THE JOLLOF WARS, healthy competitive dynamics have always been a bright spot for the continent.

The greatest opportunities often come through sport, especially on the world stage. International tournaments such as the Olympics and the World Cup are some of the few times African countries are acknowledged individually for their talents. But even then there is a temptation to bunch the region together, and write about African athletes in the same way: having all the speed, power and strength, but little of the thought, cunning, intelligence, nuance or precision. All chaos, no order. Devoid of a fine-tuned balance.

There's also a lazy tendency to assume that Africa is united in its sporting failures or successes, in a way other continents are not. Take the 2010 FIFA World Cup hosted by South Africa. The host nation got off to a great start, scoring what true believers call a 'screamer' in the opening match of the competition against Mexico. A wayward Mexican pass was picked up by South Africa's Reneilwe Letsholonyane. Showing far more care and appreciation for the ball, Letsholonyane slipped it with perfect balance to his teammate Teko Modise. Two passes in two seconds, from Modise to Tsepo Masilela and back again to Modise, ensured that Mexico's midfield was, for the briefest of seconds, frozen in place, unable to perceive time, see colour or conquer space. Triangles appeared everywhere from nowhere. All that remained was for Modise to place the ball in the path of the onrushing Siphiwe Tshabalala, bearing down on goal. Tshabalala, from the left edge of the box, barely took a touch before lashing the ball into the opposite corner of the net. Mexico's goalkeeper dived more as an act to protect his family name than to try to save the unsaveable. Amid the joyous bellow of a full stadium in unexpected jubilation came a piece of commentary that was quickly celebrated as iconic. 'Goal for South Africa!' the ITV commentator screamed – a strong, if obvious start – before he added, with no malice, just lost glee: 'A goal for all of Africa!'

Well – yes, there was some continent-wide relief that the tournament had started well for South Africa. The moment seemed to symbolise the alleviation of the pressure of being the first African country to host the World Cup. Almost as soon as FIFA announced in 2002 that the competition would be held on the continent, South Africa started carrying what would amount to years of scare stories of how the tournament would simply melt on African soil. Two months before it even began, one British newspaper warned that fans travelling to the tournament could be headed towards a 'machete race war'.

Tshabalala's goal was certainly a relief, a collective exhale for the continent. If South Africa had failed in their hosting duties, the unofficial, unspoken policy would have been that the entirety of Africa would never host the World Cup again. It would not have been treated as a unilateral failing but a reflection of an entire region, confirming all the negative biases that have long coloured the world's perception of the continent.

Still, it is impossible to imagine a commentator shouting in any circumstance 'A goal for all of Europe!' or to ever contemplate Brazilians willingly celebrating a Lionel Messi goal for Argentina.

Things that are the same cannot be rivals. South Africa are Nigeria's mortal football enemies. We have a lot of nemeses, in fact – a rota of sporting adversaries we've worked very hard to cultivate. Nothing grounds identity better than a nationally coordinated revelry in another's sporting downfall, the origins of which you have long forgotten so you lazily put down to jealousy. A form of patriotism that has its foundations in a wrongfully awarded penalty or an errant tackle decades before you were even born. A goal for *all* of Africa? We have rivalries, too.

For the best representation of this, I always think of the Africa Cup of Nations. The Cup of Nations is a lot more than just a football competition. The folklore alone – which includes stories about players faking their ages and at least two investigations into goalkeepers attempting to use juju at half-time – makes this festival of perfectly weighted sporting identity, intelligence, skill and rivalry unique. All international football tournaments are held every four years, except for this one, which is held biannually – the greatest trick the tournament ever pulled. It keeps the tension alive, the wounds never have time to heal, and the promise of revenge is palpable. In four years, Egyptians might forget their beef with Algeria, but it's hard when you have another swipe at them every other year. In total, there have been thirty-two tournaments with a ridiculous fourteen different winners, seventeen host nations, Rigobert Song and Taribo West, and at least one attempt to burn down another country's embassy in an act of vengeance.

This is about more than just sport, though. The Africa Cup of Nations is the ideal embodiment of Africa, framed to fit the only continent it could thrive on. It is an awkward, magnificent thing, forced to form as it has gone along, made to expand as new countries have expanded into their modern shapes, having to grow to meet the demands of a region unused to seeing many platforms that celebrate the individual expressions of African countries. At every Cup of Nations, countries take full advantage of the opportunity to be themselves, loud and unfiltered.

The best competitions – whether in sport or rice or another of life's elementals – are truly about time, which is why they never end. A concept which also serves well the modern history of Africa, a space you could say has fundamentally been about time. Just wait, and amid the forward progression of The Great Everything, each country's station in life will present itself – if purpose can locate opportunity, and hope finds a way of cohabitating with reality. That sequence has been the past, it will shape the future, and it will define all that is to come next.

*

Done right, and your Jollof should taste equally like a still Sunday afternoon at your parents' house and the sensation of your table being placed next to a giant speaker emitting a medley of bone-thumping noises whenever the band gets carried away. It should taste great when plated in front of you, but even better when stolen from an unguarded red cooler left on the kitchen floor, the rest of your family none the wiser about your cunning. With every mouthful you should taste the time your relay team finished last on Sports Day and you were immediately handed a bowl overflowing with strangely pink strands of soft rice as if it would heal your sorrow. It did.

It should taste as you wish to be seen. It should taste as you and yours are known.

Part Eight

What's Next?

My mother runs a primary school in Lagos, and every year they hold elections for prefects – Head Boy and Head Girl, Deputy Head Boy and Girl, Time Monitor, and so on.

The election campaign is one of the most exciting moments in the school calendar. Children barely old enough to lace their own shoes scurry optimistically around the school complex putting up posters, handing out flyers and reciting slogans. Every single student votes: from those in playgroup, where it takes real political acumen to canvass toddlers between their thrice-daily naps, to the eleven-year-olds with one foot in secondary school. So, if you're serious about winning, you have no choice but to shake every hand, teach each baby how to point at your face on a ballot, and at least entertain whatever request is put your way – a system that encourages students to build relationships across year groups.

Votes are counted publicly on election day, one by one, to demonstrate the election was free and fair. Parents are invited to come into school to watch the count and independently ensure the credibility of the final tally.

In recent years, I have been recruited to work as the unofficial campaign manager for two successful candidates: my nephew's bid for Head Boy, and the election of my niece as Deputy Head Girl. I have one more niece to get elected before I retire from front-line primary school politics. Both efforts have started with a frantic last-minute video call from a nervous child worried that their declaration speech, to be delivered the following morning at a full school assembly, won't cut it. I ask them to recite their draft. Hearing what they and their classmates come up with every year will forever be a delight: ideals that are warm and genuine, clear-eyed and earnest, no malice, just goodwill for all mankind. Peppered amongst these are what they don't know to be the idle lexicon of the professional politicians and talking-head social forecasters who populate the news their parents watch and talk about around them; catchphrases we inadvertently internalise at a young age. I will never tire of hearing a nine-year-old declare that 'our children are the future'.

'That's really lovely,' I'm always proudly moved to say. 'But what are you going to do after you're elected?' I watch over FaceTime as their faces shift to confusion. 'Better yet, what are you already doing?'

It's always tempting to lean heavily on vague notions of the future – placeholders for real, actionable ideas. You see it regularly in attempts to forecast what is ahead for Africa, in the short and the long term. There exists a reliance on either assuming impending doom or hazy pronouncements of hope on the horizon based loosely on nineteen being the median age of Africans. These predictions bypass what is important, which is what individuals, for better or worse, are building on the continent at any given time, in a multitude of fields. They don't speak to how groups are learning from the mistakes of strongmen who were once yesterday's freedom fighters; or how people are identifying where the remnants of colonialism are still causing harm, from the battles to retrieve stolen artefacts to the way Western governments and development agencies meddle; or how locally led organisations are defining popular culture both at home and for the world.

Today, activists are organising to shift governments and social norms; creatives are revolutionising culture; scientists and medical experts are offering answers as to why the pandemic did not cause a mass extinction event on the continent; and a burgeoning youth-run fintech sector is just one of the many industries working to change the accepted wisdom that the only way to make money in Africa is to work for a government or sell a natural resource.

Nothing at all is promised. But as my nephew and nieces can now explain, action is the only reliable predictor of more action. And the continent has seen plenty of it in recent years, from a generation that, ready or not, will determine what's next.

*

Two contradicting truths entwined. The movement was leaderless and women led the movement.

For two weeks in October 2020, millions of young people across Nigeria effectively encamped on the streets of major cities, declaring with an unprecedented level of solidarity across ethnicities and socio-economic groups that enough was very simply enough. They had taken all they could; suffered in a suffocating silence for too long. With their futures threatened, they came out to change the present.

The peaceful movement started as an anti-police-brutality push in opposition to the Special Anti-Robbery Squad (SARS) – a supposedly specialist unit of the Nigerian police force responsible for tackling violent crime, robberies, kidnappings, and investigating the origins of complex cybercrimes. But since its formation in 1992, SARS has attracted widespread anger for abusing its authority and committing grievous crimes of its own. The unit was regularly accused of carrying out extrajudicial killings, unlawful arrests and the indiscriminate extortion of young people.

Four months before the protests, an Amnesty International report documented over eighty cases of police brutality over three years that showed 'a pattern of abuse of power by SARS officers and the consistent failure by the Nigerian authorities to bring perpetrators to justice'. The report found that 'detainees in SARS custody have been subjected to a variety of methods of torture including hanging, mock execution, beating, punching and kicking, burning with cigarettes, waterboarding, near-asphyxiation with plastic bags, forcing detainees to assume stressful bodily positions and sexual violence'.

Women out late in the evening or dressed in 'provocative' clothing were accused of being prostitutes, while SARS's attempts at stamping out cybercrime extended little beyond stopping the cars of young men in possession of what they considered to be expensive gadgets – smartphones, laptops – and accusing them of using these items to commit unknown, sophisticated offences. No evidence that linked you to a specific crime was needed; just the suspicion that these items could, in theory, have been the key component of some crime perpetrated somewhere. That was enough to be detained. For detainees to avoid the abuse in custody that Amnesty outlined, officers routinely demanded payment on the spot, marching those with insufficient cash to nearby ATMs, draining innocent people of their finances.

Initially intended as an undercover operation, SARS abuses were common knowledge across Nigeria. As far back as 2016, human rights organisations documented 143 complaints in just six months. Still, successive governments allowed the unit to continue operating without serious oversight, despite desperate calls to disband the group. A former senior SARS official even went on national television to justify the unit's illegal methods. 'If I stop you on the road and I want to look at your phone and I want to see your Facebook, I don't think I'm committing any crime,' the officer said, despite it being a crime in Nigeria to search private property without a court order.

A line was finally drawn in October 2020 when footage of a young man being shot and killed by SARS officers in the southern Nigerian town of Ughelli went viral. 'They left him for dead on the road side and drove away with the deceased['s] Lexus jeep. I have videos,' an eyewitness tweeted.

A protest sparked up in the town a day later, and some demonstrators carried mock coffins. By the end of the week, protests had taken root in the capital, Abuja, but it was Lagos that quickly became the epicentre of the burgeoning revolution. Activists took over the Lekki Toll Gate – a busy area in the wealthy suburb of Lagos Island – making it the movement's de facto headquarters. They shut down traffic, camped overnight and crowdfunded sustenance. #EndSARS trended worldwide.

After three days of continuous protests, the impromptu #EndSARS movement showed no signs of retreating. It was growing, in fact, as the international media and the vast (and influential) Nigerian diaspora slowly caught on to a struggle that was shaping up to define a generation.

Reading the wind, the Nigerian government rushed to declare that SARS would be abolished. In the same breath, however, authorities announced the formation of a new undercover police unit: the Special Weapons and Tactics (SWAT) team that would not only take over the duties of SARS but would consist of former SARS officers. A clever rebrand that wasn't nearly clever enough. #EndSWAT trended within minutes.

The movement forged ahead – this time with specific demands that made it clear a basic logo change wouldn't suffice. These included the release of all arrested demonstrators, the establishment of an independent body to oversee the investigation and prosecution of all cases of police brutality, a psychological evaluation and retraining of all SARS officers before they could ever be redeployed, and an increase in the police's pathetically low salaries – a recognition that exploitation flourishes in desperation.

In spite of the reasonableness of the demands, the government showed no signs of engaging with a generation they had long ignored and underestimated. The movement thus expanded to encompass broader frustrations against systemic corruption and an unaccountable Nigerian ruling class whose contempt permitted a police force to operate with impunity for over a decade.

An impasse had been reached, which the government attempted to break by violently cracking down on demonstrations, deploying armed officers to disrupt marches. Yet each morning, in the face of repression, thousands of young people resolutely organised and peacefully gathered at the Lekki Toll Gate and at other sites in multiple cities, willing that famed moral arc of justice to bend in their favour.

Leaderless movements still require some mechanism to ensure the day-to-day mundanities of life are taken care of: the distribution of food and security; the drafting of public statements; liaising with international media organisations.

Fortunately for the future of Africa's largest country, a collective of women decided to lend their substantial talents and network to spearheading this generation-defining show of values.

They are the Feminist Coalition – a thirteen-strong group of young Nigerian women who had come together just four months earlier to form a grassroots organisation with the aim of building a community that could 'organise around the social, economic and political equality for Nigerian women in a more sustainable way'. They are a collective that chose a name that is a statement in and of itself in a country teeming with men that regularly use 'feminist' as an insult. They are journalists and writers; lawyers and consultants; tech entrepreneurs and crypto-savants. They are Damilola Odufuwa, Odunayo Eweniyi, Layo Ogunbanwo, Ozzy Etomi, Ire Aderinokun, Karo Omu, Kiki Mordi, Laila Johnson-Salami, Obiageli Ofili Alintah, Fakhrriyyah Hashim, Jola Ayeye, Oluwaseun Ayodeji Osowobi and Tito Ovia.

'Going through social media like everyone else, we were upset at the violence unarmed citizens were facing at the hands of police, especially as that same day a woman was shot in the face by a police officer – and we believed that without structure, the protests could turn violent and women would be the most affected,' the Feminist Coalition said. 'We've had monthly meetings since our inception in July 2020, but we had not started on any projects yet. We joke that this was a baptism by fire – we designed a logo, set up the website, got some copy assets together, set up our social media, set up the donation accounts, the request forms, the tracking sheets; Fem Co as it's known today, was literally a reality overnight. Their first meeting ended up running for 2 hours and the conclusion at the end was clear. We would help crowdsource donations for the peaceful End SARS protests. Focusing on food, water, medical, legal aid.'

Within hours, the Lagos-based group, with some members working internationally, had built a locally led civil rights organisation that rivalled most small non-profits.

You could rate their impact on fortifying the foundations of #End-SARS by how quickly they were targeted by the state, and then how effortlessly they responded. Their website was blocked, so they had to rely on social media. Restrictions were placed on their individual bank accounts, so they seamlessly switched to accepting bitcoin. Members were on the receiving end of threatening phone calls and messages. Still they rose to stand on the front lines of a struggle that, if successful, would have the biggest positive impact on men.

Undeterred, they allocated resources where needed to fuel the largest social movement in modern Nigerian history, publicly accounting for every kobo spent on supporting over one hundred peaceful protests in twenty-five states, touching every region of the country.

The Coalition was joined by a rapid-response team coordinated by two more women, podcaster Feyikemi Abudu and lawyer Moe Odele, who marshalled a team that offered legal aid to peaceful demonstrators picked up by security services. They provided private security for demonstrators as they marched and camped, and organised first aid and ambulances to treat victims of the police's violent crackdown. The women built a state within a state, showing more nation-building ability than Nigeria's ruling class have managed in decades.

The only thing they lacked, the government possesses in abundance: little care for human life.

The #EndSARS protests effectively came to an end on the night of 20 October 2020, when the Nigerian military opened fire on protesters as they gathered peacefully at the Lekki Toll Gate. It was a coordinated attack; streetlights surrounding the site were turned off, as was a large illuminated billboard that loomed over the toll gate; eyewitnesses reported seeing tear gas deployed before the shooting started. Footage from the attack was streamed live on Instagram. Amnesty International reported that at least fifteen people were killed and hundreds more injured.

Continuing the protests became untenable in the face of that level of violence. Too much life had been lost, too easily, and it would not have ended there.

But prior to the tragedy, there was hope, and that hope – not in the nation's rulers, but in themselves – by logic can only endure. For two weeks, young Nigerians had done more than painted a vision of their nation. They had built it themselves in small corners and with loud voices. A social safety net designed overnight, equipped with emergency-response capabilities to feed, heal, compromise, account, communicate and leverage, with enough left over for a DJ. They demonstrated a discipline and decency that the country's authorities were devoid of and used it for the betterment of their fellow citizens. There were no internal power grabs or attempts at siphoning off resources to favoured ethnic groups. Everyone sang their part when required, conducted by young women whose life-saving actions should go some way, among younger generations at least, to strengthening the country's push for gender equality: a reminder to any who need reminding in a deeply paternalistic society that women are not only worth listening to but following.

It would be lazy to assume that a two-week movement alone signals that the future of governance is bright. But one thing that can be said with certainty is that young Nigerians now know better. There remain no excuses to follow in the footsteps of the leaders that have overseen the nation since independence.

The #EndSARS movement built a modern, social framework whose boundaries may not have been able to contain a bygone generation. But it can shape a new social contract that will come due in time.

It was about possibilities and broadening options. It was about establishing a bare minimum. It was not about leaders. It was about leadership.

Now they know better.

*

EVERY FRIDAY FOR A YEAR they came out. Starting in February 2019, tens of thousands of young Algerians and their parents and some of their parents' parents – collectively known as the Hirak movement – shook a political system until many of its leaders fell from the branches of government they had forcibly lodged themselves in for decades. They took to the streets, chanted and waved flags. They carried small children on their shoulders so they too could get a sense at an early age of what it takes to define your country.

The first leader to find his way to the ground was the country's eighty-two-year-old president, Abdelaziz Bouteflika, the very man who hadn't spoken in public for six years but had decided to seek a fifth term in power despite the inconvenience of being physically incapacitated.

As the protests accelerated, Bouteflika was thrown overboard by the country's powerful head of the army and de facto strongman Ahmed Gaid Salah, himself closer to eighty than democracy, and a remnant of a bygone era, which is why Algerians were determined not to stop at the president. The country's ruling class was populated by too many Bouteflikas and Salahs. 'It's time to break the chains,' one activist declared.

Every Friday for a year, Algerians prised more of those chain links apart, peacefully. So peaceful were the demonstrations, they gained the nickname the Revolution of Smiles – a moniker that did nothing to undermine the seriousness of the cause. 'We are the ones that got rid of Boutef!' they chorused, reminding The Powers of their powers.

The power and effectiveness of the Hirak movement was not so much just in its considerable numbers, but in its make-up: Algerians of all ages lent their feet and voices to the cause, an intimidating spectacle for any government. This was a marked difference from the #EndSARS movements, which would, a year later, almost exclusively consist of young Nigerians. This is not to say that older generations in the country were ambivalent to the cause. They were not. But they were willing to leave the work of demonstrating to young people. Algeria's revolution attracted physical representation on the streets from every demographic. As a result, it was harder for the government to brush aside the sentiment as the preoccupations of a youth they could easily choose to ignore.

Every Friday the Hirak movement continued, even after government officials – including Bouteflika's own brother and two former prime ministers – were arrested and jailed for corruption. These public trials and convictions, though welcomed by activists, were a failed attempt at placating a crowd who knew reforming a political system would require a lot more than a handful of show trials. They could see the candidates for the pending elections – allies of the administration they had just toppled, ready to come in and resume regular order.

Every Friday the Hirak movement waited for the authorities to understand that they no longer wanted to participate in a system that was built around leaving them out. The protests forced two planned elections to be postponed. The elections that were held, ten months into the movement, returned the lowest turnout in decades, with barely 40 per cent of eligible voters casting a ballot for one of five almost-identical candidates. For a winner, the system threw up Abdelmadjid

Tebboune, Bouteflika's former number two – hardly a detour from the decades-long track.

Every Friday they turned up until the pandemic hit, and the most sustained political movement the country had ever known was forced to suspend mass protests as nationwide lockdown restrictions were introduced, prohibiting all demonstrations and outdoor gatherings.

In the months that followed, the government exploited the pandemic to arrest and imprison those they considered to be the leaders of what was also a leaderless movement. Prominent figures were picked up and tried under 'harming national unity' and other vague charges. The movement, in lockdown, couldn't respond in the numbers previously managed. Multiple activists were sentenced to up to eighteen months in prison, and hundreds more were detained as they awaited trial.

'The Algerian authorities are taking advantage of the COVID-19 pandemic to accelerate the pace of repression against Hirak activists, put its opponents in jail and silence the media,' Amnesty International reported. 'Between 7 March and 13 April alone, at least 20 activists were either summoned for interrogation by the police, or arrested and held in pretrial detention, or sentenced on charges based only on their exercise of their right to freedom of speech or peaceful assembly in different parts of the country. At least 32 people who were arbitrarily detained during the Hirak movement protests remain behind bars to date.'

It was a Monday and COVID-19 vaccines were only just starting to make their way around, yet thousands returned to the streets in February 2021 to mark the two-year anniversary of a peaceful movement that hadn't achieved everything they wanted but had done more to hold a system accountable than any other in the country's recent history. They returned to the streets, still wanting the military to give up its control over the government, and suddenly the president was announcing that he would release protesters, praising the 'blessed Hirak' for all they had done to make Algeria a better country. The protesters were not fooled by the rhetoric. They had learned that sustained pressure was required to make the government blink. They knew the government would return to cracking the whip on demonstrators.

Where #EndSARS and the Feminist Coalition demonstrated the power of leaderless movements, the Hirak movement, at its best, demonstrated the power of involving everyone. Bringing these elements together, you see a new way of organising for justice and equity that could stand a better chance at shaking from their stupor the generation of freedom fighters that plague the continent. This will require a concerted effort by a diverse citizenry willing to stand with the continent's famed youth – a lesson future movements would do well to learn.

*

NOTHING LESS THAN a state of emergency would suffice.

In October 2020, the body of Shannon Wasserfall was found in a shallow grave near Walvis Bay, a port city on Namibia's coast. The twenty-two-year-old had been missing for six months. Her remains were only discovered after her father received an anonymous text message telling him where Wasserfall's body was buried.

Her death was no aberration, but rather the latest in a string of incidents of grotesque violence against women in the country, compounding the tragedy across Namibia.

An average of two hundred incidents of domestic violence were reported per month that same year, while one in four Namibian women are survivors of sexual violence from an intimate partner – a reality that had only been made worse during the pandemic as people were forced to lock down in place with their abusers.

Wasserfall's murder was the catalyst for large-scale protests against gender-based violence throughout the country. Just a few days after her body was discovered, thousands of predominantly young women marched through the streets of the capital, Windhoek, to demand an effective shutdown of all government operations in order for authorities to focus on the singular task of tackling a pandemic of sexual violence and femicide. The movement was appropriately dubbed #ShutItDown.

From the government, the demonstrators called for the presidency to declare 'a State of Emergency in respect of Femicide and Sexual and Gendered Violence; and extensive, immediate and transparent consultation with SGBV [sexual and gender-based violence] experts on best and immediate and radical courses of action to curb violence against women and children'.

Following that, a step-by-step, comprehensive to-do list was drafted by the movement, for what the government and other civic agencies needed to achieve during this shutdown.

'Prioritise a sexual offenders registry and make it available to critical and interested bodies, particularly those working with women and children,' the plan started. 'Prioritise the establishment of sexual offences courts in order to expertly, effectively and, most importantly, sensitively deal with SGBV cases; prioritise the urgent review of sentencing laws for sex offenders and murderers, particularly pertaining to bail, suspension of sentences and severity in order to emphasize Namibia's intolerance of SGBV; prioritise the immediate expedition of all current murder and sexual offences cases in trial or under investigation.'

Of the police, the protesters called for the retraining of all officers 'to strengthen the capacity of the Force to respond to SGBV reports and allegations'. The Ministry of Education was called on to 'immediately mandate the curriculum development and implementation of a national

rape and sexual violence prevention programme in schools for implementation in 2021; immediately liaise with Civil Society Organisations
and SGBV experts to provide training to ALL teachers in respect of
SGBV; and to immediately mandate the review of all school rules, particularly those which promote slut shaming and victim blaming, and
ensure that no learner is suspended from school for speaking out against
SGBV'.

Amid all this, protesters also called for the resignation of the country's minister for gender equality, Doreen Sioka, a controversial figure who,
among other things, has proposed that women who withdraw their sexual violence cases for any reason should be jailed.

Their demands extended beyond the government and into the private sector. Private organisations were asked to conduct an 'immediate
review of sexual harassment and assault policies in all businesses to
enhance the ability for survivors to report incidents without fear and
silencing and perpetrators to face appropriate repercussions for acts of
sexual assault and harassment'.

Everything here – each individual policy recommendation specifically
tailored to each government department, authority and organisation –
was crafted and laid out within a few days of the discovery of Wasserfall's
body.

The government responded to this vast constructive effort, releasing a
statement commending the #ShutItDown movement and promising to
immediately engage with the group's detailed requests.

Namibia's prime minister, Saara Kuugongelwa-Amadhila, followed up with a lengthier announcement, outlining twenty steps the
government would take to address the prevalence of SGBV. The
measures included: setting up dedicated courts to deal with sexual
violence; a review of sentencing laws for sex offenders to ensure anyone convicted serves at least twenty-five years before being eligible

for parole; creating a database of all active SGBV cases and investigating any that appear to be stalled; contacting the survivor and the family of the victim in each pending case, to update them on the status of their case; providing psycho-social support to victims and witnesses and preparing them for trial; improving standards in DNA tracing; and reviewing school rules to promote the fight against SGBV.

The government concluded by promising to hold regular press conferences to update the country on the steps that it had taken.

It was exactly one week from the discovery of Wasserfall's body to the Namibian government releasing its most comprehensive plan to tackle gender-based violence, in response to arguably the most comprehensive plan of all the recent youth-led political movements shaping the continent. The protestors' message was that things could not continue as they were; that no nation could exist if over half its population feared for their safety whenever they stepped outside. Within days, they had organised in multiple cities and rallied behind a single, detailed agenda, which for any country, anywhere in the world, would go a long way to addressing the global pandemic that is violence against women. Above all, that young Namibians chose to shut down their country over the issue speaks to the values of those who will hopefully be at the forefront of future policy-making.

*

THE LIFE OF BOBI WINE appears to have been meticulously scripted: raised in the slums of Kampala. Polygamous father. Dozens of siblings. Music was his way out; his ride to riches.

As fame descended, everything for Wine changed while everything around him stayed the same. He remained selectively oblivious, he's admitted, to the growing inequality within his nation while he busied himself accumulating the trappings of success.

Sense was eventually slapped into Wine. Not in the clichéd figurative way that implies a stark moment of revelation without actual physical violence. But in the very literal, another-person's-tensed-palm-made-crucial-contact-with-his-face way – forcing the musician to realise that his life needed a new direction, one that included a dedication to alleviating the suffering of others.

Wine was twenty-six years old at the time of The Slap and had recently bought a Cadillac Escalade, imported into Uganda from the US. One night, as he parked outside a club in Kampala, a stranger – 'another young man my age' – frustrated by what he perceived to be an egregious display of wealth, walked up to one of the most successful musicians Uganda has ever produced and smacked him across the face. It got Wine thinking. About inequality. About the entrenched political class. About privatisation. About how stupid that Escalade must have looked to inspire an unprovoked slapping from a stranger.

Robert Kyagulanyi Ssentamu chose the stage name Bobi Wine in tribute to Bob Marley, and to suggest that his ambitions matched those of the alcoholic drink: to get better with age. The Slap gave him an opportunity to live up to that by turning his life towards a new motivation. He decided to make the switch from creating songs about the buoyant frivolities of life – nothing wrong with those, of course – to making music that spoke to the realities facing the communities and people he had grown up around. From then on, social issues drove his work and made him even more popular in the clubs and cars of Uganda – a country where 80 per cent of the population are millennials or younger, desperate for a seat at whichever table decides their futures.

Almost a decade later, now thirty-four, Wine ran for office, winning a parliamentary seat in central Uganda by a landslide in 2017. From his higher perch in politics, he could make even more noise. His growing popularity, his willingness to name the names of those in the ruling elite who were violating their duties, and his call for a youth-led revolution was a throwback to a former legendary Ugandan freedom fighter who would now become his nemesis: the current president, Yoweri Museveni.

Museveni rose to power after leading an army insurgency in 1986 that toppled a military junta, making him, at the time, somewhat of a national hero. He promised political reforms and a future for the country that would include upholding human rights. He was once hailed as an exemplar of African leadership as he worked to bring change to a fledgling nation.

But nearly four decades on, Museveni is still in power, with no signs of letting go. With a population that has a median age of nineteen, four in five Ugandans have never known another leader. At seventy-seven years old, Museveni has very little in common with those he leads. The only way he can hold on to power, his critics say, is by stifling opposition, as Bobi Wine discovered when the revolution he called for started to take shape.

Just a few years after entering parliament, Wine announced that he would be running for president. Almost immediately, the singer was hit by the full weight of the government's suppression tactics: he was banned from holding concerts, his campaign rallies were disrupted by the police, and local media organisations that wanted to interview him were quickly and aggressively disavowed of that idea. Worst of all, many of Wine's acquaintances and family members were targeted by the authorities. Dozens have been arrested and beaten, some have disappeared; a few, including his former driver, were killed.

Though Wine is considered too high-profile a target – his death or disappearance would no doubt bring with it international condemnation and the brand of populist uprising that has overthrown other leaders on the continent – he has faced brutal attacks of his own. In August 2018, Wine was picked up by security forces under the thin pretence that Museveni's motorcade had come under attack from Wine's supporters throwing stones. The singer was badly beaten in custody, by multiple officers, to the point he couldn't walk, then charged with treason. An assault, Wine says, he may never psychologically recover from.

Bobi Wine and his supporters bore this abuse for another two years, right up until the presidential election in January 2021, where in the days leading up to the vote, the internet was shut off across the country and Wine was placed under house arrest. Similar to his previous election victories, Museveni was eventually declared the winner in a vote that electoral observers reported was anything but free and fair. Driven into politics to rid his nation of a despot, Museveni has turned into a strongman of his own.

Bobi Wine and his campaign embodied the hopes of young Ugandans. He attracted more international attention than any millennial candidate in the political history of the continent.

Even if he had won, there is of course doubt as to Wine's ability to lead. As there should be with any young leader. There is nothing to say that he would have lived up to this promise – the modern history of Africa is overrun by freedom fighters who became lost when they finally caught their tail.

What will best define what comes next for the continent is not only the moment when young activists like Wine get into positions of power, but what our generation does when those times come. And those times will come.

Museveni cannot be in power forever; the mortality of our human shells will see to that. Nor can The Powers in Algeria or President Teodoro in

Equatorial Guinea or any of the other tired independence heroes dotted around the continent. These leaders understand that one of the gravest immediate threats to their positions is that their clan are increasingly being outnumbered by a young, educated electorate not enamoured by the past glories of ageing revolutionaries. An electorate, like the #ShutItDown activists in Namibia or the Feminist Coalition in Nigeria, that has the capability to not only marshal large numbers but is policy-literate and internet-savvy. We cannot be held off in perpetuity. We too will catch our tail and power will transition, but that reality cannot be taken for granted. Guard rails need to be put up now to stop history repeating itself. Joining the global trend of advocating for leaderless political movements is a positive step that shows power for the sake of it, over the cause, is not as strong of a commodity as it has been in the past. Still, decency is a garden that needs to be tended.

'What specific steps will you take then to convince people that you won't just be another freedom fighter who turns into a dictator?' VICE asked Bobi Wine on the eve of the recent presidential election.

'Museveni has always boasted of having liberated us,' Wine replied. 'I tell the people of Uganda that we must achieve this liberation all of us together as a nation so that not one single politician, not even myself, will wake up one morning and say "I liberated you." We are liberating ourselves.'

He continued: 'Looking at the Museveni of today and the Museveni of the 1980s and '90s, you will just agree with the saying that power corrupts and absolute power corrupts absolutely.'

In other words: Museveni was young once.

It's important to resolve such concerns before we elect the first batch of leaders. For it's far easier to slap sense into a twenty-something rapper than a president with unlimited power.

*

TANZANIA HAS RECENTLY DISCOVERED the fierce possibilities of inevitable change. That, with time, this too shall pass. And that change alone is not nearly enough – what fills the vacuum matters a great deal.

The opportunity came after the sudden death in March 2021 of President John Magufuli.

Magufuli – widely believed to have died from COVID-19 – was one of the continent's most powerful COVID-19 deniers. He pushed back fervently against claims that the virus was spreading in Tanzania, while at the same time promoting untested herbal remedies and rejecting even the simplest of mitigators such as masks or social distancing.

Under his orders, the Tanzanian government stopped reporting coronavirus cases and deaths early in the pandemic, around the same time most countries were implementing their first round of lockdowns. Months before he died, he falsely declared the emerging vaccines to be dangerous and potentially part of a plot to steal Africa's wealth.

Magufuli refused for Tanzania to be entered into the World Health Organization's COVAX initiative aimed at ensuring the equitable distribution of vaccines throughout the world. He wished the pandemic away by personally declaring his country COVID-free.

Dissent from the official government position was a risky endeavour. After winning the presidency in 2015, Magufuli drifted in the same direction as Uganda's Museveni, cracking down on the usual suspects: the media, opposition parties, and dissenting civic voices. Tundu Lissu, the last serious opposition leader to challenge Magufuli, was shot sixteen times in a single assassination attempt. Lissu survived and fled to Belgium, where he remained in exile for several years before returning to Tanzania to challenge Magufuli in the 2020 elections – a contest in which dozens of other potential presidential candidates were banned by the government from competing. Magufuli was declared the winner, allegedly winning over 80 per cent of the vote in elections that independent observers claimed were not free.

Tanzania's descent towards authoritarianism continued seemingly unabated, until Magufuli disappeared in March 2021. Reports quickly emerged that he was being treated for COVID-19 in Kenya and that he had been put on life support.

Magufuli would never return to Tanzania. His death was announced three weeks after his last public appearance. Tanzania's constitution dictates that, upon a president's death, the vice president completes the rest of their term. In this case it meant the ascension of Samia Suluhu Hassan and the emergence of the country's first female president.

Everything changed.

In her first official address as president, Suluhu Hassan warned against the dangers of COVID-19 and advised Tanzanians to protect themselves against the virus by wearing masks and keeping their distance. She inaugurated a presidential pandemic taskforce to study the most effective next steps for the country to take, and ordered the implementation of a vaccine distribution programme – actions that no doubt saved tens of thousands of lives. 'This pandemic has no respect for your health,' President Suluhu Hassan declared.

Her reforms extended beyond COVID-19. She reached out to opposition parties to invite them back into the political process, even appointing some former opponents to key regional roles. In her first one hundred days, the president declared that the press, whose freedoms had come under considerable attack under Magufuli, were not the proverbial enemy of the people, and promised to strengthen the media's role in holding the government to account. Suluhu Hassan also embarked on a tour of other East African nations to repair much of the damage done by the 'bulldozer' president, increased the

representation of women in civil society, and reversed policies introduced under Magufuli that saw pregnant schoolgirls automatically
expelled.

There is plenty of time left in her term – or potentially beyond – to
change course and go down the destructive path of her predecessor. For
now, however, Suluhu Hassan has shown that poor leadership is not
some inherent African quality. There is no curse. There is not a lack of
competency or will to do what is right by your country. The real scarcity
since the continent's independence era has been opportunity.

President Suluhu Hassan was intellectually and morally prepared for
the challenge – a bar her nation will require her to sustain. We must
hope for the same when other countries have the chance to break out
from under the rule of a singular figure, and a new generation of leaders
is able to take office. A future fitting for a generation who have taken to
the streets and social media, claiming to be more liberal and tolerant
than previous ones. What's vital is that in those golden moments, whoever steps in – whether it's a millennial activist like Bobi Wine or a
sixty-one-year-old former office clerk and aid worker like Suluhu
Hassan – they should rise and fulfil that promise of a brighter future
for a region with youth and time on its side.

*

PRESIDENT SAMIA SULUHU HASSAN'S ascension also serves as a
reminder that the continent still has a lot more road ahead when it
comes to electing female heads of state. So far, the continent has only
known five since the independence era: Ellen Johnson Sirleaf of Liberia,
Joyce Banda of Malawi, Ameenah Gurib-Fakim of Mauritius, Sahle-
Work Zewde of Ethiopia, and now Suluhu Hassan.

Still, over the past decade, the continent has enjoyed a significant rise in the number of elected female legislators and women selected for high-ranking government positions. Rwanda leads the world, with more than 60 per cent of its parliament and 53 per cent of ministerial positions occupied by women. South Africa, Namibia, Senegal, Mozambique, Ethiopia, Burundi and Tanzania also feature in the top-thirty countries in the world for representation of women in politics. In 2020, Egypt amended its constitution to introduce a requirement that women make up 25 per cent of parliamentary seats.

Women are also shifting away from exclusively being considered to run for what the UN refers to as 'soft portfolios' – family, children, social affairs – to departments that are traditionally run by men – defence, military. According to the UN, since 2017 'there are 30 percent more women ministers of defense, 52.9 percent more women ministers of finance, and 13.6 percent more women ministers of foreign affairs'.

The trajectory is clearly moving in the right direction. Still, representation in politics does not automatically equate to social equality or imply countries with the highest representation of women are not repressive or culturally patriarchal. Tangible results are all that matters, and early research has found a correlation between a rise in the number of elected female officials and investments in key social programmes, especially in health care, as well as a drop in infant and maternal mortality rates.

*

TANZANIA MIGHT BE HEADED for a period of peace and prosperity. To get there safely, they could look to Botswana, who might be able to offer, at least in part, a road map.

The landlocked southern African country has basked in much economic delight and political stability since its independence from the British. Botswana's victories have been so pronounced, they have been met with shock – shock! – by academics and economists that an African country could enjoy decades of relatively uninterrupted growth and prosperity. In books and journals and research papers, Botswana is routinely nicknamed the African Miracle and the African Exception, as if success is a concept alien to the continent. A recent feature in *Der Spiegel*, the biggest news magazine in Europe, suggested that Botswana only resembles Africa when you're flying above it. Offering examples of how seemingly un-African the country is, the writer points to how 'friendly, quick, and surprisingly meticulous' the airport is; taxi drivers who charge a fair price; and the high prevalence of US fast-food chains lining roads that feature European-manufactured cars.

Botswana does have a lot to be proud of. It's the continent's longest continuous democracy and has enjoyed an economic growth that is faster than almost any country in the world – maintaining the fastest growth in income per person over the last three decades. It's firmly established on the rung of upper-middle-income nations. Its history has been relatively conflict-free, ruled by leaders that have not confused themselves for their nations and have routinely known when to quit.

Nature and nurture have co-parented Botswana to where it is today. And instead of its accomplishments being used as a way to generically malign the rest of the continent, Botswana could provide a peek into the possible near-futures of African nations about to embark on a period of a stability similar to the one Botswana has enjoyed since independence.

Botswana secured its independence from a British government that was never too interested in meddling in the country's affairs. Botswana didn't suffer the racist settler policies endured across much of the rest of southern Africa, or the divide-and-rule tactics inflicted throughout West Africa. Additionally, Botswana was not designed as artificially as most other states; it is largely dominated by one ethnic group, the Tswana, who make up about 80 per cent of the population. From the start, Botswana was able to more easily work towards building a singular, cohesive national identity.

Diamonds also helped. Just a year after Botswana was freed, the country struck gems. Lots of them. Fortuitous timing, as the British would have certainly shown more interest in the country's business if these diamonds had surfaced earlier.

Botswana at independence was one of the least developed, poorest nations in the world; arid and landlocked, with few roads and very little in the way of prized goods to export. The diamond boom altered that trajectory, with successive governments smartly managing the nation's resources and making decisions for the betterment of the entire nation.

The existence of valuable natural resources does not guarantee prosperity. Often it foments easy corruption and xenophobia-fuelled conflicts over the proceeds. But as the home of the world's second-largest diamond reserves, Botswana has invested revenue in key infrastructures, especially in education and health care. Money has been put aside for rainy days as the government looks for ways to ease the nation's reliance on their little gems.

The ruling party, the Botswana Democratic Party, has been rewarded by voters at every election for their focus on development, with the country reaping rewards from that relative political stability.

The further the continent gets from the damage wrought by colonialism and the early ethnic battles and civil wars following independence, the more each country's attention will be focused on developing the common good. Political races will be less of a winner-takes-all brawl and more about ways these increasingly mature nations – that are not to blame for their make-ups – can harness their resources to positively impact the greatest number of people.

This is not something larger countries can so easily experiment with – Botswana's government is responsible for a population roughly equivalent to that of Berlin, propelled by a colonial-soft approach and diamonds from the sky. But in time, as those artificially designed national identities become stronger and the pull from hoarding for you and yours slackens, and with the natural resources littered across the continent, the conditions that helped Botswana succeed will be ripe for more countries to take advantage of.

*

You DO NOT HAVE to strain hard to hear the predictions of doom that constantly ring out about the future of Africa. Forecasters are forever foreshadowing an impending onslaught of biblical proportions – from the final death of democracy to assumptions that COVID-19 would wipe out a continent helpless to respond.

One alarm bell that is certainly worth ringing, however, is the unfolding crisis of climate change, the effects of which are already being felt throughout a continent that contributes around 3 per cent in total to the world's greenhouse gas emissions, but is on course to suffer the most from its adverse effects.

The impact of rising temperatures is hitting hard. The Global Climate Watch Index 2021 found that five African countries – Mozambique, Zimbabwe, South Sudan, Malawi and Niger – are among the top-ten nations in the world that have been impacted so far by climate.

Mozambique, for example, was struck in 2019 by Cyclone Idai – the worst cyclone in the history of southern Africa. The storm killed more than a thousand and displaced hundreds of thousands. The 120-mile-per-hour winds devastated the port-city of Beira on the east coast, bursting multiple river banks. The resultant flooding created a new inland lake the size of Luxembourg. 'The water was rising fast so we ran for the nearest tree and climbed up,' a fisherman told VICE after the storm. 'There were snakes in the water. My youngest son was exhausted and started to fall asleep. He fell out of the tree down into the current below. I went into the water after him but I got stuck in the branches of a tree and he was swept away. That was the last time I saw him.'

Just six weeks later, a second, more deadly cyclone hit northern Mozambique. Combined, the unprecedented weather events destroyed 700,000 hectares of crops. Cyclone Eloise, in January 2021, was even stronger than its recent predecessors, causing extreme flooding throughout the region.

'Warming of the surface ocean from anthropogenic (human-induced) climate change is likely fueling more powerful TCs [tropical cyclones],' the US government's National Oceanic and Atmospheric Administration says. 'The destructive power of individual TCs through flooding is amplified by rising sea levels, which very likely has a substantial contribution at the global scale from anthropogenic climate change. In addition, TC precipitation rates are projected to increase due to enhanced atmospheric moisture associated with anthropogenic global warming.'

Severe flooding from extreme rainfall, which climate scientists predict will become more regular, has also been experienced across East Africa, affecting around three million people. In 2020, Lake Victoria and the River Nile rose to their highest levels on record. And then locusts. Literal locusts. A plague of billions of locusts swept through East Africa in 2020 thanks to the cyclone winds and rains that created the perfect wet environment for them to breed, destroying crops and food supplies across Ethiopia, Kenya and Somalia.

The unexpected weather patterns will only continue to devastate communities. The Brookings Institution estimates that global warming will 'significantly decrease Africa's GDP through mechanisms such as lowered crop yields, reduced agricultural and labor productivity, and damage to human health'. An increase of 1.5 degrees Celsius, the think tank predicts, will slash the continent's GDP by nearly 4 per cent every year, over the next fifty years.

Responsibility for averting the disaster falls on the West and the biggest greenhouse gas emitters – the US, China, India, Russia – and not on a continent that contributes a negligible fraction to the warming of our planet. An Oxfam study found that the average person in Britain emits around the same amount of carbon in two weeks as a person in Burkina Faso will in an entire year.

Still, communities throughout the continent are trying to do their part. Morocco is home to the world's largest solar complex – roughly the size of San Francisco – teeming with enough solar panels to power 6 per cent of the country with clean energy. The plant is a significant step to Morocco's goal of getting 52 per cent of its electricity from renewable energy by 2030.

Over in West Africa, Togo has launched the largest solar plant in the region – a scheme that will power nearly 200,000 homes, with plans to expand the site year-on-year until every Togolese home is powered by the sun.

In April 2021, I published a feature for VICE by the writer Thomas Lewton about the Bakonzo ethnic group who live among the Rwenzori Mountains that border the Democratic Republic of Congo and Uganda. Bakonzo customs believe the god Kithasamba sits atop the snow-capped mountains, the ice and snow representing his sperm. As the snow melts, the cosmology goes, it carries life to the land below. 'The water gives us life; it fertilises our land,' a town elder told Lewton. 'After elders sacrifice to Kithasamba you see the snows shining bright, telling you that the planting season is starting. If the snows aren't visible it's a sign of calamity.'

All the signs are pointing towards calamity. Global warming is threatening the group's entire cultural beliefs and livelihood. The area is suffering from long dry spells, explained local historian Stanley Baluku

Kanzenze, and unexpected rainy seasons. The ice caps are permanently melting away, and heavy rains have brought flash flooding. 'Nature is shifting,' he noted.

The Bakanzo are desperate for a solution, fearing that climate disruptions are a sign that their gods are not pleased with them. They have found willing partners in local civic organisations, such as the Cross-Cultural Organisation of Uganda (CCFU).

As a local organisation, CCFU is fully aware of the impact global warming is having on communities in the region, as well as how to work with groups with diverse views and beliefs to help them adapt to the changing environment. 'On the one hand, you have conservationists who are interested in biodiversity and global warming; concepts which are very foreign,' said Emily Drani, founder of the CCFU. 'And on the other hand, for different reasons, a community is contributing to those objectives by caring about the forest and making sure water bodies are clean.'

Instead of pushing back against their cultural beliefs – an easy response in a country where less than 1 per cent of people still believe in traditional gods – organisations like the CCFU use local knowledge to work alongside local leaders to preserve their traditions, while at the same time ensuring they are able to respond to modern challenges such as climate change. The Bankozo have worked with the CCFU to plant over a thousand indigenous trees along the riverbanks, which will provide a protective line of defence against flooding.

In the end, these are the attempts of a local community to protect their way of life. It's a weight that is certainly too heavy for them to carry, and unless there's a substantial shift in the global approach to tackling rising temperatures, more communities across the continent will watch their beliefs, cultures and fundamental existences slowly wash away.

*

BEFORE THE WORLD BURNS, it's imperative we tell our own stories, fully, personally, in whatever ways we know how.

Few, if any, of these ways have been better – or at least more entertaining – than Nollywood, the second-largest movie industry in the world. Home to films of indeterminate length and amorphous plots, where the Big City is full of evil hucksters and each character will at some point entertain an offer for their soul; movies about pride and its vicinity to death; about the precarity of love and mothers-in-law; about getting rich or dying trying; about the whirling temptations of joining *Bad Gang*. In short: life.

Hurdles are scaled. Lessons are learned. These movies are, at their core, stories of personal triumph, where a foreign face is not required to explain the motto to protagonists responsible for their own destinies – a distinction rarely offered in Hollywood films set on the continent.

The term 'Nollywood' was coined in 2002 by *New York Times* correspondent Norimitsu Onishi, after he reported from Lagos on the burgeoning film scene. 'It seemed filmmakers were busy shooting on every street corner, frantically churning out what were then called home videos,' Onishi later explained. 'Young would-be actresses and actors came from all over the country, wanting to be discovered. Over hot pepper soup and Gulder beer at Winis, a hotel that served as a studio and the site of never-ending parties, producers and directors told me with typical Nigerian ambition and bravado that they were building the new Hollywood. I even flirted with the possibility of playing the role of an evil white man, a bit part in a production called *Love of My Life*.'

Though they have traditionally lacked a certain technical quality, the stories that populate Nollywood are of the highest definition – as fraught, clamorous, precarious and exciting as the country they project. With tales of individuals battling with the country's two most complex pressures – family and faith – the films are familiar, like comfort food.

Nollywood does not attempt to transport you to another world, but plunges you deeper into the grooves of day-to-day Nigeria, with enough servings of melodrama to justify running times that allow a viewer to start a film, break off for a nap or give a reading at a christening, and return well before a comprehensive resolution has emerged. Our real lives are not edited, so why should a Nollywood film be?

The movies are customarily made on the fly, on a relatively shoestring budget. Nollywood, Onishi writes, 'is an expression of boundless Nigerian entrepreneurialism and the nation's self-perception as the natural leader of Africa, the one destined to speak on the continent's behalf'.

Despite the heavy focus on Nigerian life – from urban match-making to rural vengeance – the films have resonated for decades across the continent and the Black diaspora because of their authenticity in depicting things as they are for an African country, in ways rarely seen in mainstream popular culture. Though Nollywood may not actively translate the mundanities of world-building in Dakar or family dynamics in Djibouti, viewers there can still appreciate the unapologetically local lens, demonstrating that success can come from centring the genuine experiences of an African country – a creative form not trying to mould itself to ensure it is palatable to an international audience.

As a result, Nollywood's road has been paved with gold: it produces over two thousand films a year, generating around $600 million annually while employing a million people.

The industry has come a long way from its humble beginnings. Nollywood found its famous form thanks to the ingenuity of Kenneth Nnebue, the screenwriter behind the fabled 1992 hit *Living in Bondage*. For the film, Nnebue decided to bypass the traditional distribution model. He instead went straight to VHS and flooded the streets, where the tapes circulated widely and the film was transported straight into millions of homes. The success of the movie – a classic tale of a man willing to risk mind and morals for money – inspired a generation of straight-to-VHS filmmakers who could churn out multiple films in a year and have them in your home within hours of wrapping.

Operations have grown considerably more sophisticated since then. With success has come better financing and distribution deals. Top of the tree sits a considerable investment from Netflix that will see the streaming service not only platform classic films but also support new productions, partnerships and creatives. Simply put: in the future, the continent's biggest story factory will be telling more stories, from a new wave of ambitious filmmakers with ambitious tales, enjoying the warmth from inside the house that pioneering artists like Nnebue built. A strong funding base should broaden the limits of Nollywood's imagination and make collaborations with filmmakers from across the continent more frequent, ensuring more stories are told to the world and showcasing more of the region's filmmaking talent. There are also plans to grow film scenes in other territories, such as Mozambique, Angola, the DRC and Ghana.

In any case, Nollywood won't need to carry the burden of storytelling alone. When I first arrived in the UK in the early 2000s, fresh off the boat from Lagos, it was not yet culturally cool to be West African. Then came Afrobeats, a genre that has done more than any other in modern times to elevate the region's cultural capital throughout the world and project what it means to be young there today.

In the late '90s, global Black identity was heavily influenced by African-American culture. Music scenes across Africa were dominated by artists rapping in faux-American accents about lifestyles extremely foreign to their own, while sporting oversized white t-shirts – the calling card of '90s American hip-hop culture. That lack of authenticity unsurprisingly struggled to find an audience.

A different path was eventually taken a decade ago by artists such as 2Baba, D'banj and P-Square, early pioneers of a new genre that sounded like the communities they were brought up in. These artists performed in their own accents, intertwining native languages with English, pidgin and any local dialect that helped get the message across.

The new genre channelled the spirit of legendary musician Fela Kuti. In the '60s and '70s, Fela triumphed with a sound that was a mix of jazz, Ghanaian highlife, and funk, which he fused to produce lengthy tracks – regularly clocking in at over fifteen minutes; longer when performed live – whose main purpose was to speak to the social ills of the day while calling as many powerful politicians a 'useless goat' as his tongue could carry. 'Make I yab them?' he would ask. His adoring crowd would scream back in the affirmative, having partly come to hear him insult the political class.

Fela's iconic 'International Thief Thief' perfectly summarises his style: blending history and international politics to give context to the post-colonial corruption that a clique of the continent's founding fathers could not shake. What Fela understood was the truth of the world around him, preaching his gospel through his own category of music: Afrobeat.

Thirty years later, millennials in the region had returned to making music about what was directly outside their windows – a switch that resonated beyond their own communities and countries, out in an international diaspora looking to connect with a continent they knew too little about.

In homage to Fela, this new birth was coined Afrobeats by the British-Ghanaian DJ Abrantee Boateng in 2011. 'This is specifically the western African sound,' Abrantee told *The Guardian*. 'Parents are really pleased, and proud, that their kids are all of a sudden embracing their culture. It didn't used to be cool, but now they're going through their parents' record collections going, "Have you got this old song by Daddy Lumba?'"

Where Fela's Afrobeat saved its energy for eviscerating politicians and a corrupt establishment, today's Afrobeats is fundamentally about having a good time. It's unapologetically joyous pop that celebrates what it means to exist proudly as yourself among your own. The type of music that makes you want to risk it all. Local compulsions blend seamlessly with international influences – hip hop, R&B, dancehall. Wizkid or Burna Boy can sing almost exclusively in Yoruba about Ojuelegba or Port Harcourt and still get their point across to a crowd in Toronto because a party is a party in any language, and good vibes are the only truly universal virtue.

Their focus on their immediate surroundings has meant artists remain flexible to changing tides. Politics may not be at its foundation, but the genre cannot, and has not, ignored the social movements that are being led by their core audience. Afrobeats stars like Falz and Davido have found their political voice and stood publicly with demonstrators. Rightly so, as Afrobeats is a genre perfectly entwined with the times: modern, fresh, global, yet anchored to a local base.

The freedom of expression that underpins Afrobeats best represents the cultural zeitgeist, a dynamic propelling new genres and content creators, giving them the confidence to produce work that reflects them and their own. This work, seen throughout the continent, is proving to be more socially liberal and tolerant, and accepting of diverse identities – with concerns ranging from protecting LGBTQ rights to pushing for broad social equality.

You can witness these demonstrations of individuality in the Lagos-based alté scene – home to young artists, musicians and performers who are bending traditional fashion norms, gender stereotypes, and centring the importance of creating work that speaks specifically to a version of themselves not dictated by others. You can see it in the depth of talent found in the twenty-something digital natives sprawled across TikTok, Instagram and the entire social-mediaverse, building broad global audiences. I spent 4 per cent of my pandemic lockdown watching sketches by Elsa Majimbo, the twenty-year-old Kenyan Instagram comedian whose acerbic takes on the world have attracted an internet following of over two million fans. What she does seems like an easy party trick on paper, but something transforms in 4k. Majimbo's props consist almost exclusively of a bag of crisps, a pair of tiny sunglasses, and a deep laugh, all of which she makes use of as the punchlines play through to monologues that circle around her constant disappointment that she is expected to engage with the human race. 'I'm not late,' she opens one video. 'I allow everyone else to arrive fast. If I say I'm five minutes away, there's a ninety per cent chance I just woke up,' she adds with a contagious cackle.

Equally addictive are the Ikorodu Bois: four teenagers who create two-minute remakes of high-budget Hollywood films using nothing but everyday rudimentary items. The souped-up cars of the *Fast and Furious* franchise are replaced by wheelbarrows; the semi-automatic weapons in *Bad Boys* are replicated with empty soft drink cans tied together. What impresses is the technical quality of their reproductions and how the scenes are perfectly sliced beat-by-beat in time with the original's action and dialogue, all arranged with basic shooting equipment. Their work – produced largely for their own amusement – regularly attracts the attention of the stars they mimic and the producers of the films they parody, as well as a wide fan base – their remake of the trailer for the Chris Hemsworth film *Extraction* has garnered over six million views on Twitter alone.

The ingenuity of the work defining the youth-led cultural and political shifts and driving change is being well documented by a thriving generation of journalists, writers, online magazines and literary journals. This work is continuing the continent's long and storied history of recording its own present, written and oral, and is journeying down the path carved out by the likes of Buchi Emecheta, Binyavanga Wainaina, Ngũgĩ wa Thiong'o, Chinua Achebe, Rajat Neogy and other literary giants. It continues the effort of magazines such as *Transition*, which gave voice to the independence movements of the '60s; and *Kwani?*, one of the first literary journals to showcase many of the continent's most revered modern writers.

Today, among many, there is the Namibian literary journal *Doek!*, and the Kenya-based *Lolwe* – two magazines that aim to publish Black writers from across the diaspora. There is the short-story haven *AFREADA*; travel journal *ìrìn*, which tells the intimate stories of African cities beyond the direction of the sun and a person's ability to buy goods in traffic; and *The Republic*, which publishes in-depth reportage on the political and social history of the continent. There is the multifaceted *NATIVE*, a culture hub and magazine that's growing into the most comprehensive chronicler of the burgeoning youth-culture scenes throughout the region. And *Zikoko!*, whose recent quizzes include 'How many pieces of Sallah meat will you get?' and 'What is your Nollywood gangster name?'

There are dozens more, and there will be countless fresh iterations in the future, with new talents. The lack of varied coverage of the continent across the world is not the fault of Africans but of a barrier that struggles to let their light through; a filter preoccupied with the same stale depictions found in popular culture and in charitable campaigns, of an Africa that never evolves; of a place incapable of gazing to the future to ask then shape: *What's next?*

*

THE SLAVE DUNGEONS WERE FULL.

Thousands of Black people were guided through the concrete tunnels; packed from wall to wall; the darkness cut by candlelight. They were treading floors pressed by millions before them. This time, however, they had come voluntarily, empowered to see for themselves where their story began. They were invited to better understand the basic mechanics of what it takes to gut a person of their identity, shackle their flesh to a new fate, and haul whatever spirit remains away like cattle to suffer.

They were there to be reminded of immense strength. *'You are the ancestors of the people that refused to die.'*

The markets were full.

Thousands of Black people had come voluntarily, to walk along beaches and meander through a grand metropolis. They were invited to meet a president, fully immerse themselves in local cultures and traditions as if they were their own, and party into the least respectable hours of the day, when fun and chaos mean the same thing.

They were there to be reminded that there was something here for them, too – if they wanted it.

In 2019, the Ghanaian government asked the descendants of enslaved Africans to come home. No matter where you were in the world, the promise was you would find in Ghana a place of rest, should you need it – temporarily or not so temporarily – or a refuge in which to reconnect with what was taken from you. President Nana Akufo-Addo declared it the Year of Return, to mark exactly four hundred years since the first slave ships arrived in the US, in 1619. Having been the site of 75 per cent of the slave dungeons in which the enslaved were kept and from which they were transported, Ghana considered it only right that the country bore the responsibility of setting the course for the journey back over the ocean.

'We open our arms even wider to welcome home our brothers and sisters in what will become a birthright journey home for the global African family,' President Akufo-Addo said in a speech in Washington. 'It was our hope that the "Year of Return" would be a joyful learning experience all round for all of us on the continent and our kith and kin from the diaspora, especially in affirming our determination that never again should the African peoples permit themselves to be subjected to such dehumanising conditions, sold into slavery, and have their freedoms curtailed.'

Though tagged as a year, the gesture had no expiration date. Any person of African descent was given the right to live in Ghana indefinitely under the country's Right of Abode law. Over a hundred Afro-Caribbeans and African Americans were granted citizenship. 'The most valuable possession that was taken away from us was our identity and our connection; it was like severing the umbilical cord,' American Rabbi Kohain Halevi said in a speech at a mass citizenship ceremony held at the presidential palace. 'But tonight, our identity, the dignity, the pride that has been absent is restored here.'

Africa has always been treated more as an idea than a place. An idea of suffering and struggle. An idea of violence. An idea of cursed leadership. An idea of a great weakness that can easily be exploited and stripped of its assets.

But for many who lost their heritage in humanity's most vile trade, a more romantic idea has endured: one of Africa as a faint dreamscape of liberation from worlds that regularly stutter when asked to affirm that their lives matter. The Year of Return attempted a seismic shift in that relationship between the continent and its distant relatives. For the half a million visitors it attracted in a single year, it turned Africa from an idea into a living space full of form and breath, capable of replacing a pencilled lineage with something resembling permanence, while grounding visitors in the delights of a present they were invited to envision owning; it promoted a spirit of remembrance, but also of celebration and of capturing an identity for yourself – a sublime notion at a time when the first spores of a global racial awakening were starting to find light. As a result, interest in visiting the continent began to grow; December 2019 became the unofficial month of return for young Black Africans and the diaspora, who flocked to Accra, Dakar, and Lagos to zanku in front of the world's biggest musicians at concerts and festivals, take tours of ancient sites, see family, and indulge until their souls and bodies were full.

Vital to its success – emotional and financial – was that it was an initiative led by an African country, devised on its terms and not one forced upon the continent. It was a collective agreement to embrace what connects – an approach that is a distant cousin of an ideology that found its feet on these exact same shores during the last great battle for freedom, thanks to Ghana's independence hero and first president, Kwame Nkrumah.

Nkrumah was the continent's most passionate proponent of Pan-Africanism, a belief that Africa and its global descendants should break down any divisions and unify under a common purpose of prosperity. Nkrumah championed the liberation of the entire continent from colonialism, providing considerable support to Ghana's neighbours looking to follow his country's lead and break free. It was his hope that, with freedom, Africa would embrace a shared vision of the future.

Before him, Pan-Africanism had its roots in the early-twentieth-century work of African-American intellectuals like W. E. B. DuBois, and Jamaica's Marcus Garvey, founder of the Universal Negro Improvement Association. But for the ideology to become reality, the message needed to be carried forward by the freedom fighters now responsible for the continent's post-colonial life. Nkrumah had friends in the cause, a posse of powerful firsts: Kenya's inaugural president, Jomo Kenyatta; Tanzania's first leader, Julius Nyerere; and the DRC's Patrice Lumumba, among others. However, the elation and distraction of the opportunity to build independent nations from scratch, and the challenges that presented, worked against the realisation of their dream – as the best political minds across Africa were focused inwards, on making the new countries they had fought for work.

Decades later, Ghana is realising a modern version of Nkrumah's vision to reconnect across borders, a value-add in an era when the domineering global ideology is to demand we build bigger physical and psychological border walls to protect *our way of life* from *them*.

A request to appreciate the idiosyncrasies that make up Africa's complex ecosystem of cultures and identities is not an attempt to put up those same walls in any form. Quite the opposite. It's wishing instead that a collective rejection of the stereotypes that have dogged the continent ever since the White Men In Khaki drew their fictitious map will encourage the world, as the Year of Return did, to engage with the continent as it actually exists – not with an idea, but with its genuine form, regardless of whether you're someone capable of tracing your ancestry to those fateful voyages, or an aid agency looking to change the course of an unfolding crisis, or a screenwriter itching to pen an Africa-set tale, or you're simply trying for a brief trip. Engage with all of it: each language and climate; each political and social framework; each nation trying to form its identity specifically. Engage with the majestic game animals, and communities bursting with kin like mine whose idea of the wild is a small town still to be touched by a reliable Wi-Fi network.

African countries should determine whatever comes next. Any clues will come shaped as action, and in its short history, the continent has never been afraid to take bold steps. In their first post-independence constitutions, Mali, Guinea and Ghana included clauses that would have handed over their sovereignty to a single entity known as the Union of African States, if one was ever formed. Today, there is little appetite or need to go that far. Instead, the cross-nation solidarity of recent youth-led social and creative movements offers a glimpse of a future where the continent pools knowledge and experience to advance individual nations for the benefit of their respective peoples; a new era at odds with the traditions of a fading political old guard who are unable to construct modern digital states, no matter how hard they fought for the old ones. Key to colonialism was pitting people against each other, through divide-and-conquer. Pan-Africanism and the Year of Return, however, push constructive collectivism, building a shared future that also respects and accommodates nuance and difference.

Perhaps, then, African countries will choose to face what's next together – where appropriate – and embrace more unity between individual sovereign states. A continent motivated by a collective rejection of the designed ethnic divisions of the past may choose to shape itself into something that, when glimpsed under that famous yellow sun, looks curiously, productively, like a country.

But until then.

Acknowledgements

To God be the glory, to Him I am most grateful. My life to now has been a continuous series of God's blessings that almost always find their way to me in the shape of people. Here are some of those people.

Above all, my parents: Olufemi Faloyin and Olutosin Nkemoyem Okwesa. They are my very best friends, the greatest thing that has ever happened to me, and the fact of my life I am most grateful for. Thank you for your love and support and prayers, and for giving me more space than I deserve to follow my heart.

To my sisters and day-ones: Vero, Temitope and Yewande. There is no doubt that I have been an exceptional younger brother to you all, and you have done well to reciprocate that love. Thank you for being my great constants and for the remarkable examples you have set. To my nephew, Feranmi, and my nieces, Sekemi and Olivia, in whom I am most pleased and so very proud. Dedicating this book to the eight people above was the easiest decision I will ever make.

I am thankful for my grandparents – Oladipo Faloyin, Olufumilayo Lashore, Oluremilekun Odeinde, Frank Okwesa, and Martina Anele – for following through on their respective visions, at speed, with a level of bravery that has made the journey of my life unreasonably smooth.

If you learn one thing from this book, let it be that the size of my extended family is comparable to that of a medium-sized industrial town. I desperately wish I had the space to fully express my gratitude to every aunty – especially my aunties! – uncle and cousin that make up my foundations. Just know that I love you all, and please accept my gratitude grouped in the city you live in. So my deepest thanks to my family in Lagos, Ibadan, Ifé, Ilorin, Osamala, London, New Jersey, Manchester, New York, California, Texas, Chicago and Atlanta. *This is Family Business / And this is for everybody standin' with us.*

To Chineze Okwesa, my guardian in more ways than I could ever imagine, thank you for supporting and guiding me for longer than my memory can stretch; to Bimbola Osibogun for ensuring I never go hungry in body and spirit; to Morayo and Bimbola Adisa for pushing me to write this book and for keeping us all in check; to Damilare Oyefeso for teaching me to chop life before life chops me; to Timi Aborisade for being the big brother I always wanted; to Titilayo Odofin for never being too far away; and in loving memory of Aramide, Deji, and Ayo.

For reasons I will never understand, Karolina Sutton responded to an email I sent on the 19th of August 2020 that wasn't so much a coherent outline for a book, but a series of vibes roughly shaped into sentences. Replying at all was generous, but agreeing to be my agent is an act of kindness I will never forget. Thank you for making this dream a reality. To the rest of the team at Curtis Brown: Caitlin Leydon, Claire Nozieres and Lolu Ojo; and to Amelia Atlas at ICM. Peppa Mignone, what a delightful coincidence, thank you for the good vibes.

From my very first conversation with my UK editors at Harvill Secker, Elizabeth Foley and Ellie Steel, I knew they would be the perfect partners for this adventure. Thank you for the respect, wisdom, and care with which you have approached this task, and for indulging my more insane ideas.

My immense gratitude to my US editor, Matt Weiland, for your enthusiasm and encouragement from the beginning, for your incredible insights, and for publishing Binyavanga Wainaina all those years ago.

Thank you to Mia Quibell-Smith, Sophie Painter, Kishan Rajani, Gemma Wain, Tom Atkins, and everyone at Vintage, Penguin Random House and W. W. Norton who have had a hand in turning a Google doc into a real-life book.

I am incredibly lucky that Nicole Eminian possesses an infinite stockpile of kindness – a collection that has shored me up in times of doubt. Thank you for fighting my enemies, real and imagined, and for being an incredible pal. To Emily Little, whose creative eye has extended into designing a delightful friendship. Thank you for always reaching out and your steady commitment to believing in me.

There isn't really anything I can say to fully capture all that Amandine and Iain Rorison-Powell have done in support of this book, and me. They have opened their lives to welcome me in, and with it offered the most perfect place of peace. I am beyond grateful, now and always, for winning this particular lottery. To more mischief, starter pizza, and the exact right amount of vibes. *Buku Buku Buku Buku.*

To Nick Marshall, my friend and brother. You remain certain that I know what I'm doing despite all the evidence to the contrary. Thank you for making this and all the great landmarks of our lives such a joy. It seems we really are in this for life, and I can't wait for all the adventures to come with you, Clara and Lily. My love and gratitude to Chris Darch for patiently sticking with me until we can finally get those season tickets side by side. You and Jen have quite simply been too good to me for way too long.

Tom Owen: to state the obvious, you are a far more talented writer than I could ever dream to be, and a better friend. Thank you for never hesitating to edit both my words and life. I am forever grateful to you, and I promise I will find a way to pay you back in Vegas.

My deep gratitude to Robert Beaven, who for two decades has picked up my calls at all odd hours of the day and night. Your steady reassurances are a blessed gift and a wonderful companion. And nothing but love and thanks to my most clever OG pals Georgia Sawyer, Amon Warmann, Tom Huws, Emma Philp and Matt Hill.

To Gordon and Jenny Opie, who embody the forever fact that teachers are life's great game-changers. This book would not have been possible without your guidance at the most important time.

I am immensely thankful to every single person in East London, but especially Miranda Thompson and Harriet Seabourne for their unwavering support, steady visions in moments of doubt, and never saying no to da club.

Gratitude FC to Charlie Woodall, Alex Solomon, Nick Sheffield, Ed Lamaison, Arthur Everett, Adam Ryman and Toby Lamb for supporting Book FC, and for year after year of being the most remarkable support system, almost by the hour, for the big and little things. You are by far the greatest team the world has ever seen.

If strangers have approached you on the street and tried to sell you this book, you were almost certainly speaking with Dan Lee or Adam Lees, the most wonderful, loyal friends/hype men a man could ask for. Charlie Armstrong, thank you for being the sane one.

To Tom Reid and Elisabeth Mecz, whose abundance of love and care has transcended seas and time zones; to Emily Pointer, Pat Pakulska and Alex Taylor for always checking in and pushing me forward with such joy; and to A Block, the Friday Email and #Manure2015 gang. Dan Strang would make a big deal out of not being mentioned, so this is me mentioning Dan Strang. (Thanks, Dan.)

Ask me for advice and I will tell you to go to work every day with people who are far more talented than you. This book, physically and creatively, would not have been possible without the support of my friends and colleagues at VICE. To Wiegertje Postma for hiring me and then proceeding to be the most remarkable mentor and friend. Ik ben voor altijd dankbaar. To Elektra Kotsoni for teaching me how to write and edit with clarity and purpose and joy. My gratitude to Hannah Ewens for rushing in to ease my worries and detangle the mysteries of writing a book; to Ruby Lott-Lavigna for your encouragement at every step; to Tshepo Mokoena for always having my back; and to my office parents, Bruno Bayley and Ellis Jones. My love and appreciation always to Tayo Yusuff, Jamie Clifton, Zing Tsjeng, Alex Miller, Phoebe Hurst, Simon Childs, Sirin Kale, Nana Baah, Emma Garland, Daisy Jones, Lauren O'Neill, Ryan Bassil, Jack Cummings, Max Daly, Joe Bish, Angus Harrison, Tim Hume, Mohammed Rasool, Alex Hoffman, Rose Donohoe, Bianca Ferrari, Marsha Cooke and Matthew Champion. Joel Golby: drip.

Finally, to the citizens of the fifty-four countries that make up Africa. For moving forward despite it all and for proudly telling your own tales when nobody else would listen. Your lives matter.

To God be the glory.

Notes

Part One: Lagos

A version of this section first appeared on VICE.com.

Part Two: By the Power Vested in Me, I Now Pronounce You a Country

p. 25   'The map was large and wrong . . .' Thomas Pakenham, *The Scramble for Africa*, Abacus, 1991.

p. 26   'The drawing loomed large . . .' T. J. Bassett, 'Cartography and Empire Building in Nineteenth-Century West Africa', *Geographical Review*, 84(3), 1994, pp. 316–335.

p. 26   'The men who had gathered there . . .' Hilke Fischer, '130 years Ago: Carving Up Africa in Berlin', DW, 25 February 2015, https://www.dw.com/en/130-years-ago-carving-up-africa-in-berlin/a-18278894.

p. 27   'The inflow of the white race . . .' John Westlake, *Chapters on the Principles of International Law*, Cambridge University Press, 1894.

p. 29   'To regulate the conditions most favourable . . .' Pakenham, *The Scramble for Africa*.

p. 30   'the representative of the United States, who wanted . . .' Protocol of 31 January 1995, Parliamentary Paper, c. 4361, 209.

p. 31   'Still, they clearly needed to find a way . . .' George Shepperson, 'The Centennial of the West African Conference of Berlin, 1884–1885', *Phylon*, 46 (1), 1985, pp. 37–48.

p. 32   'After negotiations, the conference . . .' G. N. Uzoigwe, 'Reflections on the Berlin West Africa Conference, 1884-1885', *Journal of the Historical Society of Nigeria*, 12(3/4), 1984, pp. 9–22.

p. 32   'Yet even then, at the tail end of the nineteenth century . . .' T. Ranger, *The Invention of Tradition Revisited: The Case of Colonial Africa*, in T. Ranger and O. Vaughan (eds), *Legitimacy and the State in Twentieth-Century Africa*, Palgrave Macmillan, 1993.

p. 32   'The world had, perhaps, never witnessed a robbery . . .' Patrick Gathara, 'Berlin 1884: Remembering the Conference that Divided Africa', Al Jazeera, 15 November 2019.

p. 33   *'Before the Berlin Conference had finished its deliberations . . .'* W. E. B. DuBois, 'The African Roots of War', *Atlantic Monthly*, May 1915.

p. 34   *'It did something much worse . . .'* Patrick Gathara, 'Berlin 1884: Remembering the Conference that Divided Africa', Al Jazeera, 15 November 2019, https://www.aljazeera.com/opinions/2019/11/15/berlin-1884-remembering-the-conference-that-divided-africa.

p. 37   'The first country to be created after the Berlin Conference . . .' Frederick Starr, 'The Congo Free State and Congo Belge', *Journal of Race Development*, 1(4), 1911, pp. 383–99; Daniel De Leon, 'The Conference at Berlin on the West-African Question', *Political Science Quarterly*, 1(1), 1886, pp. 103–39.

p. 37   'The Belgian government didn't want the colony . . .' Jason Burke, 'Face-Off over the Congo: The Long Rivalry between Kinshasha and Brazaville', *The Guardian*, 17 January 2017.

p. 38   'The newly established Congo Free State did not go well . . .' 'The Tale of Two Congos', *Washington Post*, 21 May 1997.

p. 38   'Any Congolese who refused to work was shot dead . . .' BBC News Africa, 'Congo and The Scramble for Africa', *History of Africa*, episode 19, 2020, https://www.youtube.com/watch?v=W0v_SwObQns.

p. 39   'With the same energy as rival grifters . . .' Matthew Craven, 'Between Law and History: The Berlin Conference of 1884–1885 and the Logic of Free Trade', *London Review of International Law*, 3(1), 2015, pp. 31–59.

p. 39   'with France and Britain . . .' Geo History, 'Colonization of Africa', December 2018, https://youtu.be/Fbb7nbIUUEM.

p. 39   'Before the conference, the French . . .' H. W. Koch, 'The Anglo-German Alliance Negotiations: Missed Opportunity or Myth?', *History*, 54(182), 1969, pp. 378–92.

p. 39   *'Our possession on the West Coast . . .'* Norman Dwight Harris, 'French Colonial Expansion in West Africa, The Sudan, and the Sahara', *American Political Science Review*, 5(3), 1911, pp. 353–73.

p. 40   *'Gambia was to comprise 10 kilometres . . .'* 'The Partition of Africa; Germany Dissatisfied with the Anglo-Belgian Treaty', *New York Times*, 17 June 1894.

p. 41   'The British were old hands at this business . . .' Robert Dennis Fiala, 'The Anglo-German Agreement over Portugal's African colonies, 1898', MA Thesis, University of Nebraska at Omaha, 1963.

p. 41   'Unlike the French, the British government . . .' Emile de Groot, 'Great Britain and Germany in Zanzibar: Consul Holmwood's Papers, 1886–1887', *Journal of Modern History*, 25(2), 1953, pp. 120–38.

p. 41   'To do this in West Africa, Britain leaned on the United African Company . . .' C. H. Firth, 'The British Empire', *Scottish Historical Review*, 15(59), 1918, pp. 185–89; 'Africa: British Colonies', Encyclopedia.com, https://www.encyclopedia.com/social-sciences/encyclopedias-almanacs-transcripts-and-maps/africa-british-colonies#A; Stephen Luscombe, 'Africa and the British Empire', The British Empire [website], https://www.britishempire.co.uk/maproom/africa.htm [accessed 11 October 2021].

p. 42   'On the other side of the continent . . .' Daniel Brückenhaus, 'Identifying Colonial Subjects: Fingerprinting in British Kenya, 1900–1960', *Geschichte Und Gesellschaft*, 42(1), 2016, pp. 60–85.

p. 42   'This was all secured by the British East African Company. . .' B. Turyahikayo-Rugyema, 'The British Imposition of Colonial Rule on Uganda: The Baganda Agents in Kigezi (1908-1930)', *Transafrican Journal of History*, 5(1), 1976, pp. 111–33.

p. 42   'which soon realised that it was expensive to run countries . . .' Editors of Encyclopaedia Britannica, 'German East Africa', *Encyclopedia Britannica*, https://www.britannica.com/place/German-East-Africa [accessed 11 October 2021].

p. 42   'Meanwhile in southern Africa . . .' John S. Galbraith, 'The British South Africa Company and the Jameson Raid', *Journal of British Studies*, 10(1), 1970, pp. 145–61; Robert Porter, 'The Consolidated Gold Fields of South Africa', in *Consolidated Gold Fields in Australia: The Rise and Decline of a British Mining House, 1926–1998*, ANU Press, 2020, pp. 5–14.

p. 42   'forcing ethnic groups to hand over their territories . . .' John Donaldson, 'Marking Territory: Demarcation of the DRC-Zambia Boundary from 1894 to the Present Day', Doctoral Thesis, Durham University, 2010, http://etheses.dur.ac.uk/328/.

p. 42   'An 1891 border agreement with . . .' Harold G. Marcus, 'A Background to Direct British Diplomatic Involvement in Ethiopia, 1894–1896', *Journal of Ethiopian Studies*, 1(2), 1963, pp. 121–32.

p. 43   'The British also took what would become . . .' Mesfin Wolde Mariam, 'The Background of the Ethio-Somalian Boundary Dispute', *Journal of Modern African Studies*, 2(2), 1964, pp. 189–219.

p. 43   'In an attempt to placate the Afrikaners . . .' Justin Parkinson, 'Why Is Cecil Rhodes Such a Controversial Figure', BBC News, 1 April 2015, https://www.bbc.co.uk/news/magazine-32131829.

p. 43   'The result of all this village-storming and treaty-signing . . .' Faisal Abdel Rahman Ali Taha, 'The Sudan-Zaire Boundary', *Sudan Notes and Records*, 58, 1977, pp. 73–84.

p. 44   'Compared to everyone else, Italy was not . . .' Michael Pretes, 'Africa: Italian Colonies', Encyclopedia.com, 22 September 2021, https://www.encyclopedia.com/social-sciences/encyclopedias-almanacs-transcripts-and-maps/africa-italian-colonies.

p. 44   'After the opening of the Suez Canal in 1869 . . .' H. R. Tate, 'The Italian Colonial Empire', *Journal of the Royal African Society*, 40(159), 1941, pp. 146–58.

p. 44   'Arrive, manipulate, negotiate with a European adversary . . .' Jeffrey Herbst, 'The Creation and Maintenance of National Boundaries in Africa', *International Organization*, 43(4), 1989, pp. 673–92.

p. 45   'Unfortunately, they wrongly identified the Akwayefe . . .' Max Fisher, 'The Dividing of a Continent: Africa's Separatist Problem', *The Atlantic*, 10 September 2012.

p. 45   'both West African nations have tried . . .' G. Pascal Zachary, 'After South Sudan: The Case to Keep Dividing Africa', *The Atlantic*, 11 July 2011.

p. 45   '*In those days, we just took a blue pencil . . .*' Pakenham, *The Scramble for Africa*.

p. 46   'Uganda and the DRC share a border . . .' 'Uganda, DR Congo Head Off Dispute as River Alters Border', *The East African*, 7 September 2009.

p. 46   '*We never had an official boundary* . . .' 'Changing River Course Alters Uganda-DR Congo Border', *The Independent*, 11 November 2019.

p. 46   'Oil has been discovered . . .' Vision Reporter, 'Fishermen Caught in Battle for Rukwanzi Oil', *New Vision*, https://www.newvision.co.ug/news/1188240/fishermen-caught-battle-rukwanzi-oil.

p. 47   'The interior structure of modern Africa . . .' Pierre Englebert, Stacy Tarango and Matthew Carter, 'Dismemberment and Suffocation: A Contribution to the Debate on African Boundaries', *Comparative Political Studies*, 35(10), 2002, pp. 1093–1118.

p. 47   '*I had a bundle of printed treaties* . . .' Adekunle Ajala, 'The Nature of African Boundaries', *Africa Spectrum*, 18(2), 1983, pp. 177–89.

p. 49   '*Boundaries were drawn across well-established lines* . . .' Anthony Asiwaju, *Western Yorubaland under European Rule, 1889–1945: A Comparative Analysis of French and British Colonialism*, Longman, 1976.

p. 50   'Later, in 1971, when Idi Amin . . .' Ajala, 'The Nature of African Boundaries'.

p. 50   '*The long-ago partition of one small ethnic group* . . .' Alberto Alesina, Janina Matuszeski and William Easterly, 'Artifical States', *Journal of the European Economic Association*, 9(2), pp. 246–77.

p. 50   'The only thing worse than having an arbitrary border . . .' Saadia Touval, 'Treaties, Borders, and the Partition of Africa', *Journal of African History*, 7(2), 1966, pp. 279–93.

p. 57   'Reckoning with their current state . . .' Elliott Green, 'On the Size and Shape of African States', *International Studies Quarterly*, 56(2), 2012, pp. 229–44.

p. 58   '*It was unfortunate that the African States have been broken up* . . .' Speech given by Tafawa Balewa on the occasion of the creation of the Organization of African Unity (OAU) at Addis Abba, Ethiopia, on 24 May 1963.

p. 58   'that the Organisation of African Unity . . .' L.T., 'Why Africa's Borders Are a Mess', *The Economist*, 17 November 2016.

p. 59   'In an attempt to salvage Africa's fledgling harmony . . .' African Union Border Programme, *Delimitation and Demarcation of Boundaries in Africa General Issues and Case Studies*, Commission of the African Union, Department of Peace and Security, 2013; Stelios Michalopoulos and Elias Papaioannou, 'The Long-Run Effects of the Scramble for Africa', Vox EU, 6 January 2012, https://voxeu.org/article/long-run-effects-scramble-africa.

p. 59   'It also wasn't clear how nations would go about . . .' H. R. Tate, 'The French Colonial Empire', *African Affairs*, 34(157), 1940, pp. 322–330.

p. 59   'The colonial powers had created such a mess . . .' John Markakis, 'The Organisation of African Unity: A Progress Report', *Journal of Modern African Studies*, 4(2), 1966, pp. 135–53.

p. 60   '*I am not unaware that, when our colonisers set boundaries* . . .' Speech given by Philibert Tsiranana on the occasion of the creation of the OAU at Addis Abba, Ethiopia, on 24 May 1963.

p. 60   'We must take Africa as it is . . .' Speech given by Modibo Keita on the occasion of the creation of the OAU at Addis Abba, Ethiopia, on 24 May 1963.

p. 60   'Finally, it simply wasn't in the personal interests . . .' Saadia Touval, 'The Organization of
African Unity and African Borders', International Organization, 21(1), 1967, pp. 102–27.

p. 61   'Unity can only be based on the general consent . . .' Julius Nyerere, 'Why We Recognised
Biafra', Observer, 28 April 1968.

p. 62   'Just weeks after both regions won independence . . .' 'South Sudan is collapsing thanks to
corruption of over oil', VICE News, 1 March 2020, https://youtu.be/qi37th_N3Ck.

p. 62   'they merged together to form a united Somalia . . .' Joshua Keating, 'When Is a Nation Not
a nation? Somaliland's Dream of Independence', The Guardian, 20 July 2018.

p. 62   'Based on the totality of evidence collected . . .' Chris Mburu, Past Human Rights Abuses in
Somalia: Report of a Preliminary Study Conducted for the United Nations (OHCHR/
UNDP-Somalia), 2002.

p. 62   'In 1991, northern Somalia, under the name Somaliland . . .' Ismail Einashe and Matt Ken-
nard, 'In the Valley of Death: Somaliland's Forgotten Genocide', The Nation, 22 October 2018.

p. 63   'Then there's the case of the world's . . .' 'South Sudan May Be Heading towards Genocide',
Vox, 29 December 2016, https://youtu.be/LkWldwFdTPo.

p. 63   'Before then, there was a deep divide . . .' Jennifer Williams, 'The Conflict in South Sudan',
Vox, 9 January 2017, https://www.vox.com/world/2016/12/8/13817072/south-sudan-
crisis-explained-ethnic-cleansing-genocide.

p. 63   'Kiir accused Machar in 2013 of plotting a coup . . .' 'South Sudan Just Ended Its Civil War
– For Now', VICE News, 4 April 2020, https://youtu.be/84fjG22fCrE.

p. 64   'The current state of South Sudan . . .' 'Interviewing South Sudan's Minister of Information
– VICE on HBO', VICE News, 17 October 2017, https://www.youtube.com/
watch?v=VpelbIt4xcY.

p. 64   'A study in 2011 by a group of Harvard and NYU professors . . .' Alberto Alesina, Janina
Matuszeski and William Easterly, 'Artifical States', Journal of the European Economic Association, 9(2), 2011, pp. 246–77.

Part Three: The Birth of White Saviour Imagery or How Not to Be a White Saviour While Still Making a Difference

p. 71   'Hidden behind that link . . .' Kony 2012 [video], 5 March 2012, https://www.youtube.
com/watch?v=Y4MnpzG5Sqc.

p. 78   'White Savior Industrial Complex . . .' Teju Cole, 'The White-Savior Industrial Complex', The
Atlantic, 21 March 2012.

p. 79   'there is a longstanding frustration with the West's . . .' Robert Mackey, 'African Critics of
Kony Campaign See a "White Man's Burden" for the Facebook Generation', New York
Times, 9 March 2012.

p. 80   *'My major problem with this video . . .'* Rosebell Kagumire, 'Kony2012; My response to Invisible Children's campaign', Rosebell Kagumire [blog], 8 March 2012, https://rosebellkagumire.com/2012/03/08/kony2012-my-response-to-invisible-childrens-campaign/.

p. 81   *'Kony continues to rely on child soldiers . . .'* Ethan Zuckerman, 'Unpacking Kony 2012', Ethan Zuckerman [blog], 8 March 2012, https://ethanzuckerman.com/2012/03/08/unpacking-kony-2012/.

p. 81   *'A community in northern Uganda . . .'* David Haglund, 'Northern Ugandans React to the Kony 2012 Video', *Slate*, 14 March 2012, https://slate.com/culture/2012/03/kony-victims-are-angered-by-the-kony-2012-video.html.

p. 81   *'It's part of a long tradition of Western advocacy'* Max Fisher, 'The Soft Bigotry of Kony 2012', *The Atlantic*, March 2012.

p. 82   *'The real star of Kony 2012 isn't Joseph Kony . . .'* Dinaw Mengestu, 'Not a Click Away: Joseph Kony in the Real World', Warscapes, 12 March 2012, http://www.warscapes.com/reportage/not-click-away-joseph-kony-real-world.

p. 82   *'The continent was fighting back against . . .'* Kate Cronin-Furman and Amanda Taub, 'Solving War Crimes with Wristbands: The Arrogance of Kony 2012', *The Atlantic*, 8 March 2012.

p. 86   *'An estimated one million people died . . .'* Asmerom Kidane, 'Mortality Estimates of the 1984–85 Ethiopian Famine', *Scandinavian Journal of Social Medicine*, 18(4), 1990, pp. 281–86.

p. 86   *'The segment features the journalist Michael Buerk . . .'* 'Ethiopia's Famine: Remembering 30 Years On', BBC News, 25 October 2014, https://youtu.be/6SVByPiF6iQ.

p. 89   *'outraged by what I saw . . .'* George W. Bush Institute, 'How a TV Show Changed Music and Africa', *The Catalyst*, 7, 2017, https://www.bushcenter.org/catalyst/africa/geldof-changing-africa.html.

p. 90   *'I thought, it's not enough to put a pound . . .'* Ibid.

p. 91   *'It was the number-one single . . .'* Michael Hann, 'Band Aid: In Defence of Its Legacy', *The Guardian*, 15 November 2014.

p. 93   *'I quickly realized that politics is numbers . . .'* George W. Bush Institute, 'How a TV Show Changed Music and Africa'.

p. 94   *'I pointed out to Geldof the lyrics . . .'* Fuse ODG, 'Why I Had to Turn Down Band Aid', *The Guardian*, 19 November 2014.

p. 95   *'In truth, my objection to the project . . .'* Fuse ODG, 'Why I Had to Turn Down Band Aid'.

p. 95   *'The song's racism lives on in the banal way . . .'* Aron Brady, 'Saving Africa, Yet Again, with a Song', Al Jazeera America, 18 November 2014, http://america.aljazeera.com/opinions/2014/11/band-aid-30-bob-geldoffebolaafrica.html.

p. 95   *'Political science professor Laura Seay . . .'* Lara Seay, 'They Know it's Christmas', *Washington Post*, 17 November 2014.

p. 95   *'There exists a paternalistic way of thinking about Africa . . .'* Bim Adewunmi, 'Band Aid 30: Clumsy, Patronising and Wrong in So Many Ways', *The Guardian*, 11 November 2014.

p. 96   'Singer Emeli Sandé, who performed in Band Aid 30 . . .' 'Emeli Sande: We Need a New
         Band Aid Song', ITV, 23 November 2014, https://www.itv.com/news/2014-11-23/
         emeli-sande-we-need-a-new-band-aid-song.

p. 96   'Where Band Aid is effective . . .' Tina Daheley and Dell Crookes, 'Bob Geldof: I Don't Care
         about Criticism of Band Aid 30', BBC News, 8 December 2014, 8 December 2014, https://
         www.bbc.co.uk/news/newsbeat-30374106.

p. 96   'As he reiterated as recently as 2020 . . .' Berny Torre, 'Geldof War on Flakes', Daily Star, 7
         April 2020.

p. 97   'There is a moment in particular about halfway through the series . . .' Jason Hehir (dir.), The
         Last Dance [TV documentary].

p. 99   'a forced relocation policy that systematically . . .' Laurence Binet et al. (eds), Famine and
         forced relocations in Ethiopia 1984–1986, Médicins Sans Frontières International Move-
         ment, January 2005/November 2013.

p. 100   'A BBC investigation in 2010 . . .' Martin Plaut, 'Ethiopia famine aid "spent on weapons"',
         BBC News, 3 March 2010, http://news.bbc.co.uk/1/hi/world/africa/8535189.stm.

p. 102   'A substantial number of the advertisers . . .' Jorgen Lissner, 'Merchants of Misery', New Inter-
         nationalist, 1 June 1981.

p. 105   'The world does not need any more white saviours . . .' Tweet by David Lammy (@David-
         Lammy) on 27 February 2019.

p. 106   'A few months after the Dooley row ignited . . .' David Lammy, 'Africa Deserves Better from
         Comic Relief', The Guardian, 24 March 2017.

p. 107   'The Ugandan government scrambled . . .' 'Visible Uganda', 14 April 2012, https://www.
         youtube.com/watch?v=fu34IsZb0qU.

p. 108   'out of a collective frustration at the rampant abuses . . .' 'Our Story', No White Saviors, https://
         nowhitesaviors.org/who-we-are/story/ [accessed 17 December 2021].

p. 109   'see the larger disasters behind it . . .' Cole, 'The White-Savior Industrial Complex'.

Part Four: The Story of Democracy in Seven Dictatorships

For further reading on this chapter, see Nic Cheeseman, Democracy in Africa: Successes, Failures, and the Struggle for Political Reform, Cambridge University Press, 2015; and Nic Cheeseman and Jonathan Fisher, Authoritarian Africa: Repression Resistance, and the Power of Ideas, Oxford University Press, 2021.

p. 121   'General Barre took power . . .' George James, 'Somalia's Overthrown Dictator, Mohammed
         Siad Barre, Is Dead', New York Times, 3 January 1995.

p. 122   'Somalia and Moscow would make it official . . .' Aryeh Yodfat, 'The Soviet Union and the
         Horn of Africa: Part Two of Three Parts', Northeast African Studies, 2(1), Michigan State
         University Press, 1980, pp. 31–57.

p. 122   'Somalia decided in 1977 . . .' Mesfin Wolde Mariam, 'The Background of the Ethio-Somalian Boundary Dispute', *Journal of Modern African Studies*, 2(2), Cambridge University Press, 1964, pp. 189–219.

p. 123   'Barre accepted Washington's offer . . .' Michael Getler, 'Somali Leader Voices Optimism After Talks', *Washington Post*, 12 March 1982.

p. 123   'General Barre was back and as strong as ever . . .' Don Oberdorfer, 'The Superpowers and the Ogaden War', *Washington Post*, 5 May 1978.

p. 127   'To achieve this wider goal . . .' A. J. Christopher, '"Divide and Rule": The Impress of British Separation Policies', *Area*, 20(3), 1988, pp. 233–40.

p. 128   'This invented system meant that the colonialists could . . .' Richard Morrock, 'Heritage of Strife: The Effects of Colonialist "Divide and Rule" Strategy upon the Colonized Peoples', *Science & Society*, 37(2), 1973, pp. 129–51.

p. 128   'To keep these disparate groups from working together . . .' 'Nigeria as a Folony', *Encyclopedia Britannica*, https://www.britannica.com/place/Nigeria/Nigeria-as-a-colony [accessed 11 October 2021].

p. 129   'What this hostile whirlwind of authority created . . .' Max Siollun, 'How First Coup Still Haunts Nigeria 50 Years Later', BBC News, 15 January 2016, https://www.bbc.co.uk/news/world-africa-35312370.

p. 137   'Already in the basement were twelve Black churchgoers . . .' 'Charleston church shooting: Suspected gunman arrested', BBC News, 18 June 2015, https://www.bbc.co.uk/news/world-us-canada-33190735.

p. 138   'In the days after the shooting . . .' John Ismay, 'Rhodesia's Dead – but White Supremacists Have Given It New Life Online', *New York Times*, 10 April 2018.

p. 138   'the green-and-white flag of a country. . .' Zach Beauchamp, 'The Racist Flags on Dylann Roof's Jacket, Explained', Vox, 18 June 2015, https://www.vox.com/2015/6/18/8806633/charleston-shooter-flags-dylann-roof.

p. 138   'British colonialists had come to accept the inevitability. . .' Kenneth Good, "Settler Colonialism in Rhodesia', *African Affairs*, 73(290), 1974, pp. 10–36.

p. 138   'Unlike much of West Africa, southern Africa . . .' Julie Bonello, 'The Development of Early Settler Identity in Southern Rhodesia: 1890–1914', *International Journal of African Historical Studies*, 43(2), 2010, pp. 341–67.

p. 139   'The British government demanded . . .' Rupert Cornwell, 'A Life in Focus: Ian Smith – Last White Leader of Rhodesia, now Zimbabwe, who Fought to Preserve Minority Rule', *The Independent*, 2 February 2019.

p. 139   'Smith was extremely committed to this white nationalist creed . . .' Dan van der Vat, 'Ian Smith', *The Guardian*, 21 November 2007; 'Ian Smith', *The Economist*, 22 November 2007.

p. 140   '*Within Britain itself, we were landed with a socialist government* . . .' Ian Smith, *The Great Betrayal*, John Blake Publishing, 1997.

p. 140   '*We think you should be able to tell the world* . . .' John Ismay, 'Rhodesia's Dead – But White Supremacists Have Given It New Life Online', *New York Times*, 10 April 2018.

p. 141   'Mugabe had been imprisoned in 1964 . . .' David Smith, 'How Mugabe Became Africa's Fallen Angel', *The Guardian*, 6 September 2019.

p. 142   'However, life in Zimbabwe would turn . . .' Samantha Power, 'How to Kill a Country', *The Atlantic*, December 2003.

p. 144   'He slipped into violent tyranny as his nation weakened . . .' Allen Cowell, 'Robert Mugabe, Strongman Who Cried, "Zimbabwe Is Mine", Dies at 95', *New York Times*, 6 September 2019.

p. 145   'South Africa remains painfully segregated . . .' Justice Malala, 'Why Are South African Cities Still So Segregated 25 Years after Apartheid?', *The Guardian*, 21 October 2019.

p. 145   'South Africa was declared . . .' Katy Scott, 'South Africa is the World's Most Unequal Society', CNN, 10 May 2019, https://edition.cnn.com/2019/05/07/africa/south-africa-elections-inequality-intl/index.html.

p. 145   'There even exists what is essentially a white-only town . . .' Dennis Webster, '"An Indictment of South Africa": Whites-Only Town Orania Is Booming', *The Guardian*, 24 October 2019.

p. 149   'Kagame was raised in a refugee camp . . .' Bert Ingelaere, 'Rwanda's Forever President', *New York Times*, 2 August 2017.

p. 149   'His family were among the thousands of ethnic Tutsis forced . . .' 'Rwanda genocide: 100 days of slaughter', BBC News, 4 April 2019, https://www.bbc.co.uk/news/world-africa-26875506.

p. 151   'few countries over the past twenty years . . .' Nicholas Kulish, 'Rwanda Reaches for New Economic Model', *New York Times*, 23 March 2014.

p. 151   'Under Kagame, the nation's economy . . .' Sam Desiere, 'The Evidence Mounts: Poverty, Inflation and Rwanda', *Review of African Political Economy*, 28 June 2017.

p. 151   'Rwanda is currently rated . . .' World Bank Group, *Doing Business 2020: Comparing Business Regulation in 190 Economies*, World Bank, 202o, https://openknowledge.worldbank.org/bitstream/handle/10986/32436/9781464814402.pdf.

p. 152   'Clinton called him one of the . . .' Arthur Assime, 'Clinton: Why I Admire Kagame', *New Times*, 26 September 2009.

p. 152   'There is a reason the *New York Times* . . .' Jeffrey Gettleman, 'The Global Elite's Favorite Strongman', *New York Times*, 8 September 2013.

p. 153   'Kagame's legacy is not completely clean . . .' Anjan Sundaram, 'Rwanda: The Darling Tyrant', *Politico*, March/April 2014.

p. 153   'Human rights organisations have spent years chronicling . . .' David Himbara, 'The African Leader Obama Shouldn't Invite', *Politico*, 3 August 2014.

p. 153   'The tentacles of what is alleged to be a sophisticated . . .' Antonio Cascais, '20 years under Rwanda's "benevolent dictator" Paul Kagame', DW, 17 April 2020, https://www.dw.com/en/20-years-under-rwandas-benevolent-dictator-paul-kagame/a-53159121.

p. 153   'One of his biggest critics, Paul Rusesabagina . . .' Abdi Latif Dahir, 'Rwanda Hints It Tricked "Hotel Rwanda" Dissident into Coming Home', *New York Times*, 6 September 2020.

p. 153   'The most important human rights problems . . .' United States Department of State, '2013 Country Reports on Human Rights Practices: Rwanda', 27 February 2014, https://www.refworld.org/docid/53284a805.html [accessed 16 December 2021].

p. 154   'I actually wish Rwanda did it . . .' Aislin Laing, 'Rwanda's President Paul Kagame "Wishes" He Had Ordered Death of Exiled Spy Chief', The Telegraph, 24 January 2014.

p. 154   'In power for two decades . . .' Chris McGreal, 'Is Kagame Africa's Lincoln or a Tyrant Exploiting Rwanda's Tragic History?', The Guardian, 19 May 2013.

p. 155   'In a lengthy New Yorker profile . . .' Philip Gourevitch, 'The Life After', New Yorker, 4 May 2009.

p. 169   'Obiang Nguema Mbasogo is the president of Equatorial Guinea . . .' Douglas Yates, 'Dynastic Rule in Equatorial Guinea', African Journal of Political Science and International Relations 11, 2017, pp. 339–59.

p. 170   'President Nguema has run Equatorial Guinea . . .' Simon Baynham, 'Equatorial Guinea: The Terror and the Coup', World Today, 36(2), 1980, pp. 65–71.

p. 171   'A cult of personality flourished under Macías . . .' Teodoro Obiang Nguema Mbasogo, Ma vie pour mon people, Editions Jaguar, 2002.

p. 172   'An official state radio station was made . . .' "Equatorial Guinea's "God"', BBC News, 26 July 2003, http://news.bbc.co.uk/1/hi/world/africa/3098007.stm.

p. 172   'By the end of 1980 the new government . . .' Douglas Yates, 'Dynastic Rule in Equatorial Guinea'.

p. 173   'Equatorial Guinea struck oil . . .' 'Oil Production in Africa as of 2020, by Country', Statista, https://www.statista.com/statistics/1178514/main-oil-producing-countries-in-africa/.

p. 173   'The government makes little pretence . . .' Sarah Saadoun, 'The Anniversary That Shouldn't Be: 40 Years of President Obiang in Equatorial Guinea', Human Rights Watch, 3 August 2019,https://www.hrw.org/news/2019/08/03/anniversary-shouldnt-be-40-years-president-obiang-equatorial-guinea.

p. 173   'It is called a "state secret" . . .' Adam Withnall, 'The Brutal Central African Dictator Whose Playboy Son Faces French Corruption Trial', The Independent, 12 September 2016.

p. 173   'The US-based Riggs Bank . . .' Anthony Daniels, 'If You Think This One's Bad You Should Have Seen His Uncle', The Telegraph, 29 August 2004.

p. 174   'Teodorin was never elected vice president . . .' Julie Zeveloff, 'Meet the Playboy Son of an African Dictator, Who Just Got in Trouble with the Justice Department', Business Insider, 21 October 2011, https://www.businessinsider.com/teodoro-nguema-obiang-mangue-equatorial-guinea-playboy-life-2011-10.

p. 174   'the French government launched an investigation . . .' Angelique Chrisafais, 'Son of Equatorial Guinea's President Is Convicted of Corruption in France', The Guardian, 27 October 2017.

p. 174   'Teodorin's spending in 2017 . . .' Jason Burke, 'French Trial Reveals Vast Wealth of Equatorial Guinean President's Son', The Guardian, 2 January 2017.

p. 174   'He was charged with money laundering . . .' Alonso Soto, 'New Cabinet Paves Way for Successor to World's Longest-Serving President', Bloomberg, 20 August 2020, https://www.bloomberg.com/news/articles/2020-08-20/new-cabinet-paves-way-for-successor-to-longest-serving-president.

p. 177   "'What did I do to you?" is a remarkable question . . .' Kareem Fahim, Anthony Shadid and Rick Gladstone, 'Violent End to an Era as Qaddafi Dies in Libya', *New York Times*, 21 October 2011.

p. 177   'The only excuse for Muammar Gaddafi . . .' Peter Beaumont and Chris Stephen, 'Gaddafi's Last Words as He Begged for Mercy: "What Did I Do to You?"', *The Guardian*, 23 October 2011.

p. 178   'The fundamental essence of Gaddafi's . . .' Neil MacFarquhar, 'An Erratic Leader, Brutal and Defiant to the End', *New York Times*, 21 October 2011.

p. 178   'So confident of his all-mighty glory . . .' 'The Times Obituary: Muammar Gaddafi', *The Times*, 20 October 2011.

p. 178   'The disjointedness of his chaos . . .' Max Fisher, 'How Gaddafi Fooled Libya and the World', *The Atlantic*, 20 October 2011.

p. 178   'Political parties were, of course, banned . . .' Simon Tisdall, 'Gaddafi: A Vicious, Sinister Despot Driven Out on Tidal Wave of Hatred', *The Guardian*, 23 August 2011.

p. 179   'His eccentricities became part of his lore . . .' Tarik Kafal, 'Gaddafi's Quixotic and Brutal Rule', BBC News, 20 October 2011, https://www.bbc.co.uk/news/world-africa-12532929.

p. 179   'Odd peculiarities do not keep you in power . . .' Reuters Staff, 'Gaddafi Rule Marked by Abuses, Rights Groups Say', Reuters, 22 February 2011, https://www.reuters.com/article/us-libya-protest-abuses-idUSTRE71L1NH20110222.

p. 181   'Gaddafi chose not to go quietly into the night . . .' Kim Sengupta, 'A Fiery Message from Gaddafi: My Enemies Deserve to Die', *The Independent*, 2 September 2011.

p. 181   'He promised to do this "house by house" . . .' Jon Lee Anderson, 'King of Kings', *New Yorker*, 31 October 2011.

p. 182   '*Sanctions have been in place* . . .' 'Zimbabwe sanctions should end to boost post-Mugabe economy, UN experts urge', ACNUDH, https://www.ohchr.org/SP/NewsEvents/Pages/DisplayNews.aspx?NewsID=22451&LangID=E [accessed 17 December 2021].

p. 182   '*Last year, President Trump extended painful economic sanctions* . . .' Tweet by Emmerson Mnangagwa (@edmnangagwa) on 7 January 2021.

p. 183   '*There is nothing patriotic* . . .' Tweet by Marco Rubio (@marcorubio) on 6 January 2021.

Part Five: There Is No Such Thing as an African Accent and Binyavanga Wainaina Is Still Right

p. 195   'Wainaina addressed one of his open letters . . .' Binyavanga Wainaina, 'An Open Letter to Madonna', *The Guardian*, 12 April 2013.

p. 196   '*Granted, Madonna has adopted two children* . . .' Elliot Ross, 'Madonna earns the wrath of Joyce Banda – a full statement', Guardian Africa network, 11 April 2013, https://www.theguardian.com/world/2013/apr/11/malawi-madonna.

p. 196   'most celebrated work started as an angry email . . .' Matt Weiland, in 'In Memoriam: Binyavanga Wainaina', Literary Hub, 24 May 2019, https://lithub.com/in-memoriam-binyavanga-wainaina/.

p. 196   'It wasn't the grimness that got to me . . .' Binyavanga Wainaina, 'How to Write About Africa II', *Bidoun*, 21, Summer 2010.

p. 197   'Always use the word "Africa" or "Darkness" . . .' Binyavanga Wainaina, 'How to Write About Africa', *Granta*, 92, 2 May 2019.

p. 201   'The portrayal of Africa and Africans in the film . . .' Richard Brody, 'Adam Sandler's "Blended" Is a Failure for the Ages', *New Yorker*, 23 May 2014; A. O. Scott, 'When Single Parents Collide on a Safari', *New York Times*, 22 May 2014.

p. 206   'described in her 2009 TED talk . . .' Chimamanda Ngozi Adichie, 'The Danger of a Single Story', TED, 7 October 2009, https://youtu.be/D9Ihs241zeg.

p. 207   'Chadwick Boseman had to fight . . .' Kirsten Acuna and Anjelica Oswald, 'Marvel Was Originally Unsure of Black Panther Having an African Accent – but Chadwick Boseman Pushed Back', Insider, 28 August 2020, https://www.insider.com/black-panther-chadwick-boseman-marvel-accents-2018-8.

p. 209   'Wakanda is no more or less imaginary . . .' Jelani Cobb, '"Black Panther" and the Invention of "Africa"', *New Yorker*, 18 February 2018.

p. 210   'It felt to me like a deal-breaker . . .' Karen Attiah, 'Opinion: Why Chadwick Boseman's Fight for African Accents in "Black Panther" Was So Important', *Washington Post*, 1 September 2020.

p. 210   'The language of Wakanda . . .' John Eligon, 'Wakanda Is a Fake Country, but the African Language in "Black Panther" Is Real', *New York Times*, 16 February 2018.

p. 214   'a broad space that African-American writer . . .' Adam Serwer, 'The Tragedy of Erik Killmonger', *The Atlantic*, 21 February 2018.

p. 216   'From Paul Cuffee's attempts in 1811 . . .' Carvell Wallace, 'Why Black Panther is a defining moment for Black America', *New York Times*, 12 February 2018.

p. 217   'You know, you got to have the race conversation . . .' Ibid.

p. 219   'It's worth remembering that Wakanda . . .' David Jesudason, 'Is Hollywood ready to stop stereotyping Africa?', BBC Culture, 4 March 2021, https://www.bbc.com/culture/article/20210304-is-hollywood-ready-to-stop-stereotyping-africa.

p. 220   'In *Black Is King*, Beyoncé's visual album . . .' Angelique Jackson and Audrey Cleo Yap, 'How Beyoncé's "Black Is King" Takes Her Embrace of Blackness to a New Level', *Variety*, 4 August 2020.

Part Six: The Case of the Stolen Artefacts

p. 229   'They told a spectacular lie . . .' Dan Hicks, *The Brutish Museums: The Benin Bronzes, Colonial Violence and Cultural Restitution*, Pluto Press, 2020.

p. 229   'giant walls snaked through the Kingdom of Benin . . .' Mawuna Koutonin, 'Benin City, the Mighty Medieval Capital Now Lost without Trace', *The Guardian*, 18 March 2016.

p. 229   'described by the *Guinness Book of Records* . . .' *Guinness Book of Records 1974*, Guinness World Records, 1974.

p. 229 'For centuries, the Kingdom of Benin . . .' National Geographic Society, 'The Kingdom of Benin', National Geographic Resource Library, https://www.nationalgeographic.org/encyclopedia/kingdom-benin/ [accessed 11 October 2021].

p. 229 'there was 1691, and the Portuguese sea captain . . .' Kylie Kiunguyu, 'African Marvels: The Walls of Benin', This Is Africa, 13 March 2019, https://thisisafrica.me/politics-and-society/african-marvels-the-walls-of-benin/.

p. 229 'Great Benin, where the king resides . . .' Kuljit Chuhan, 'The Empire of Benin and Its Cultural Heritage', Revealing Histories, http://revealinghistories.org.uk/colonialism-and-the-expansion-of-empires/articles/the-empire-of-benin-and-its-cultural-heritage.html.

p. 230 'The walls split the city into hundreds of neighbourhoods . . .' Jonathan Jones, 'Spoils of War', The Guardian, 11 September 2003.

p. 230 'The city and its surrounding villages . . .' 'Benin's African fractals', Edo Connect, https://www.edoconnect.com/post/2019/07/09/benins-african-fractals [accessed 1 October 2021].

p. 230 'Many of the court's daily operations were formalised . . .' Benjamin Sutton, 'Long in Exile, the Looted Benin Bronzes Tell the Story of a Mighty African Kingdom', Artsy, 21 February 2019, https://www.artsy.net/article/artsy-editorial-long-exile-looted-benin-bronzes-story-mighty-african-kingdom.

p. 231 'artisans [who] have their places carefully allocated . . .' Lourenço Pinto, quoted in A.F.C. Ryder, Benin and the Europeans (1485–1897), Humanities Press, 1970.

p. 231 'The Kingdom of Benin had another trick . . .' Toyin Falola, 'The Real Wakanda – Inside the Lost City of Benin', History Answers, 9 March 2019, https://www.historyanswers.co.uk/people-politics/the-real-wakanda-inside-the-lost-city-of-benin/.

p. 231 'These priceless artefacts, known collectively . . .' Alex Marshall, 'This Art Was Looted 123 Years Ago. Will It Ever Be Returned?', New York Times, 23 January 2020.

p. 232 'James Phillips died in January 1897 . . .' Alexander Herman, 'Britain's Pillaging of the Benin Bronzes Begs for a Reasonable Resolution', Art News, 21 December 2018, https://www.theartnewspaper.com/2018/12/21/britains-pillaging-of-the-benin-bronzes-begs-for-a-reasonable-resolution.

p. 233 'The King of Benin has continued to do everything . . .' James Phillips, quoted in Thomas Uwadiale Obinyan, 'The Annexation of Benin', Journal of Black Studies, 19:1, 1988, pp. 29–40.

p. 235 'A diary entry by a British soldier . . .' Hicks, The Brutish Museums.

p. 235 'After dispersing the natives . . .' Felix N. Roth, 'A Diary of a Surgeon with the Benin Punitive Expedition', Journal of the Manchester Geographical Society, 14, 1898, pp. 208–21.

p. 235 'All the stuff of any value found in the King's palace . . .' Alex Marshall, 'This Art Was Looted 123 Years Ago: Will It Ever Be Returned?', New York Times, 29 October 2021.

p. 236 'Their signature move was to slice . . .' Mike Dash, 'Dahomey's women warriors', Smithsonian Magazine, 23 September 2011.

p. 236 'At their peak, there were six thousand . . .' Michael Bamidele, 'The Story of the Fearless Women Warriors of Dahomey', The Guardian [Nigeria], 14 June 2020.

p. 236 'A priest in 1861 claimed to have witnessed . . .' Dash, 'Dahomey's women warriors'.

p. 237   'Dahomey was extremely proud of its warriors ...' Fleur Macdonald, 'The Legend of Benin's Fearless Female Warriors', BBC Travel, 27 August 2018, https://www.bbc.com/travel/article/20180826-the-legend-of-benins-fearless-female-warriors.

p. 239   'The target of the military operation was Maqdala', Richard Pankhurst, 'The Napier Expedition and the Loot from Maqdala', *Présence Africaine*, 133/134, 1985, pp. 233–40.

p. 239   'In an effort to maintain his stronghold ...' Richard Pankhurst, 'Maqdala and Its Loot: A Brief History', Link Ethiopia, https://www.linkethiopia.org/article/maqdala-and-its-loot-a-brief-history/.

p. 240   'Tewodros was cornered, helpless and dazed ...' V&A's Ethiopian Treasures: A Crown, a Wedding Dress and Other Loot', BBC News, 4 April 2018, https://www.bbc.co.uk/news/world-africa-43642265.

p. 240   'Desperate and increasingly isolated, the emperor ...' Richard Pankhurst, 'Maqdala and Its Loot'.

p. 240   'Throughout his reign, Emperor Tewodros II ...' Daniel Trilling, 'Britain is Hoarding a Treasure Nobody Is Allowed to See', *The Atlantic*, 9 July 2019.

p. 241   'One eyewitness account noted that Tewodros's corpse ...' Richard Pankhurst, 'The Napier Expedition and the Loot from Maqdala'.

p. 241   '*The easterly wind gradually grew stronger ...*' Henry Morten Stanley, *Coomasse and Magdala: The Story of Two British Campaigns in Africa*, Sampson Low, Marston, Low & Searle, 1874.

p. 242   '*Any Herero found inside the German frontier ...*' David Olusoga, 'Germany Comes to Terms with Its Forgotten Namibian Death Camps', *The Guardian*, 15 January 2017.

p. 242   'Germany's colonial presence in Africa ...' Ewelina Ochab, 'The Herero-Nama Genocide: The Story of a Recognized Crime, Apologies Issued and Silence Ever Since', *Forbes*, 24 May 2018.

p. 243   '*My intimate knowledge of many central ...*' Jan-Bart Gewald, 'The Great General of the Kaiser', *Botswana Notes and Records*, 26, 1994, pp. 67–76.

p. 243   '*I do not concur with those fanatics ...*' Quoted in Horst Drechsler, *Let Us Die Fighting*, Zed Press, 1980.

p. 243   'Trotha disregarded this touching protest ...' Norimitsu Onishi and Melissa Eddy, 'A Forgotten Genocide: What Germany Did in Namibia, and What It's Saying Now', *New York Times*, 28 May 2021.

p. 244   'Herero women were required to collect ...' Tim Whewell, 'Germany and Namibia: What's the Right Price to Pay for Genocide?', BBC News, 1 April 2021, https://www.bbc.co.uk/news/stories-56583994.

p. 244   '*As its last option ...*' 'The search in Germany for the lost skull of Tanzania's Mangi Meli', BBC News, 13 November 2018, https://www.bbc.co.uk/news/world-africa-45916150.

p. 244   '*Any occasion to rescue a large number of skulls ...*' Ibid.

p. 245   '*The town burnt furiously ...*' Kwame Opoku, 'When Will Britain Return Looted Ghanaian Artefacts? A History of British Looting of More than 100 Objects', AfricAvenir, https://www.africavenir.org/nc/news-details/article/kwame-opoku-when-will-britain-return-looted-ghanaian-artefacts-a-history-of-british-looting-of-mor.html [accessed 1 October 2021].

p. 246   'General Wolseley, declared British troops ...' Ibid.

p. 246   'The first room visited was one which . . .' Ibid.

p. 247   'First, the British left the Asante with a bill . . .' Ibid.

p. 257   'Let's start where there is broad agreement . . .' Felwine Sarr and Bénédicte Savoy, The Restitution of African Cultural Heritage. Toward a New Relational Ethics, trans. Drew S. Burk,
November 2018, http://restitutionreport2018.com/sarr_savoy_en.pdf.

p. 258   'The declaration opens by condemning theft . . .' 'DOCUMENT: Declaration on the
Importance and Value of Universal Museums', in Ivan Karp et al. (eds), Museum Frictions:
Public Cultures/Global Transformations, Duke University Press, 2006, pp. 247–49.

p. 258   'In a speech to Parliament . . .''Abyssinian War – Prize – The Abana's Crown and Chalice',
Hansard, 207, 30 June 1871, https://hansard.parliament.uk/Commons/1871-06-30/
debates/0e763636-72ee-4a5c-bb3f-f6b19e10922f/AbyssinianWar%E2%80%94Prize%
E2%80%94TheAbanaSCrownAndChalice [accessed 1 October 2021].

p. 259   'with the crown described as a . . .' Tristram Hunt, 'Maqdala 1868' [blog], 4 April 2018,
https://www.vam.ac.uk/blog/museum-life/maqdala-1868.

p. 261   'a fundamental part of the existential fabric . . .''Culture Minister Visits British Museums on
Debut Visit to the UK', Embassy of the Federal Democratic Republic of Ethiopia, London,
29 March 2019, https://www.ethioembassy.org.uk/culture-minister-visits-british-museums-on-
debut-visit-to-the-uk/.

p. 261   'Museums know so little about what they hold . . .' Hicks, The Brutish Museums.

p. 262   'There remains something essentially valuable . . .' Tristram Hunt, 'Should Museums Return
Their Colonial Artefacts?', The Guardian, 29 June 2019.

p. 267   'Thomas Dermine, declared that any items . . .' Thomas Dermine, 'As a Belgian Politician, I
Feel a Responsibility to Restitute Stolen Artifacts to the Congo. Here's Why My Fellow
Citizens Should, Too', Artnet, 23 July 2021, https://news.artnet.com/opinion/belgium-
restitution-1991446.

p. 268   'The DRC is used to the slow-trickle return . . .' Ciku Kimera, 'The Battle to Get Europe to
Return Thousands of Africa's Stolen Artifacts Is Getting Complicated', Quartz Africa, 29
November 2019, https://qz.com/africa/1758619/europes-museums-are-fighting-to-keep-
africas-stolen-artifacts/.

p. 269   'We are aligned with the spirit and soul . . .''A Message from Director Hartwig Fischer', British
Museum [blog], 5 June 2021, https://blog.britishmuseum.org/a-message-from-director-
hartwig-fischer/.

p. 271   'New York's Metropolitan Museum of Art . . .' Daniel A. Gross, 'The Troubling Origins of
the Skeletons in a New York Museum', New Yorker, 24 January 2018.

p. 271   'France, meanwhile, has chosen to embark . . .' Kate Brown, 'In a Groundbreaking Report,
Experts Advise French President Macron to Begin the "Restitution" of Looted African Art',
Artnet, 20 November 2018, https://news.artnet.com/art-world/french-restitution-policy-
macron-1399429.

p. 271   'In 2017, President Emmanuel Macron addressed . . .' Bénédicte Savoy, 'The Restitution
Revolution Begins', Art News, 16 February 2018, https://www.theartnewspaper.
com/2018/02/16/the-restitution-revolution-begins.

p. 272   'Savoy and Sarr concluded . . .' Sarr and Savoy, *The Restitution of African Cultural Heritage. Toward a New Relational Ethics.*

p. 273   'Prior to its release, Stéphane Martin . . .' Alex Greenberger, 'Outgoing Leader of Paris's Musée du Quai Branly: Report Urging Repatriation of African Objects Is "Self-Flagellation"', ArtNews, 2 January 2020, https://www.artnews.com/art-news/news/stephane-martin-musee-quai-branly-repatriation-1202674176/.

p. 274   'By now, the report had called for museums . . .' Farah Nayeri, 'France Vowed to Return Looted Treasures. But Few Are Heading Back', *New York Times*, 22 November 2019.

p. 274   'The government seemed to be shifting back . . .' Vincent Noce, 'France retreats from report recommending automatic restitutions of looted African artefacts', Art News, 5 July 2019, https://www.theartnewspaper.com/2019/07/05/france-retreats-from-report-recommending-automatic-restitutions-of-looted-african-artefacts.

p. 275   '*The question of restitution is being increasingly debated . . .*' Nayeri, 'France Vowed to Return Looted Treasures'.

p. 276   'After the BLM protests, Belgium took steps . . .' Steve Wembi, 'Belgium Toppled Statues of Its Racist Former King. Then What?', VICE, 25 May 2021, https://www.vice.com/en/article/v7evpm/belgium-toppled-statues-of-its-racist-former-king-then-what.

p. 277   'The line stretched out the door . . .' Jason Farago, 'Artwork Taken from Africa, Returning to a Home Transformed', *New York Times*, 3 January 2019.

p. 277   'Mwazulu Diyabanza has been nicknamed . . .' Leah Feiger, 'Colonizers Stole Africa's Art; This Man Is Taking It Back', VICE, 22 September 2020, https://www.vice.com/en/article/y3z77y/a-real-life-killmonger-is-trying-to-decolonize-european-museums.

p. 279   'Regardless, it has taken an immense demonstration . . .' Tarisai Ngangura, 'The Colonized World Wants Its Artifacts Back', VICE, 7 December 2020, https://www.vice.com/en/article/5dpd9x/the-colonized-world-wants-its-artifacts-back-from-museums-v27n4.

p. 279   'the organisation Digital Benin is working . . .' Digital Benin, https://digital-benin.org/ [accessed 11 January 2022].

p. 280   '*Part of what happened to Africa . . .*' Ngangura, 'The Colonized World Wants Its Artifacts Back'.

Part Seven: Jollof Wars: A Love Story

p. 293   'Jollof rice, you could say . . .' Ozoz Sokoh, 'The Wide World of Jollof Rice', Food & Wine, 10 May 2021, https://www.foodandwine.com/grains/rice/the-wide-world-of-jollof-rice.

p. 294   'Without needing to seek too hard . . .' Jiji Ugboma, 'The Jollof Wars', Eater, 6 August 2020, https://www.eater.com/21274028/jollof-wars-social-media-rivalry-ghana-nigeria-styles-history-west-africa.

p. 296   'Enslaved Africans carried within themselves . . .' Jessica Harris, *High on the Hog: A Culinary Journey from Africa to America*, Bloomsbury, 2011.

p. 296   'The Negro is a born cook . . .' Michael Twitty, 'Ole Missus vs. Mammy: Who Owns Southern
Food?', VICE, 29 June 2016, https://www.vice.com/en/article/xym7wj/ole-missus-vs-mammy-
who-owns-southern-food.

p. 296   'Elizabeth Swanson, the wife of a Virginia governor . . .' Patricia Mitchell, 'The African
Influence on Southern Cuisine', Food History, https://www.foodhistory.com/foodnotes/
leftovers/african/infl/01/ [accessed 23 November 2021].

p. 296   'From Africa came the staples . . .' Osayi Endolyn, 'Fried Chicken Is Common Ground',
Eater, 3 October 2018, https://www.eater.com/2018/10/3/17926424/fried-chicken-is-
common-ground.

p. 296   'From Africa came rice, including red rice dishes . . .' Jocelyne Sambira, 'Slave Trade: How
African Foods Influenced Modern American Cuisine', UN Africa Renewal, https://www.
un.org/africarenewal/web-features/slave-trade-how-african-foods-influenced-mod-
ern-american-cuisine [accessed 23 November 2021].

p. 297   'which the South served with a side of economic revolution . . .' Dora Mekouar,
'How Enslaved Africans Influenced American Diet', VOA News, 15 March 2019, https://www.
voanews.com/a/how-enslaved-africans-helped-invent-american-cuisine-/4814817.html.

p. 297   'Those from the rice crucible . . .' Jessica Harris, High on the Hog.

p. 297   'Away from the direct heat, the involuntary labour . . .' Kelley Fanto Deetz, 'How Enslaved
Chefs Helped Shape American Cuisine', Smithsonian Magazine, 20 July 2018.

Part Eight: What's Next?

p. 310   'Today, activists are organising to shift governments . . .' Aanu Adeoye, '2020 Was the Year
Young People Across Africa Demanded Change', VICE, 29 December 2020, https://www.
vice.com/en/article/88am3b/2020-was-the-year-young-people-across-africa-
demanded-change.

p. 313   'The peaceful movement started . . .' Tolu Olasoji and Leah Feiger, 'Nigeria Is Fighting Its
Own Battle Against Police Brutality', VICE, 15 October 2020, https://www.vice.com/en/
article/7k9z9b/nigeria-is-fighting-its-own-battle-against-police-brutality.

p. 313   'an Amnesty International report documented . . .' 'Nigeria: Time to end impunity: Torture
and other human rights violations by special anti-robbery squad (SARS)', Amnesty International, 26 June 2020, https://www.amnesty.org/en/documents/afr44/9505/2020/en/
[accessed 23 November 2021].

p. 314   'Initially intended as an undercover operation . . .' Valentine Iwenwanne, 'Protesters in
Nigeria Demand a Proper End to Police Unit That Tortures Detainees', VICE, 12 October
2020, https://www.vice.com/en/article/4ayk4d/sars-police-unit-nigeria-dissolve-torture.

p. 314   'A line was finally drawn in October 2020 . . .' '"SARS killing in Ughelli": Nigeria Police
SARS kill boy inside Ughelli? See wetin make e boil for police brutality', BBC Pidgin, 4
October 2020, https://www.bbc.com/pidgin/tori-54396330.

p. 316   'Fortunately for the future of Africa's largest country . . .' Vincent Desmond, How Women Powered Nigeria's #ENDSARS Movement, *Elle*, 18 November 2020.

p. 316   *'Going through social media like everyone else . . .'* The Feminist Coalition, 'In Our Own Words: The Feminist Coalition', 18 December 2020, https://feministcoalition.medium.com/in-our-own-words-the-feminist-coalition-61bc658446dd.

p. 317   'Within hours, the Lagos-based group . . .' Ruth Maclean, 'In Nigeria, "Feminist" Was a Common Insult. Then Came the Feminist Coalition', *New York Times*, 12 March 2021.

p. 319   'Every Friday for a year they came out . . .' 'The Youth-Led Protests That Forced Algeria's President to Not Run Again', VICE, 13 March 2019, https://youtu.be/tacTOgBEN70.

p. 319   'The first leader to find his way to the ground . . .' Adam Nossiter, 'It's Time to Break the Chains. Algerians Seek a Revolution', *New York Times*, 24 March 2019.

p. 320   'Every Friday the Hirak movement continued . . .' Adam Nossiter, 'Algeria Cancels Presidential Election, Setting Up New Impasse', *New York Times*, 2 June 2019.

p. 320   'The protests forced two planned elections . . .' Ahmed Rouba, 'Algeria Election: Why Voters Were Urged to Boycott Parliamentary Poll', BBC News, 12 June 2021, https://www.bbc.co.uk/news/world-africa-57439768.

p. 320   'the lowest turnout in decades . . .' 'Turnout at Lowest in 20 Years in Divisive Algerian Parliamentary Elections', France 24, 13 June 2021, https://www.france24.com/en/africa/20210613-turnout-at-lowest-in-20-years-as-algeria-votes-in-parliamentary-elections.

p. 321   'In the months that followed, the government exploited . . .' 'Algeria to Ban Unauthorised Protests in Move Seen as Targeting Popular Hirak Movement', France 24, 10 May 2021, https://www.france24.com/en/africa/20210510-algeria-to-ban-unauthorised-protests-in-move-seen-as-targeting-popular-hirak-movement.

p. 321   'It was a Monday and COVID-19 vaccines . . .' Eric Goldstein, 'Algeria's Hirak Protest Movement Marks Second Anniversary', Human Rights Watch, 23 February 2021, https://www.hrw.org/news/2021/02/23/algerias-hirak-protest-movement-marks-second-anniversary.

p. 322   'In October 2020, the body of Shannon Wasserfall . . .' Eoin McSweeney, 'Anti-Femicide Protesters Call for a State of Emergency in Namibia', CNN, 19 October 2020, https://edition.cnn.com/2020/10/19/africa/namibia-gender-based-violence-protests-intl/index.html.

p. 322   'Her death was no aberration . . .' Lisa Ossenbirk, 'Why Are Anti-Femicide Protesters Taking to Namibia's Streets?', Al Jazeera, 13 October 2020, https://www.aljazeera.com/news/2020/10/13/why-are-anti-femicide-protesters-demonstrating-in-namibia.

p. 322   'An average of two hundred incidents of domestic violence . . .' Esther Ogola, 'Namibia SGBV: Shannon Wasserfal's death sparks protests against femicide', BBC News, 19 January 2021, https://www.bbc.co.uk/news/av/world-africa-55709472.

p. 323   'thousands of predominantly young women marched . . .' 'Dozens Arrested in Namibia's Anti-Femicide Protests, TRT, 10 October 2020, https://www.trtworld.com/africa/dozens-arrested-in-namibia-s-anti-femicide-protests-40467.

p. 323   'Following that, a step-by-step, comprehensive to-do list . . .' Henning Melber, "#ShutItAll-Down in Namibia – the Fight against Gender-Based violence', The Conversation, 29 October 2020, https://theconversation.com/shutitalldown-in-namibia-the-fight-against-gender-based-violence-148809.

p. 323   'Of the police, the protesters called for the retraining . . .' Nobantu Shabangu, '#ShutIt-Down: Ongoing Namibian Protests Call for End to Gender-Based Violence', Okay Africa, 12October2020,https://www.okayafrica.com/namibia-shutitdown-protests-fight-against-gender-based-violence/.

p. 324   'The government responded to this vast constructive effort . . .' Ndapewoshali Shapwanale, 'Namibia Weighs Demands for Rape Crackdown after Street Protests', Reuters, 13 October 2020, https://www.reuters.com/article/us-namibia-women-protests-trfn-idUSKBN 26Y0ZY.

p. 325   'raised in the slums of Kampala . . .' 'Bobi Wine: Uganda's "ghetto president"', BBC News, 22 February 2021, https://www.bbc.co.uk/news/world-africa-55572903.

p. 325   'As fame descended, everything for Wine changed . . .' David Peisner, 'Uganda's "Ghetto President": How Bobi Wine Went from Dancehall Grooves to Revolutionary Politics', Rolling Stone, 25 April 2020.

p. 326   'Sense was eventually slapped into Wine . . .' David Pilling, 'Uganda's Bobi Wine embodies the rise of African youth', Financial Times, 28 August 2018.

p. 326   'Robert Kyagulanyi Ssentamu chose the stage name Bobi Wine . . .' Abdi Dahir, '"Everything Is Worth Freedom": Uganda's Opposition Leader Faces the Future', New York Times, 11 April 2021.

p. 326   'Almost a decade later, now thirty-four . . .' Patience Akumu, 'Uganda's Young Voters Are Hungry for Change – and for Bobi Wine', The Guardian, 13 December 2020.

p. 327   'His growing popularity, his willingness . . .' Abdi Dahir Latif, 'Jailed, Exiled and Silenced: Smothering East Africa's Political Opposition', New York Times, 27 November 2020.

p. 327   'Museveni rose to power after leading an army insurgency . . .' Sally Hayden, 'Young Ugandans Want Change from the Only President They've Ever Known', VICE, 15 January 2021, https://www.vice.com/en/article/dy8w9q/young-ugandans-want-change-from-the-only-president-theyve-ever-known.

p. 329   'What specific steps will you take . . .' Julia Steers, 'Young Ugandans Want Change from the Only President They've Ever Known' [video], VICE, https://youtu.be/i_sxUDxmPOU.

p. 330   'Magufuli – widely believed to have died from COVID-19 . . .' Julia Steers, Martin Mwaura and Stacey Naggier, 'Inside the Country That Was Ruled by COVID-Deniers', VICE, 28 April 2021, https://www.vice.com/en/article/akgdnj/tanzania-covid-john-magufuli.

p. 330   'Under his orders, the Tanzanian government stopped . . .' Sammy Awami, 'Tanzania President Raises Doubts over COVID Vaccines', Al Jazeera, 27 January 2021, https://www.aljazeera.com/news/2021/1/27/tanzania-president-denounces-covid-vaccines.

p. 330   'Tundu Lissu, the last serious opposition leader . . .' Samuel Gebre, 'Tanzania's Opposition Leader was Shot 16 Times. Now He's Challenging the President', VICE, 15 October 2020,

https://www.vice.com/en/article/y3zaag/tundu-lissu-tanzania-election-opposition-leader.

p. 331   'In her first official address as president . . .' Chrispin Mwakideu, 'Tanzania: President Samia Suluhu Hassan's 100 Days in Office', DW, 26 June 2021, https://www.dw.com/en/tanzania-president-samia-suluhu-hassans-100-days-in-office/a-58015991.

p. 331   'Her reforms extended beyond COVID-19 . . .' Priya Sippy, 'Tanzania's new leader is making up for lost time in the fight against Covid', Quartz Africa, 29 June 2021, https://qz.com/africa/2006013/tanzania-president-samia-hassan-issues-new-covid-19-restrictions/.

p. 331   'the president declared that the press . . .' Apolinari Tairo, 'President Samia Commits to Supporting Media in Tanzania', East African, 29 June 2021.

p. 331   'Suluhu Hassan also embarked on a tour . . .''100 Days of Samia: Her Moves Usher in New Era of Bipartisan Politics, Growth', East African, 28 June 2021.

p. 332   'Still, over the past decade, the continent has enjoyed . . .' Inter-Parliamentary Union, 'Women in Politics: 2021', United Nations, 2021, https://www.ipu.org/women-in-politics-2021; Nayé Bathily, 'Africa Takes Historic Lead in Female Parliamentary Speakers', World Bank, 13 February 2020, https://blogs.worldbank.org/nasikiliza/africa-takes-historic-lead-female-parliamentary-speakers.

p. 333   'Rwanda leads the world . . .' Zipporah Musau, 'African Women in Politics: Miles to Go before Parity Is Achieved', UN Africa Renewal, 8 April 2019, https://www.un.org/africarenewal/magazine/april-2019-july-2019/african-women-politics-miles-go-parity-achieved.

p. 333   'Botswana's victories have been so pronounced . . .' Charles Manga Fombad, 'The Enhancement of Good Governance in Botswana: A Critical Assessment of the Ombudsman Act, 1995', Journal of Southern African Studies, 27(1), 2001, pp. 57–77.

p. 334   'Botswana is routinely nicknamed the African Miracle . . .' 'The African Exception', The Economist, 28 March 2002.

p. 334   'A recent feature in Der Spiegel . . .''Gescheiter Staat', Der Spiegel, 2 January 2020.

p. 334   'It's the continent's longest continuous democracy . . .' Dipa Patel, 'Botswana – An African Economic Miracle', LSE, 28 January 2020, https://blogs.lse.ac.uk/internationaldevelopment/2020/01/28/botswana-an-african-economic-miracle/.

p. 334   'Nature and nurture have co-parented Botswana . . .' Ellen Hillbom, 'Diamonds or Development? A Structural Assessment of Botswana's Forty Years of Success', Journal of Modern African Studies, 46(2), 2008, pp. 191–214.

p. 334   'Botswana secured its independence . . .' Alexander McCall Smith, 'Beguiled by Botswana', New York Times, 16 November 2003.

p. 336   'You do not have to strain hard . . .' Ngozi Okonjo-Iweala, 'Africa Can Play a Leading Role in the Fight against Climate Change', Brookings Institution, https://www.brookings.edu/research/africa-can-play-a-leading-role-in-the-fight-against-climate-change/#footnote-8.

p. 336   'contributes around 3 per cent ...' Robin McKie, 'Global Heating to Inflict More Droughts on Africa as well as Floods', *The Guardian*, 14 June 2019.

p. 336   'on course to suffer the most from its adverse effects ...' C. M. Wainwright et al., 'Extreme Rainfall in East Africa, October 2019–January 2020 and Context under Future Climate Change', *Weather*, 76, 2021, pp. 26–31.

p. 336   'The impact of rising temperatures is hitting hard ...' 'How Africa Will Be Affected by Climate Change', BBC News, 15 December 2019, https://www.bbc.co.uk/news/world-africa-50726701.

p. 336   'Mozambique, for example, was struck in 2019 by Cyclone Idai ...' Landry Nintereste, 'Cyclone Idai Shows the Deadly Reality of Climate Change in Africa', *The Guardian*, 21 March 2019.

p. 336   'The storm killed more than a thousand ...' Neha Wadekar, 'The Cyclones Destroyed Everything. Climate Change Will Likely Make Things Worse', VICE, 21 July 2021, https://www.vice.com/en/article/dyv5zj/the-cyclones-destroyed-everything-climate-change-will-likely-make-things-worse.

p. 337   'Just six weeks later ...' Ed Ram, '"You're Killing Us": Mozambique's Deadly Cyclones Are Only Getting Worse', VICE, 19 March 2020, https://www.vice.com/en/article/v74qxa/mozambique-deadly-cyclone-idai-climate-change.

p. 337   '*Warming of the surface ocean from anthropogenic* ...' 'Climate change is probably increasing the intensity of tropical cyclones', ScienceBrief, 26 March 2021, https://news.sciencebrief.org/cyclones-mar2021/.

p. 338   'Morocco is home to the world's largest solar complex ...' Climate Investment Fund, 'Solar Plant the Size of San Francisco Powers Morocco's Sunlit Ambitions', Climate Home News, 22 January 2019; Hassan Nfaoui, 'How Can Morocco Achieve 52 Percent of its Electricity from Renewable Energy in 2030?', Renewable Energy World, 29 September 2016, https://www.renewableenergyworld.com/baseload/how-can-morocco-achieve-52-percent-of-its-electricity-from-renewable-energy-in-2030/#gref.

p. 338   'I published a feature for VICE ...' Thomas Lewton, 'These People Are Losing Their Gods to Climate Change' VICE, 12 April 2021, https://www.vice.com/en/article/v7e4zy/these-people-are-losing-their-gods-to-climate-change.

p. 340   'The term "Nollywood" ...' Norimitsu Onishi, 'How the Times Named "Nollywood"', *New York Times*, 11 February 2016.

p. 341   'Nollywood, Onishi writes ...' Norimitsu Onishi, 'Nigeria's Booming Film Industry Redefines African Life', *New York Times*, 18 February 2016.

p. 341   'The industry has come a long way ...' Lizelle Bischoff, 'From Nollywood to New Nollywood: The Story of Nigeria's Runaway Success', The Conversation, 28 September 2015, https://theconversation.com/from-nollywood-to-new-nollywood-the-story-of-nigerias-runaway-success-47959.

p. 342   'investment from Netflix that will see the streaming service ...' Lanre Bakare, 'Out of Africa: How Netflix's Ambitions Could Change the Continent's Cinema', *The Guardian*, 12 March 2021.

p. 342   'Simply put: in the future, the continent's biggest . . .' Katie Simmonds, 'Bigger than Hollywood: The Quiet Ascent of New Nigerian Cinema', Canon, https://www.canon.co.uk/view/nollywood-hollywood-nigerian-cinema/.

p. 342   'A strong funding base should broaden the limits . . .' Charles Igwe, 'How Nollywood Became the Second Largest Film Industry', British Council, 6 November 2015, https://www.britishcouncil.org/voices-magazine/nollywood-second-largest-film-industry.

p. 342   'Then came Afrobeats, a genre that has done . . .' Aaron Cohen, 'A Brief History of Afrobeats', Teen Vogue, 19 July 2019.

p. 343   'A different path was eventually taken . . .' Dan Hancox, 'The Rise of Afrobeats', The Guardian, 19 January 2012.

p. 343   'Thirty years later, millennials in the region . . .' Jon Pareles, 'The Legacy of Fela Kuti's Music of Resistance: Hear 15 Essential Songs', New York Times, 10 June 2020.

p. 344   'Where Fela's Afrobeat saved its energy . . .' Mary Pettas, 'Fela Kuti and the Legacy of Afrobeat', The Culture Trip, 6 February 2017, https://theculturetrip.com/africa/nigeria/articles/fela-kuti-s-afrobeat-legacy/.

p. 347   'In 2019, the Ghanaian government asked . . .' Ineye Komonibo, 'How Afrobeats Helped Pave the Diaspora's Road Back Home', Refinery29, 4 February 2020, https://www.refinery29.com/en-gb/afrobeats-the-year-of-the-return.

p. 347   'No matter where you were in the world . . .' Stephanie Busari and Leona Siaw, 'Ghana Is Being Heralded as the Next Big Tourist Destination. Here's Why', CNN, 7 February 2019, https://edition.cnn.com/travel/article/ghana-year-of-return-tourism-intl/index.html.

p. 348   'We open our arms even wider . . .' Nana Akufo-Addo, quoted in Meghan McCormick, 'Ghana: Come For The Celebrities, Stay To Be A Part Of Something Bigger', Forbes, 9 January 2019.

p. 349   'Nkrumah was the continent's most passionate . . .' Jessica Ankomah, 'How Ghana's "Year of Return" Sparked a Pan-African Phenomenon', The Culture Trip, https://theculturetrip.com/africa/ghana/articles/how-ghanas-year-of-return-sparked-a-pan-african-phenomenon/.

p. 349   'Nkrumah championed the liberation . . .' Adom Getchew, 'A Fuller Freedom', The Nation, 29 October 2019.

p. 349   'Before him, Pan-Africanism had its roots . . .' Peter Kuryla, 'Pan-Africanism', Encyclopedia Britannica, https://www.britannica.com/topic/Pan-Africanism [accessed 11 October 2021].

p. 349   'Nkrumah had friends in the cause . . .' Matteo Grilli, 'Making Sense of Decades of Debate about Nkrumah's Pan-African Ideas', The Conversation, 4 March 2020, https://theconversation.com/making-sense-of-decades-of-debate-about-nkrumahs-pan-african-ideas-132684.